INTERNATIONAL ADMINISTRATION:

Its Evolution and Contemporary Applications

D0882092

INTERNATIONAL ADMINISTRATION:

edited by

Its Evolution and Contemporary Applications

ROBERT S. JORDAN

STATE UNIVERSITY OF NEW YORK AT BINGHAMTON

New York

OXFORD UNIVERSITY PRESS

London   1971   Toronto

PREFACE

The idea of a book on international administration came out of nearly ten years of teaching a graduate seminar on the subject under the Consortium of Universities in Washington, D.C. This opportunity was made possible through the cooperation of Thomas H. Carroll, late president of George Washington University, while I was serving as his assistant; A. M. Woodruff, dean of George Washington University's School of Government, Business, and International Affairs; and Ernest Griffith, dean of the School of International Service, American University. It was apparent to me from the outset that the availability of teaching materials was so limited that the graduate student (not to speak of the undergraduate), if he were not in a major international city such as Washington, could not do effective research, or even learn much about, international administration. Furthermore, with the growth of multinational activities of both a functional and non-functional character, it has become more necessary for teachers of international organization and administration as well as of public and comparative administration, to have available to them a book which discusses the origins of international administration as such and also which contains suggestions as to how the techniques of international administration are being adapted to serve the major contemporary needs of peace-keeping, politico-military regionalism, and economic regionalism.

The general question of *how* to do something—as well as *what* to do—is as much a function of international politics as it is of national politics. But whereas domestically there has evolved a variety of means by which bureaucracies carry out their purposes, and a variety of national administrative traditions to serve national needs, such has not been the case internationally to nearly the same extent. The primacy of the state as the major political force in world affairs has been one reason for this situation. The need to evolve the means by which states *can* work out their varying interests without resorting to force has become one of the most important challenges of contemporary diplomatic practice.

The secretariat tradition, as it evolved in European international politics after the formation of the Congress of Vienna and the Holy Alliance, and through the work of the British Committee of Imperial Defense, represents a vital thread in the creation of the international civil service of the League of Nations (the first "continuing conference"), and thereafter in the political organs of the United Nations. After World War II, another thread can be found in the way the regional security and economic organizations that grew up in the West as a consequence of the Cold War arranged themselves. In addition, the experience of Britain and France in administering their colonies, especially in the closing decades of the colonial era, has provided another thread, less international, perhaps, but more functional. This colonial experience has influenced not only the choice of means, but also has provided the human expertise for those contemporary international organizations engaged in economic and social activities.

This book, then, is intended to give the teacher and student of international affairs, international organization and administration, or public and comparative administration, useful material concerning the origins of international administration as it is practiced today. This may help them to perceive the continuity of efforts to achieve a means of responding through multinational activities to the changing conditions of international life which has—and can have—such an influence for making the future of mankind brighter rather than dimmer.

I am grateful for the inspiration of Professor Harold Sprout of Princeton University, who encouraged me to go to St. Antony's College, Oxford, as a graduate student, and to the former Warden of St. Antony's College, F. W. D. Deakin, who made it possible for me to study the origins and contemporary applications of the British Cabinet secretariat tradition under the supervision of Professor Norman Gibbs, to whom this book is dedicated. The continuing interest of Professor Max Beloff of All Souls College, Oxford, in my desire to write about the relationship of the British Cabinet secretariat tradition to international administration is also appreciated. Jeffrey Lennard, while an undergraduate at George Washington University, performed a very professional service in assisting me in preparing the manuscript for publication. David Fishback, another undergraduate, laid the groundwork bibliographically for me to undertake this project, and Miss Eva Maestas typed part of the manuscript. My former colleague at Oxford and George Washington universities, J. Kenneth McDonald, provided valuable criticism of Chapter 2. Finally, it would be remiss of me not to mention the encouragement given by Miss Ruth Russell, formerly of The Brookings Institution and now of Columbia University, to bring the idea for this book to reality.

Binghamton, N.Y.   R. S. J.
August 1971

CONTENTS

PROLOGUE

Observations on the Life of an International Civil Servant   3
RICHARD W. VAN WAGENEN

PART ONE   The Evolution of International Administration

1 The Influence of the British Secretariat Tradition on the
Formation of the League of Nations   27
ROBERT S. JORDAN

2 The Evolving Concept of the International Civil Service   51
ROBERT RHODES JAMES

3 The Legacy of British and French Colonial Rule   74
DAVID J. MURRAY and JOHN BALLARD

4 Functional Agencies and International Administration   98
RICHARD SYMONDS

PART TWO   The Application of International Administration

5 International Administration of Peace-keeping Operations   123
LARRY L. FABIAN

6 Political-Military Regionalism and International
Administration   168
FRANCIS A. BEER

7 Economic Regionalism and International Administration:
The European Communities Experience   187
LAWRENCE SCHEINMAN

8 The National Bureaucracies of the EEC Member States and
Political Integration: A Preliminary Inquiry   228
WERNER FELD

EPILOGUE

The International Civil Servant in Law and in Fact   245
DAG HAMMARSKJÖLD

Bibliography   272

The Contributors   288

Index   291

INTERNATIONAL ADMINISTRATION:

Its Evolution and Contemporary Applications

PROLOGUE

Observations on the Life
of an International Civil Servant

RICHARD W. VAN WAGENEN

Where is it that everybody is a foreigner and nobody is a foreigner? On the staffs of international organizations, where tens of thousands today practice international administration. The international civil servant may not be "a new human category," as Georges Langrod claims, but he *is* "indispensable" and he *will* have a profound influence on the future.

This Prologue reflects briefly upon the reflections of Loveday.[1] His classic volume draws upon more years of experience as an international civil servant than I can claim. Mine have been spent with the World Bank Group, an organization in some ways narrower and in some ways broader than his League of Nations. These reflections will not, however, be bounded by that experience.

Even among the non-political international organizations, the Bank Group is not typical. Two reasons for this stand out: its governing bodies use weighted voting, and its main operation (the World Bank, or International Bank for Reconstruction and Development) is largely independent of governments in a finan-

---

1. Alexander Loveday, *Reflections on International Administration* (Oxford: Clarendon Press, 1956).

Views expressed by the author are his own. They do not necessarily reflect those of the World Bank.

cial sense. It is also financially independent of the United Nations, even though it is a specialized agency associated with the UN. Moreover, its staff is in a sense quite business-oriented, as compared with those of other international organizations. The Bank will not invest in any project that does not stand high in the priority list of development needs of the receiving country, no matter how large the return to the investor might be. But neither this constraint nor the fact that the Bank Group is a non-profit operation prevents it from using the methods of business, as distinguished from the motives of business. Most staff members feel stronger kinship with national organizations such as the Swedish International Development Authority (SIDA) or the Canadian International Development Agency (CIDA) or the U.S. Agency for International Development (AID) than with any private international banker. Of course they feel still closer kinship with regional development organizations such as the Inter-American Development Bank (IDB) and the Asian Development Bank (ADB). The test of Bank staff respect for and affinity with another agency is whether it actually produces economic advance in the developing countries.

Any student of International Organization will recognize the hazards in writing this Prologue, because analytically it is a squeeze between the obvious and the abstruse. Also, it is written from a viewpoint—that of a U.S. citizen, native-born. This nationality provides about a third of the professional staff and a quarter of the non-professional staff of the Bank Group at present. (This unusual reversed ratio is a result of international recruitment of "locally recruited" personnel, especially secretaries.)

SIMILARITIES AND DIFFERENCES

Did Loveday tell it like it was? Essentially he did, with perspective and balance, covering the life of the League of Nations and the first decade of the United Nations. Without trying to summarize his views, comments are offered here upon a few that are of special interest today. These focus on the distinctive features of an international civil service. (The "usual" or "normal" national civil service is the type with which comparisons will be made. This lets us exclude those countries where more than one "nation" lives under a single legal system — Belgium, Yugoslavia, and Nigeria, for example, not to mention the Hapsburg Empire.)

The *similarities* overwhelm the differences between national and international administration. But this is no less true of comparisons among all forms of organizational life, private as well as public (civilian as well as military), except for universities. In organizations of about the same size, the circumstances of daily life and the kinds of people on the staff are very much the same. The "principles" of administration apply, with minor variations.

Morale is at the core, and Loveday is accurately vague in emphasizing the "spirit of the institution" as its binding element. As with any teamwork situation, staff relations depend much more upon individual characteristics than upon group characteristics if the members are in close and continuous contact. To say it unscientifically, people get along well with a "decent fellow," no matter where his decency came from.

If Loveday's reflections have a fault, it is that he tends to lump together the similarities and differences without a fine enough distinction. He is right in saying that "industry, a sense of humour, judgment, justice, and kindheartedness" are "essential to success in any walk of life." But he selects some other qualities as being *especially* needed by an international civil servant which, I think, are not. They are equally essential "in any walk of life": "intellectual capacity," "determination," "constructive imagination," "capacity for leadership," "administrative ability," "nervous energy," and "specialized knowledge." He does list, however, some qualities we would both agree are particular assets to an international administrator: diplomacy, "convivencia" (its absence would mean "caos" in an international staff but only irritation in a national staff), and objectivity. To stay out of a deep morass, we should not go beyond Loveday's statement that the qualities needed "do not differ widely from those that go to make up a good national official, but their order of importance and relative values are somewhat different." It helps a little to add Egon Ranshofen-Wertheimer's observation that a "poor national official is in all likelihood also a poor international administrator. But a good national official will not necessarily make a good international civil servant" because he must think and act contrary not only to his political and social instincts but also to his national instincts. This is more true in a political international organization than in a mainly non-political one, where "national instincts" seldom if ever get in the way because decisions do not affect national safety or ideology.

One of the few generalizations I would venture is that a good fundamental education, acquired academically or otherwise, means even more to success on an international than on a national staff. By "fundamental" I mean the skills of communication that might be called "The Four G's": listening, speaking, reading, and writing. Communication is a more sensitive problem in an international civil service, where there is less tolerance for error.

The *differences* must be inspected more closely than the similarities; otherwise we would miss the point as badly as a cell biologist without a microscope. They almost all result from two facts: the staff must be drawn from several nationalities, and the headquarters must be located in somebody's territory. My observations focus on a headquarters-based rather than a field-stationed civil service, but it should be kept in mind that in the Bank Group virtually all the seventy-five nationalities on the professional staff include members who travel to the field.

Loveday illuminated all the obvious and many of the subtle

differences arising from the fact that most staff members live and bring up their families in a foreign country and that their office life is shared year after year with more people *not* of their nationality than *of* it. We cannot go into all these differences here, but it is interesting to touch upon half a dozen of them that have changed notably since the time he wrote about the League period.

The League was European-dominated and the Secretariat was overwhelmingly European. This would be unthinkable today in a "universal" international organization such as the UN or the Bank. They are instead Western-dominated, though not as completely as Conor Cruise O'Brien claims in his colorful observations.

Popular attitudes toward "foreigners" have notably changed in some countries, especially in the U.S. Increased contact is a prerequisite of attitude-change, according to social psychologists. This is making its impact, conscious and subconscious. The Bank is an extreme example, perhaps because a good proportion of its professional staff spends a fifth of the year in a variety of underdeveloped countries on a more than casual basis—one week in one and four weeks in another. Some even spend a third of the year abroad on such short visits. This gives contact with people in their own cultures, not in artificial surroundings.

Objectivity and neutrality are as central attributes of an international civil service as ever, but they are not sufficient by themselves in this modern day of positive action at the international level. The UN's main task is still security against international violence, but in doing this job and others it has much more of an "operating" function than the League. This is even more apparent in functional organizations like the FAO and the Bank. As it was then and always shall be, world peace is the main goal, so that *if* Pope Paul VI is correct in his implication that "development is the new name for peace," the eyes of the modern development agencies are on the target. All three UN

Secretaries-General have declared, in their own words, that economic and social development is an essential condition of peace. Development work does need initiative, drive, and the practical capacity to operate in the field. So do UN peace-keeping operations and lesser forms of "presence." Neutrality is certainly required, but Dag Hammarskjöld's distinction between neutrality toward fact and neutrality toward action asserts that neutrality of one sort is not a bar to operations. (He made this point a decade ago in his Oxford speech, which appears as the Epilogue to this volume.) David Morse put it more plainly and forcefully when he said, after many years as its Director-General, that the ILO was "objective yet not neutral."

The loyalty issue is not so prominent as it used to be, either when the Fascist and Nazi members truly disfigured the body of the League in its last years or when this issue occupied center stage at the UN during the McCarthy period in the U.S. One reason is that today a greater portion of all international civil servants work on essentially non-political problems.

Professional life is more secure now for an international civil servant than when Loveday wrote—for two reasons. First, the major organizations are not only much larger than they were in League and early UN days, but there are more of them and they are undoubtedly more permanent. Second, a greater proportion of international staffs are in the more marketable professions (engineers, agriculture specialists, economists, etc.). These men are able to move anywhere—to other international or national, public or private, philanthropic or business opportunities.

The social isolation that Loveday deplored at length is also reduced by now. Staff members and families both share the increase in electronic communication that has come to every developed country where headquarters are located, and the staff member himself travels in addition. Nevertheless, isolation is one of the difficulties of international life that remains.

WHAT DIFFERENCE DO THE DIFFERENCES MAKE?

Life in an international civil service breeds unusual problems of morale. Quite apart from morale questions, certain special adjustments are needed to make an international administration work well. Both deserve attention.

Morale

High morale fuels any organization, and Loveday rightly puts heavy emphasis upon it. Damage is mainly caused by expatriation, but so are certain benefits.

First, on the *negative* side is the feeling of isolation (already mentioned) that overtakes families. The degree depends upon such things as the strength of their home ties, their sense of adventure, and their stage in the family cycle. Families with children are caught between a rock and a hard place if their compatriots are scattered about in a large city and its suburbs. If they do not want their children "Americanized" or "Romanized," they feel they have to send them to a nearby international school in the host country or else far away to a school in the home country. To support the latter choice is, of course, the purpose of the staff education allowance common in an international civil service. Yet even these measures do not protect the children from the ubiquitous mass media where they live. The family may tend to fragment because the younger members adapt better to the surroundings than the older. Or, as Mottram Torre points out, this social isolation may draw the family more closely together—except that a couple without children may fare worse because at home the husband and wife led separate professional lives and in the new country they are forced together.

Something that has been neglected by observers is the mitigating effect of the rather common mixed-nationality marriages found in an international staff. No matter where one partner is employed, the other will be expatriated, and perhaps it is no less psychologically healthy to have both living outside their national ambits than only one. Does a Thai whose wife is French do better to live in Bangkok, Paris, or Washington? In any case, it is only in a small city or town that a large group of expatriates can manage *both* a social life among themselves and resistance to absorption. There, they can form a sizable group in close neighborhood. Even in large cities it is noticeable that the senior members of expatriate families usually do not fear cultural absorption, or else they feel proof against it. Yet they try strenuously to keep options open for their children, especially by preparing them for higher education at home if they come from a developed country.

Second, and related to the twinges of isolation, is a feeling of civic impotence. No vote means no voice, to a large extent, and this loss is all the more acute because people attracted to international organizations are often precisely those with a strong sense of civic responsibility and a desire to participate. Citizens of the headquarters country may vote and carry on most kinds of public activity, but even they feel certain political restraints.

A third morale-depressant can be the insecurity mentioned earlier. The main cause is disconnection from career ladders at home. One critical time is said to be about age thirty-five. Yet today this is not really a crisis of security but rather a choice between two securities: either in the international civil service or at home. The choice was not frequently offered in Loveday's time, when international organizations were scarce and the major one was insecure itself. About age fifty-five is another time of crisis, when the staff member usually arrives at the highest level he will reach in the service. If he does not happen to like that level as a prospect for the next ten years, he must decide whether he can do better at home before it is too late. After retirement it does not matter so much, unless he has grown too far away from home people and places. A more obscure insecurity of the expatriate, at least in the U.S. where three of the major headquarters are located, is that his sons are subject to the military draft and that his death (or even divorce) means that his family must leave the country. Insurance is not on sale for these contingencies.

On the *positive* side, expatriation may carry some benefits. Above all is the respect earned by the international civil service because of its motivation and objectives. If I must step onto *some* treadmill, a man may ask himself, how do I know which mill is grinding out a commodity worth my life's work? More will be said about this at the end of the Prologue.

The standard of living is higher for many expatriates coming to developed countries from the less developed, and no lower for most of the others. In some cases the "real" advantage is substantial, because any dollar surplus that might be saved from salary is multiplied when converted into the home currency for investment or the support of relatives.

Career failure can be muted for some staff members of an international civil service more easily than elsewhere because of the peculiar "geographical distribution" feature. Using the Bank as an example, nationality means quite a bit in recruitment, but some claim that it means nothing one way or the other with regard to progress up the ladder. This is not entirely true. There are pressures outside the service, such as national prestige, that push for a reasonable distribution in the upper echelons. This is characteristic of an organization such as the UN, where national distribution is under a quota. But it is also true for the Bank, which is not cursed with any quota system but which has a determined policy to overcome the inevitable Anglo-Saxon image resulting from the availability of U.K. and U.S. citizens when it was created in the mid-forties.

While there is internal staff pressure against national monopoly and duopoly, staff pressure for promotion by merit is even greater. In the World Bank Group (for example) it is not a matter of policy that department directors must be nationals of various countries. Yet an observer will note that in fact the 31 departments are headed currently by 12 nationalities, with only about half the department heads being U.S. or U.K. citizens. Also, in the higher ranks a vertical chain of 3 of the same nationality does not happen to exist except in one of the 31 departments. Even in the lower ranks such a chain is very unusual. Thus a "rare" nationality would appear to have an advantage in promotion if qualifications are almost equal.

This carries a corollary twist—for two kinds of nationality, failure is less hard on morale. A staff member from the two or three most numerous groups can take some of the pain out of slow promotion by the excuse that his nationality is over-represented. At the other end, the least-represented countries are likely to be the least developed, and a staff member of such a nationality is apt to have educational deficiencies or lack of confidence or some other handicap that he can use to rationalize failure, much as racial minorities in some places are able to use discrimination. But in between—for staff members neither from the U.S. nor U.K. nor France, nor Afghanistan nor Botswana nor Guatemala, for example—this comforting psychological parachute is replaced in the career man's knapsack by a baton.

Adjustments

What sort of special adjustments are needed to make an international administration work? It must be said right away that these are not as great as many would think. The one real exception is the speech impediment of most organizations: they have more than one working language. The mixture of nationalities and cultures is no great problem. It seems to keep the staff constantly alert and aware of potential troubles before they arise.

Students and practitioners generally concede that mixed

nationality makes for a more effective international civil service, and Loveday strongly concurs. It may be a nuisance, as some like to say, but it has three main advantages. One is the impact that different viewpoints make upon decisions. These are viewpoints that come from first-hand understanding of developing countries that goes beyond mere factual knowledge. Another is the constant practice it gives the staff in relating to other nationals at headquarters, so that their sensitivity is sharpened for the field. The greatest advantage, however, is the credibility a multinational staff gives to the whole organization when it deals with any part of the world. Besides, mixed nationality is required by mixed governance and financing and by national prestige!

In any case, the nationality mixture puts an extra dimension into the game, like a wild card in poker. It adds one more circuit to the social wiring diagram. We should examine the consequences at some length.

For one thing, staff members are not interchangeable, as they usually are in a national civil service. They cannot take assignments without giving thought to ethnic or nationality considerations. Suspicion or prejudice are sometimes too deep to be waived by an international armband. Indians cannot be used on Pakistan. An Israeli cannot work on an Arab country. A South African or a Portuguese cannot work in a black African country without difficulty. Some other antipathies are muted; for example, U.S. staff members can work in Latin America. Inside the staff, these people all work together as individuals, vertically and horizontally, composing a tribute to the human capacity for role-playing and to the infectious attachment of one person for another. A few restrictions appear in practice as to who can say certain things at certain times with credibility because of the nationality of the speaker, but in those rare cases it is easy enough to find another member of the staff to say them.

Naturally, a chauvinist would be troublesome and ineffective, but his corners quickly round off after joining a staff with a tradition such as the Bank's. What about the man at the other end of the scale—the cosmopolitan, or rootless person, whom Loveday and Wilfred Jenks and others discount? I can throw little light on this, but the Bank does have a neutral Swiss who says he is neutral even about Switzerland! Sometimes a sort of sublimation occurs. The staff member cannot vote in the U.S. or in his home country. If there is an important election coming up in one of the countries he is responsible for following, he may well become more interested in Chile or Ceylon politics than the politics of the U.S., where he lives, or the politics at home.

Working relationships in the international civil service need special attention at the personal level. Whatever the size and color of the wheels, they must be round enough to mesh. To achieve this is a challenge to the organization's leadership, which must pull the staff ahead by making the goals vivid and attractive, and then requiring high performance. This can be done more easily in an organization of limited purpose than in an all-purpose one—easier in WHO or ILO or the Bank or the Fund than in the UN, for example. "Economic development" may not be a clear concept, but it is sharper than "peace and justice." Leadership is easier in the Bank for another reason as well. The Bank president is the initiator of almost all action, while in the UN the General Assembly, the Security Council, and the other Councils and Commissions act more independently of the Secretary-General.

It is said with much truth, nevertheless, that a multinational staff has a built-in tendency toward fragmentation. Some nationality bonds are thicker than others. National groups have an interest in the success of their members and in the recruitment of first-rate countrymen and, of course, in the advancement of compatriots to really influential positions on the staff. Some national groups in the Bank staff used to hold social meetings of their members quite regularly, but this dwindled as the staff grew larger. Only one group has come to my attention that apparently keeps track of its nationals' salaries and by doing this makes appointment of new staff members from that country a little more complicated. Another nationality group has a reputation for maintaining a mild information network within the staff. There may be others, but to locate them would call for an inquiry deeper and less misleading than the informal and lively one Hernane Tavares de Sá has published about the UN Secretariat ("the UN's vital center of power").

On the whole, there seems to be no national clannishness at the Bank that outshines cliques formed by able members within national civil services—the Rhodes Scholars, the graduates of the national defense college or its equivalent, and versions of the British "old school tie," for example. The important thing is that there is no infection from cliques that undermines staff morale, even though an occasional suspicion of favored treatment may arise. This is remarkable when one considers that an international staff has no common cultural background and no symbols transmitting emotional voltage. Instead, it is "an institution derived from an exclusively rational recognition of the need for its existence," as a pseudonymous UN Secretariat member once wrote. A strong *organizational tradition* seems to be "a more potent influence toward staff discipline and conformity than is a marked degree of ideological homogeneity," Robert Cox recently observed. Loveday puts it this way: "What matters most is the spirit of the institution, and the capacity of the administration to win the trust of the staff."

Are the normal personality clashes more frequent, or more aggravated, in an international civil service? I believe not, because differences in manner and in style of approach are *expected* in a way that they are not in a national civil service. The expectations may be the wrong ones because the stereotypes do not fit, but at least some "difference" is foreseen at the outset. Preconceived images about nationality actually serve the useful function of warning a man that there must be *other* nationality characteristics, unknown to him, buried in various other staff members. Therefore he is apt to tolerate superficially bad behavior from others that would be resented if it came from his own countrymen. If a person fits the stereotype (an emotional Irishman or a mercurial Italian), many staff members are not surprised. But if he does not fit the stereotype, this can be taken as education instead of irritation. Anyhow, stereotypes are constantly being erased. I have known on the staff non-volatile Latins, an Englishman whose sense of fair play was feeble, and even an explosive Dutchman.

This dimension is all the more slippery because of cultural groups *within* nations and because of class distinctions within cultural groups. Loveday really was referring to classes, I think, when he wrote: "What is important in the case of the great majority of the staff, apart from language, is not their nationality, but the cultural group from which they spring." All this leaves a colleague today without as many clues to compatibility as he could have sensed as a European among Europeans in Loveday's time and sphere.

It is tempting to stop at the standard observation that everyone is different and that affinities are made by professional and social interests and matters of taste, regardless of nationality. While this is true, it implies that an international civil service is really no different from a national civil service. At that level of generalization there is no argument, but the level is not a very informative one. Perhaps the Bank and similar functional organizations are simply not very illuminating on this point. The staff is so busy and so many are usually absent from headquarters on mission that perhaps the normal rubbing of personalities is not enough to chafe and irritate deeply. Perspective from afar smooths out ruts, bumps, and consciousness of status.

One of Loveday's most emphatic points is that feelings of superiority that one nationality might have over another must be erased from the mind. This is true, but he did not mention the corollary that any feelings of national inferiority must also be erased from the mind. Persistent deference, characteristic of some cultures, invites adverse judgments from certain other cultures. If the feeling of inferiority itself continues, it may eventually be over-corrected by a masking belligerence. If that happens, the inferiority feelings can be sensed by others more strongly, and effectiveness is reduced. Loveday is right when he notes that people have *real* handicaps and also unreal *beliefs* about their handicaps.

Conflict of loyalty could still be a problem at the UN, which was created to engage in highly political activities and also has a broader spectrum of national membership than the Bank Group. Among the non-political organizations, the Bank has shown that staff members are not visibly upset with each other in times of crisis—Indians and Pakistanis when the 1965 war broke out, or Arabs and Israelis in 1967—and I doubt whether anyone held those national troubles against any staff member or felt called upon to diminish the stature of that man's country through him or through the Bank's operations.

In fact, the loyalty question seems rather out of date. Social psychologists have long known that there is in practice no great problem about multiple loyalties—dividing "loyalty" into various levels and segments. Loyalty of a staff member to his international organization does not conflict with loyalty to his country except in rare cases where a direct confrontation might be forced. Solidarity builds up in spite of the tendency to fragment that was mentioned earlier, as staff members come to identify personally with the organization. It is true (as Sidney Bailey has written) that "the qualities of international loyalty come, to a considerable extent, from continuing contact with other people." Perhaps "conflict of interest" is a more accurate and modern way to designate the pull that can exist between strict objectivity and the shading of decisions a little toward one's own country. So as to avoid any possibility of embarrassing a staff member, he is not allowed in the Bank to work directly on the country of his citizenship. This does not waste him, however, as a handy source of expertise about the affairs of his own country or those in which he has lived for some years.

Staff conflict of interest could conceivably come in connection either with one of the Bank's executive directors or with the Embassy. The only national delegates who work full-time at the Bank are the executive directors and their alternates. They are of course not staff members. The board of 20 votes the interests of the 114 member countries. It would be by staff contact with an executive director who is a countryman, or with the Embassy, that a conflict-of-interest incident could occur; but all parties know their roles, and there has apparently been little if any overstepping. I find it easy to agree with James Morris, who observed the Bank's work for several months in the field and at headquarters and then wrote in 1963: "There seem to be no national rivalries at H Street, no bickering loyalties or subterfuges of patriotism." There could conceivably be also, in an operation like the Bank Group (which includes the International Finance Corporation), a commerical type of conflicting interest, since business investments are the core of IFC activity. The collective decision-making process used in the Bank Group, however, helps to guard against this unlikely possibility.

All in all, no special adjustment to the conflict-of-interest or loyalty hazard needs to be made, apart from notifying each new staff member of the provisions of the Charter (or its equivalent) that he must not seek or receive instructions from any external authority.

Administrative form and process have to be adjusted a little to the needs of an international civil service. Loveday has underlined the governing distinction: there is no ministry on top of the administration. This means there is no cabinet, legislature, or judiciary. Thus the international staff member "must be much more than a civil servant carrying out instructions received from a minister or a parliament," wrote Loveday. But he continued: "His most important task is to promote understanding among the very persons from whom he may later receive instructions." The latter is still true of the UN itself, and of the other specialized agencies to a lesser degree. It is not so true of the Bank Group, whose rather hard-earned tradition of independence from governments protects the "working" staff from having to adapt decisions to the political wind. The Bank borrows and lends funds, its decisions concern only one subject (economic development), and its board cannot make a loan that the head of the staff has not proposed. The tradition is strong enough so that governments do not expect to have any real administrative control. Even though the Bank Group's operations in general must be acceptable to several groups, official and unofficial, in several countries, there is no direct supervision by any government agency. For this very reason of independence, more self-discipline is required of the staff than would be required in a national civil service.

Communication within a bureaucracy is always of prime importance. This is especially true in an international civil service because of the greater chance for static. This arises directly from language differences. The Bank is quite trouble-free, with English as the only official language. Yet even an American would have to seek both literal and cultural translations from a Commonwealth colleague when he received a letter of recommendation summarizing a candidate's personality: "He is a good off spinner and a dependable bat." How much more so the Korean with dictionary in hand!

Only profound study would reveal which particular style of national administration, or combination of styles, is best adapted to international administration, with first attention paid to the degree of delegation practiced under each. Styles in current international organizations are blends, but a version very much like the U.S. system prevails at both the UN and the Bank. The Bank's administration, at least, is liberally salted with British pragmatism and flexibility. Above all it has been strongly influenced by business administration practices. Perhaps the

French-Latin public system, with its clearcut directives and hierarchy, would be easier to operate with a staff that is not nationally homogeneous, because it does not require flawless teamwork; yet it might tend to become slow and rigid.

Administrative style is not entirely an individual matter. Loveday ventured that "administrative capacity . . . is perhaps the one quality required of an international official—apart from linguistic ability—which seems to be commoner amongst the nationals of some states than amongst the nationals of others." I feel more certain of Leon Gordenker's "obvious hypothesis" that persons "trained in certain political systems" may be more adaptable to the "ideal norms of an international civil service" than others. To mention one extreme, the Japanese system would not work well anywhere but in a near-perfectly homogeneous culture. In any case, Bank staff members quickly become administrative relativists, recognizing perforce that the Bank's own style of work is one among many. Perhaps this is bred by field contact with such a wide variety of systems, among them those that Gunnar Myrdal calls the "soft state." Fortunately, the systems are mostly left in the field and only the relativism is brought back to headquarters. This attitude of tolerance fits Loveday's profound conviction that "administrative liberalism," constantly pursued by the leaders of an international civil service, is necessary for high morale. By that I do not believe he meant looseness or softness. Rather, he meant the British flexibility to which he was accustomed. This has the serious flaw, however, that one man's flexibility is another man's arbitrariness.

Three adjustments in what is usually called personnel administration can be mentioned.

Recruitment for an international civil service has obvious extra difficulties: locating candidates, especially in prosperous countries and in countries with a low educational level; reaching them for interviewing without unconscionable expense; and above all, evaluating their suitability for international work.

An essay on the last of these points would be mostly a series of questions. An international organization has the usual problems of balancing intellect, personality, leadership qualities, articulateness, etc., but in addition it is faced with all the variables underlying each of these items that arise from an array of cultures. How do you judge a very young man's potential leadership from a record that shows only how well he has done among his countrymen? How judge articulateness during an interview with a man whose culture prizes reticence and brevity? How compare in personality a confident Greek with a Burmese cultivated in humility? How correct for the fact that the Burmese is being interviewed by a Colombian or the Greek by a German, or vice versa? What about the relation, during interview, between a former colonial civil servant and an applicant from his former colony? Objectivity is of the essence, but it is not enough. The complexity resembles charting the captain's cigar-glow as he paces the bridge of his tossing ship on a stormy night. Yet no computer can handle an interview. Loveday feels sure of one thing in this connection: that character must be put above intellect, as success depends "more on the personality of its officials, on their ethical outlook, and their instinctive behavior than on their intellectual attainments." This helps a little, but mainly it underlines his real conclusion: "There is no high road to success." All this leads to the practice of conservatism by careful organizations like the Bank, and Loveday agrees that the only way to be nearly certain about a recruit is to try him out in some capacity. The Bank does this with many consultants in the field, and they become probably the largest source of mature specialists who are appointed to the staff.

A system of narrow job specifications is fatal to an international civil service that is serious about recruiting staff from its less developed member countries. As Loveday became convinced, "The solution of the geographical problem appropriate in most cases lies in recruiting young, looking for brains and character rather than experience, and teaching the recruits their job in the office. This cannot be done when the system of narrow job specifications prevails." A modern operating organization such as the Bank recruits more of these generalists than some would expect, then trains many of them on the job. Most are recruited through a Young Professionals Program. This way, freedom from job specifications for generalists is achieved and yet the advantages of job specifications for non-generalists are not lost. The Bank must recruit many experienced specialists for its project appraisal and supervision work and for keeping platoons of consultants on the right path; this does require a number of rather narrow job specifications.

Assessing the performance of staff members is crucial. It is an especially hard task in an international civil service, for the same reasons that make assessing a potential recruit so complicated. In one sense it is easier than recruitment because there *is* a relevant performance to look at. In another sense it is harder, because of cases such as this hypothetical one: a non-Western national based at headquarters (Western) does his work in three or four different countries during the first year; that year is his probationary period, so the first eight or ten months is the critical time. How much allowance should be made for the strangeness of the headquarters and field surroundings, including possibly a language handicap? If the probationary period is judged strenuously and the recruit is dropped, an elaborate face-saving scheme has to be devised, since the dismissal is obvious unless a better position awaits him elsewhere. Even in cases where such a maneuver is not needed, the expense of shipping family and household furniture from the other side of the world has to be doubled and lost. On the other hand, if the probationary period is judged with liberality the consequences may be worse, both for the man's career in the long run and for the staff in general at all times. A humane dismissal at any point is complicated except for U.S. and Canadian citizens stationed in Washington or New York, Frenchmen stationed in Paris, and the like.

In sum, an international civil service has a harder time finding and keeping only the right staff members than its national counterparts do, and it has a greater investment in each person who is brought onto the staff.

WHAT DIFFERENCE DOES IT ALL MAKE?

There are three good reasons for undertaking a particular life work—one has no choice, or it is enjoyable, or it is important. The first has to be disregarded. The second is a matter of taste: whether a career (to be enjoyable) should be interesting, exciting, easy, prestigious, profitable, challenging, or whatever, is too subjective to analyze. Combinations of any two or all three might be ideal. Only the third is worth analyzing.

"Importance" is an excellent reason for working in a multilateral agency these days, whether or not the work is highly enjoyable. One has to beware of examining his objectives too closely in any occupation for fear of finding that they are riding loose from anchor or sky-hook. But one can have less fear of looking his goals in the face when he works in an international civil service than in most vocations.

Why is it important? Without fanning Andrew Boyd's "pure flame of idealism [that] seldom shines so pure through years of departmental duty," many hold the effort to promote "peace, justice and progress" (in the General Assembly's words) to be an end in itself.

But beyond that lies a still more remote end: a real breakthrough along the lines of functionalist theory. The functionalist believes that if and when consensus is ever reached for setting up international bodies with real political power, operating under enforceable law covering a great part of the world—and many think this is already well advanced in Western Europe—it will have been achieved largely through the "non-political" work of international organizations over a long, habit-forming period. The international civil servant is helping to form that habit. He is helping to legitimize an "International Establishment" manning effective political institutions. The better or luckier his performance, the sooner may come the breakthrough. This may come partly by way of "bureaucratic interpenetration," as in Europe. It may come in part by "task expansion" achieved through trained sensitivity that tells a staff just "how far to go too far" (as Ralph Townley put it). Or the catalyst may simply be a few modest agents of irreversible "system transformation." For any of these the international civil servant could claim a big share of the credit.

Some would prefer the analysis of I. L. Claude, who points out that as the economic programs of international organizations "have been turned towards the problem of passive provocation, the conventional theory of functionalism has been stood upon its head." In either case, the international staff member who fights on the economic development front pushes a gradual advance at the international level, which is today the crucial one.

Writing of politics and public administration at the state and local levels in the U.S., after many years as perhaps the country's most astute participant and observer, Louis Brownlow concluded: "I have become convinced that in all but extremely exceptional instances the level of performance, once raised, never drops back all the way." What if this happens to be true at the international level as well?

Besides, the second good reason comes through—it's enjoyable.

PART ONE

The Evolution of International Administration

"The two World Wars are prominent among the factors responsible for transforming the range and nature of British government over the past fifty years—at the least, they have set the pace and the exact form of a development that otherwise might have come about differently. The problems and conditions may often have been remote from those of peace; the experience gained, and the methods adopted, irrelevant to peacetime needs. But the machinery of administration, and administration itself, appear differently as a result."

John Ehrman

1

The Influence of
the British Secretariat Tradition on
the Formation of the League of Nations

ROBERT S. JORDAN

It is interesting to note, as Richard Symonds does in Chapter 4 of this book, that the high point of the evolution of functional international organizations came prior to World War I. The conviction that functionalism could be a way of keeping the fruits of economic and social progress from becoming despoiled by nationalistic and international political rivalries had been shattered by 1919. The tremendous growth of technology and the universalization of the nationalistic impulse that had evolved in Europe had prevented a truly "apolitical" approach to functional international cooperation from surviving the disaster of that war.

It is also noteworthy that the evolution of one of the most effective means of achieving some measure of multinational coordination and possible amelioration of international political rivalries took place in the same period that the "pure" form of functionalism was in vogue. This occurred as a consequence of the great colonial—or imperial—expansion of Great Britain into the non-European world by the end of the nineteenth century. One result of this expansion was the Boer War in South Africa. In the wake of the generally poor performance of Britain in this

The author is grateful for the assistance of Jeffrey Lennard in gathering research material for this chapter.

27

war, and because of the growing awareness in London that the Empire needed more systematic overseeing, a means of coordinating Britain's military affairs was introduced, called the secretariat method.

As Britain's overseas involvements expanded, and the variety of conditions under which Britain could find itself embroiled militarily multiplied, innovative forms of administration to handle policy-making requirements took on more and more of an institutional character. What would begin as an improvisation, such as supplying a secretary or clerk to "look after things" for an ad hoc committee or working group, gradually, over the years of the first decade and a half of this century, evolved into a coherent concept of governmental procedure. This procedure, later on, was adapted to meet the needs of Allied war-making in World War I. From that experience, the method served as the central concept of the formation of the international civil service of the League of Nations.

By the same token, after a commitment was made to form an international civil service which would serve the main policy-making organs of the League of Nations, the first Secretary-General began to take those intermediate steps which would define the kind of civil service that could help to cope with the worldwide responsibilities of the League. The precedent which Britain had set in evolving a strong career secretariat for the Committee of Imperial Defense, War Council, Dardanelles Committee, and War Cabinet, was applied on an international level, carrying through the Allied Supreme War Council, the Supreme Council at the Paris Peace Conference, and then into the Secretariat of the League in an ever-strengthened form. The British influence, in sum, was controlling.

Ironically, in the view of Sir Maurice Hankey (later Lord Hankey), the person most responsible for achieving it, this precedent of a strong centralized secretariat should not have been carried over into a multinational organization. His view was not accepted. Thus, a particular mode of national administration, stemming from Britain's imperial role in protecting its dominions as well as its colonies, became an important contribution to the development of a form of international administration which was designed to help prevent a recurrence of warfare among the industrial states of Europe.

THE COMMITTEE OF IMPERIAL DEFENSE

Initially, the idea of a "secretariat" grew out of the British notion that there should be a bureaucratic cadre of non-political officials who would serve whatever "government of the day" the sovereign empowered to rule. Generally speaking, this cadre was not to be involved in policy-making—a political function—but rather in policy-implementing—an administrative function.

The immediate circumstances, however, which gave rise to the formation of a group of civil servants into a secretariat that would serve the needs of a governmental policy-making body, came from the external responsibilities of government, rather than from domestic sources. Just after the turn of the century, in 1902, the prime minister decided to set up a Committee of Imperial Defense (CID) as a subcommittee of the Cabinet, and in 1904 a small section of career civil servants and some military career officers was formed to coordinate its work. Professor Franklyn Johnson has offered an explanation as to why this development had not taken place earlier within the full Cabinet itself to take care of overall policy-making needs:

> A weakness of cabinet government of the late nineteenth century was the lack of agenda or minutes. This was an especially serious failing because of the technicalities and delicate relationships among the strategic factors which accompany military activities, and their general lack of interest to politicians, who find it easy to overlook such problems in the absence of memoranda and records. Thus perhaps it was only natural that the need for an elaborate cabinet secretariat should first appear in the defence sphere, and then, under the pressure of a great military effort,

the secretariat of the Committee of Imperial Defence should become a part of the cabinet machinery.[1]

It was not until 1916 that the secretariat system was introduced for the Cabinet generally. Before that, the Cabinet did not work from a formal agenda and there were no minutes kept of its deliberations and decisions. It had, however, been long-established practice for the prime minister, the "first among equals" in the Cabinet, to report its proceedings to the sovereign. This was not, of course, in any way a substitute for the lack of a permanent record of the Cabinet's activities.

In the relatively neglected sphere of defense affairs during the first decade of the twentieth century, the Committee of Imperial Defense carried on its work with the increasingly valuable—and valued—help of its small secretariat. The secretary to the CID, because of the nature of his work, possessed a significant potential for direct influence over much of the business of the Committee. Under certain circumstances, this influence could acquire political overtones if the secretary were to wander outside of the nebulous boundary of his professional neutrality. This happened in 1907 when Sir George Clarke, the first secretary to the CID, was pressured to resign because he had openly advised the prime minister to oppose the construction of Dreadnoughts. This was an issue of great political and strategic significance at that time. Aside from the fact that the decision went against him, it was recognized that he had compromised his ability to deal effectively with many powerful naval leaders.

It was clear that a secretary who performed a coordinate role had to always maintain unobstructed channels to all the governmental bodies, groups, and leading individuals in the

---

1. Franklyn A. Johnson, *Defence by Committee: The British Committee of Imperial Defence, 1885–1959* (London: Oxford University Press, 1960), p.13. For Lord Hankey's view of this book, see Stephen Roskill, *Hankey, Man of Secrets*, Vol. I, 1877–1918 (London: Collins, 1970) pp. 138–42.

policy-making process. While he might be asked his opinion on some issue—and he often was—he should not have, according to the tradition which was built up, taken stands on issues in such a way as to interfere with his access to and credibility with those persons and organs that he was serving.

Sir Charles Ottley succeeded Sir George Clarke (later Lord Sydenham) in 1907, and in 1908 Hankey joined him as his assistant. Both of these men were from the navy (Hankey being a Marine), which dispelled the lingering suspicion in naval quarters about the impartiality of the CID's Secretariat. In 1912 Hankey succeeded to the secretaryship, holding this post—and that of secretary to the Cabinet as well after 1916—until his retirement in 1939.[2]

It would be inaccurate to infer that the CID Secretariat had little power just because it was to behave in policy-making in a politically neutral manner. From its beginning, the Secretariat had the ability to initiate matters, and this can be a strong power indeed. The terms of reference, based on the *Esher Report*, provided that the Secretariat could "consider all questions on the subject and anticipate"[3] the informational requirements of the prime minister. As Lord Hankey was to put it, retrospectively and quite candidly:

> The Government Departments looked at everything through departmental spectacles, and generally referred to us only questions in which their own business was crossed by or dependent on that of other departments. In these circumstances we secre-

2. For a brief review of the evolution of the CID Secretariat, and the later career of one of Hankey's trusted lieutenants, Sir Hastings Ismay (later Lord Ismay), see Robert S. Jordan, *The NATO International Staff/Secretariat, 1952–1957, A Study in International Administration* (London: Oxford University Press, 1967), esp. Part I.

3. Quoted in Johnson, op. cit., p. 65. The Esher Report's full title was, *War Office (Reconstitution) Committee: Report of the War Office (Reconstitution Committee)*, Part I, dated 1904. Lord Hankey retained his appointment as a royal marine through most of his career, even though his assignment was more that of a civil servant. His salary was not paid by the navy, however.

taries soon discovered that we must find out ourselves what
our work should be and then persuade either the Prime Minister
himself or some department to refer it formally to us. In practice
most of the initiative was taken by the staff of the Committee.[4]

Turning now to the Committee itself, we should note that
its hallmark was flexibility of membership. The CID was a
means by which the military leaders could communicate more
or less systematically with the political leaders about security
questions. As requirements dictated, the membership of the
CID would change, but always under the chairmanship of the
prime minister. He decided who should sit on the Committee.
This was important, because the Committee was always advisory only—it, of itself, did not take the political decisions
that lay at the heart of government. These were taken by the
Cabinet under the leadership of the prime minister. But continuity and permanence of the CID Secretariat, in the face of
the evanescent nature of the Committee membership, tended
to give the secretary and his assistants an influence which
otherwise would have been improbable. The Secretariat was
"the cornerstone of the whole edifice."[5]

Initially, the secretary to the CID was authorized several
assistant secretaries, two junior officers each from the army,
navy, and Indian army, and from one or more colonies. These
persons succeeded William Tyrell, a Foreign Office official
who had been asked to keep minutes of the CID. Tyrell was
described by Lord Hankey as "a part-timer who did not pretend
to know the job."[6]

From these beginnings, the place of the secretariat in the

4. Lord Hankey, The Supreme Command 1914-1918, Vol. I (London:
George Allen and Unwin, 1961), p. 52.
5. Quoted from the Esher Report in ibid., p. 46.
6. Quoted in Johnson, op. cit., p. 56. Sir William Tyrrell (later First Baron)
had been senior clerk in the Foreign Office 1907–18, private secretary to Sir
Edward Grey 1907–15, assistant under-secretary of state for foreign affairs
1918–25, permanent under-secretary at the Foreign Office 1925–28, and ambassador in Paris 1928–34. From his career it is evident that he was no "minor
clerk," as it might be inferred from Hankey's comment.

machinery of British government grew in importance to such an extent that the secretariat function, as mentioned earlier, was built into the work of the Cabinet itself during World War I. It was no longer possible for the Cabinet, aside from the sub-committee which was the CID, to continue the informal and diffuse methods of the past. To meet the total needs of total war, authority and responsibility had to be defined by the primary policy-formulating bodies and the executive agencies of the government to a greater degree than ever before had been necessary. By the time of Hankey's retirement, it was clear that his long tenure could be seen as a transition period between the days of informality and the "gifted amateur" ruling Britain, and the coming into existence of the modern state requiring a large bureaucracy of professionals. It simply would be impossible today, even for a man as "omnicompetent" as Hankey (as one observer described him) to hold all the main policy-making threads in his hands or in those of his secretariat. Lord Hankey, during his tenure of office, witnessed the development of Britain as a modern administrative state.

The secretariat system also was important to the successful prosecution of World War I. L. S. Amery, who had been a member of the CID Secretariat, put it: "As for Hankey he had, in his quiet unobtrusive way, helped to prepare us for war, and had, in effect, both devised and continually oiled the machinery which won it."[7] Even more complimentary—almost adulatory —was the comment in 1919 of Lord Riddell, a man who was not a leader but who was close to the leading figures of the time:

> The truth is that Hankey is one of the best-tempered, most agree-able, kindest men I have ever met—a real Christian in every sense of the word—as well as one of the most efficient.[8]

7. The Rt. Hon. L. S. Amery, C. H., *My Political Life, VII: War and Peace 1914–1929* (London: Hutchinson, 1953), p. 172.

8. Lord Riddell, *Lord Riddell's Intimate Diary of the Peace Conference and After, 1918–1923* (New York: Reynal and Hitchcock, 1934), p. 69.

In light of the fact that Hankey was able to maintain himself in the seat of power for so long, it must also be assumed that he had qualities of tough-mindedness and tenacity of purpose. He also, apparently, was a man who loved his work, as he freely admitted:

> . . . the Committee was brought formally into existence by a Treasury Minute dated May 4, 1904. When I opened my newspaper at breakfast and read this item of news I remarked to my wife that the secretaryship of the new Committee was the post of all others to which I would aspire, adding that it was never likely to happen, and if it did, only late in life as the crown to my career. Little did I think that within less than eight years I was destined to realize my ambition, much less that I should hold the post for more than a quarter of a century, and that it would lead me into the vortex of national, Imperial, and international affairs during one of the most eventful periods in the Empire's history.[9]

THE WAR COUNCIL AND WAR CABINET

In November 1914, with the onset of World War I, Prime Minister Asquith set up the War Council, which was composed of many of the same persons who sat on the CID. And, consistently, the Secretariat of the CID assumed the responsibility for the work of the War Council. There was a difference, however, between the functions of the CID and the War Council. The Council, which existed alongside the full Cabinet, was a more fluid body that proffered its advice only when asked to do so and then mostly on new departures of wartime strategy or about combined operations. In 1915 the War Council was replaced by the Dardanelles Committee, which soon in effect became the War Committee. The Secretariat of the War Committee, however, although deeply enmeshed in the problems of the British government as regards the waging of the war, still was serving an advisory and consultative body rather than a

9. Hankey, op. cit., p. 46.

decision-making or executive body. This aspect was in the tradition of the CID.

In contrast, when Prime Minister Lloyd George formed his War Cabinet in December 1916, the Secretariat's responsibilities changed by virtue of the altered role of the War Cabinet from that of the previous bodies. The War Cabinet was an executive body which was derived from the Cabinet itself. It was intimately involved in the prosecution of the war.

In the course of the war Britain had become increasingly engaged in working out collaborative relationships with its allies, especially with France, and later with the United States. As a consequence the Secretariat, once established, immediately began to take on not only an internal role but also a rapidly expanding international role as well. Furthermore, along with others, Hankey was becoming more concerned about the kind of peace that should be obtained even while the war was yet to be resolved.

Hankey's influence—apart from that of the Secretariat generally—on key decisions in the conduct of the war, is illustrated by an observation by L. S. Amery: ". . . Hankey, in close touch with junior officers in the Admiralty . . . took it upon himself to state the case for convoys with overwhelming force in a memorandum early in February. Lloyd George caught fire at once, and never let the Admirals alone till they finally gave way in April, and very soon became whole-hearted converts to the new method."[10] Amery also reveals how important the other secretaries could be in their work at this time:

> In January Hankey turned me on to act for him as secretary of the Inter-departmental Committee which had been set up by the late Government to study the question of the territorial changes outside Europe which we should aim at in the terms of

10. Amery, op. cit., p. 120. Roskill's account of this episode, drawing on a wide range of sources, including Hankey's own papers, confirms the key role Hankey played in this crucial decision of wartime grand strategy (see Roskill, op. cit., pp. 356 ff.).

peace, or might secure by exchanges with our own Allies. The secretary of such a committee, if he has any skill at drafting, and is supported by the chairman, can usually get what he wants, or most of it, for the simple reason that no one is prepared to take the trouble to recast the document from beginning to end. Consequently even the most drastic amendments usually end in a compromise that leaves the main argument substantially unaffected.[11]

Without a doubt, one of the major features of the secretariat system was the use of subcommittees. Lord Hankey thought that the parceling-out of the work of the CID, and later the War Council and the various successor bodies, was one of his greatest contributions to good governmental management. Subcommittees, for example, could be useful to coordinate affairs among government departments or matters which might overlap departments. They also could help in dealing in greater detail with particular problems than the full Committee (or Cabinet) may have found would justify their collective attention.

Under the War Cabinet, the system of delegation to committees and subcommittees was extended considerably. Even at that, from its formation in December 1916 to its dissolution in October 1919, the full Cabinet held more than 650 meetings, with over 500 persons who were not members of the War Cabinet and the Secretariat attending these meetings at different times.[12] The volume of business for the Secretariat must have been enormous.

It was at this time, after the evolution of the wartime planning function from the War Council, through the Dardanelles Committee and the War Committee, to the War Cabinet, that the "Cabinet Office" was created. Its duties, as written up by Hankey in a Rules of Procedure, were: (1) to record the pro-

---

11. Amery, ibid., p. 102. Insofar as this reflects sharp practices, this comment may reflect the fact that Hankey might not have entirely trusted Amery.

12. Cab. 37/161/14, as given in *The Records of the Cabinet Office to 1922*, Public Record Office Handbook #11 (London: H.M.S.O., 1966), p. 3.

ceedings of the War Cabinet; (2) to transmit relevant extracts from the minutes to departments concerned with implementing them or otherwise interested; (3) to prepare the agenda paper, and to arrange the attendance of ministers not in the War Cabinet and others required to be present for discussion of particular items on the agenda; (4) to receive papers from departments and circulate them to the War Cabinet and others as necessary; and (5) to attend to the correspondence and general secretarial work of the Office.[13]

Even though Hankey came to move among the highest level wartime Allied decision-makers, there has been some disagreement as to whether the machinery which made this possible could be explained through institutional evolution, as had been suggested, or through the personal career of Lord Hankey, as has also been suggested. As Professor John P. Mackintosh put it:

> The view that the Committee of Imperial Defence was the true ancestor of the War Council of 1914 and later of the War Cabinet comes largely from the writings of Lord Hankey. . . . This is largely a matter of pride of parentage, for there are evident connections—the main one being the Secretariat under Hankey— but for the purposes of the historian the important point is that before 1914 the Committee of Imperial Defence met occasionally and played a minor advisory role, while Lloyd George's War Cabinet was the executive body meeting every day and running the war. The latter took over the powers and outlook of the peacetime Cabinet and added some of the practices of the old Committee of Imperial Defence.[14]

Lord Hankey would put it somewhat differently: "both before and during World War I we were always working, by trial and error, after nearly 100 years of freedom from major war, to build up a really reliable system. The big point was that at last we had in the C.I.D. the nucleus of a workable system."[15]

13. Ibid., p. 4. For a thorough and authorized history of Lord Hankey's career during this period, see Roskill, op. cit.

14. John P. Mackintosh, *The British Cabinet* (London: Stevens and Sons, 1962), p. 272n.

15. Quoted by Johnson, op. cit., p. 73.

THE IMPERIAL WAR CABINET AND
IMPERIAL WAR CONFERENCE

The dominion governments, reflecting Great Britain's world-wide commitments, had sometimes been consulted about questions of a political or strategic nature even before the outcome of World War I. For example, representatives of the dominions had from time to time participated in meetings of the CID. This tradition of consultation was institutionalized by Prime Minister Lloyd George shortly after he came to office. He requested that the dominion governments should be involved in "a series of special and continuous meetings of the War Cabinet in order to consider urgent questions affecting the prosecution of the war. . . ." [16] The gathering together of this group, on a continuing consultative basis, came to be known as the Imperial War Cabinet. It was concerned with the planning of naval and military operations and of other broader issues affecting the Empire that the war had engendered.

In contrast, the Imperial War Conferences, under the chairmanship of the Secretary of State for the Colonies, was concerned with matters not directly connected with the war but which affected the Empire. The Conferences went on from 1917 to 1921. One can point to the Commonwealth Conferences held today as successors to these Imperial Conferences.

Noteworthy in the experience of the Imperial War Cabinet were the periodic meetings of dominion prime ministers with the British prime minister. Because the war came to a close fairly soon after this practice had developed, the procedures for its institutionalization were not fully developed. However, the prime ministers did take up at their last session the question of the representation of the dominions at the Paris Peace Conference, which opened in January 1919. Canada, Australia, South Africa, New Zealand, and India agreed that their own

16. *The Records of the Cabinet Office to 1922*, op. cit., p. 4 (quotation from CD. 9005).

delegations at the Peace Conference should be included in the British Empire Delegation, which was seen as an extension of the Imperial War Cabinet. Significantly for our purposes, the War Cabinet Office provided most of the staff for the secretariat of the British Empire Delegation, with some of the staff coming from the dominions.

In summary, the records of the Imperial War Cabinet, the various meetings in London of dominion prime ministers, and the work of the British Empire Delegation were all served by the "Cabinet Office" of the War Cabinet.

THE PARIS PEACE CONFERENCE

Regardless of the nature of the origins of the Cabinet Office— whether it was established due to institutional evolution or personal leadership—the secretariat function had become central not only to Britain, but also, by 1919, to the conduct of Allied affairs and, especially as far as the future was concerned, to the making and keeping of peace. Because of the central position of Hankey in coordinating the British role in the wartime coalition, it was only natural that he and his secretariat would remain alongside the prime minister as the process of peace-making began. In a sense, this aspect of proximity played into the situation which had evolved during the war. The emphasis had been on *coordination* among the Allied states rather than joint execution of common projects. The secretariat style lent itself to this situation. It was good for planning and coordination, but not for execution. For example, a precedent for the League was described thus:

> [The Allied organizations'] powers were advisory, and they had no control over the resources of the different governments. The control was a national control. . . . The function of the Allied organisations was to make plans for the exercise of the national controls. It was their task to assemble the statistics and other

> data needed as a basis for correct decisions, to agree upon the
> accuracy of this information, to study it with the help of experts,
> and to recommend plans of action for the adoption of the several
> governments. Each government, however, was always free to
> reject any recommendation, if it was deemed contrary to the
> national interest. The Allied organisations, therefore, merely
> were machinery devised to secure effective co-operation among
> the nations fighting Germany for the purpose of utilising their
> full strength, with the least waste in carrying on the war. [17]

More and more, ad hoc groups composed of representatives
of each Allied state were formed to deal with specific problems,
and this practice brought with it an increasing requirement
for secretariat support. The Wheat Executive, formed in 1917
in London by Britain, France, and Italy, is an example. Its responsibility was to develop a comprehensive plan for the supply
of wheat and to supervise the plan's execution. The Executive
was composed of representatives of each participating country.
Similar terms of reference were set for the Allied Maritime
Transport Council. The Council's secretariat was non-national,
charged to serve the organization as a whole, but the Council
was assisted by national staff members as well.

Because of the combination of the prime minister's decision-
making habits and the growth of these Allied groups, the Cabinet Office Secretariat had become more involved in international affairs than perhaps otherwise would have been the case.
The result was that within the British delegation to the Peace
Conference there arose some disagreement about which part
of the government—the Cabinet Office or the Foreign Office—
should serve the policy-making needs of the delegation. Part
of this disagreement stemmed from a general feeling of mistrust
over the role which professional diplomats, employing "traditional diplomacy," had played in the pre-1914 years, with what
appeared to be disastrous consequences. This had led to a feel-

17. George Rublee, "Inter-Allied Machinery in War-Time," *The League of
Nations Starts: An Outline by Its Organizers* (London: Macmillan & Co., 1920),
pp. 30–31.

ing of grievance on the part of the professional diplomats, as expressed for example, by Sir Harold Nicolson: "It is quite true that there was no time for much consultation: it is also true that there was little desire."[18]

He went on to observe, "haphazard methods [were] adopted for co-ordination between the Plenipotentiaries and the Delegation as a whole. We were seldom told what to do. We were never told what our rulers were doing."[19] This was because the machinery of coordination had been set up by the Cabinet Offices under Hankey's direction. It operated very efficiently, but not in the service of the Foreign Office.

Hankey thus served the prime minister's needs; furthermore, he was the only person to attend continuously the meetings of the Big Four (Lloyd George, Clemenceau, Orlando, and Wilson). He had had experience in this situation, having headed the British Section of the Supreme War Council, which had been established near the end of the war. He thus had had an opportunity to meet his approximate counterparts in the French, Italian, and American governments.

When the Peace Conference was held in Paris, it became inevitable that the French would be the hosts, and M. Clemenceau would be chairman, with the General Secretariat under French direction. This was generally considered to be unfortunate, for the French secretary was not as able as was Hankey. From the British view, this was a drawback which for a time directly affected the ability of the Conference to proceed to its main task. As Nicolson put it:

> This defect in the Secrétariat Général was gradually remedied by the hearty British efficiency of Sir Maurice Hankey. Yet in the early stages it constituted a serious drawback. And for this reason. A really brilliant Secretary, a Gentz or a Massigli, might have remedied the omission of an agreed programme by the con-

18. Harold Nicolson, *Peacemaking 1919* (New York: Grosset and Dunlap, 1965), p. 110.
19. Ibid., p. 111.

stant preparation of intelligent agenda papers. M. Dutasta was too flurried for any such acts of vision or responsibility. He took subjects in their order of temporal urgency, not in their order of actual importance. As a result, the first six weeks of the Conference were wasted in the discussion of *actualités* and were not devoted to the central purposes for which it had been convoked.[20]

The basic problem, of course, was that in distinction to the work of its predecessor, the Supreme War Council, the Conference could not take its agenda from events as they unfolded. Rather, the conferees needed the larger issues formulated for them. Only a strong secretariat, composed of persons with experience in working at the highest levels of governmental policy-making, and the professional self-confidence of a Hankey, could have overcome this deficiency.[21]

Another deficiency, as revealed above, was that the Secretariat, being composed of nationals from the participating states, had a tendency to suffer from a lack of strong centralized direction. This was a problem not only of language—each secretary having to have his work translated into the other official language—it was also a matter of national style. The success of the Peace Conference Secretariat, composed as it was of persons seconded from their governments, could not obviate the problem.

But, ironically, Hankey, who was able to work effectively

20. Ibid., p. 120.
21. Sometimes this assistance might have been counter-productive, as Amery describes: "Lloyd George, not having read the brief so carefully prepared for him, might start most eloquently arguing the very case we were concerned to oppose. Hankey would scribble a note in his large, legible hand which Lloyd George would glance at without interrupting the flow of his argument. Presently he would blandly explain that he thought he had done full justice to a view which, however, the British Government did not share, and would now expound our own real attitude. Meanwhile Hankey would draft a resolution which Lloyd George would then read out as representing the fully considered proposal which he had brought with him." (Amery, op. cit., pp. 178–79).

under these circumstances, and who strongly recommended that the secretariat function in the League should be headed by a single person, did not support a strong centralized international secretariat for the League political organs. He favored the retention of national secretaries, although working under a single Secretary-General. As he said: "It is . . . better to have a single secretary if one can be found who is acceptable to all. The authors of the Covenant did well to establish a single Secretary-General."[22]

Sir Eric Drummond, the first League Secretary-General, summarized the different views:

> The first was that the Secretariat should be composed of national delegations of the various members of the League. Each delegation would be paid for by the Government of the country from which it comes and be responsible soley to that Government. The practice which had prevailed at international conferences previous to the foundation of the League of Nations would thus be continued, while the duties of the Secretary-General would be largely confined to the co-ordination on special occasions of the services of the national delegations on the Secretariat, and to the centralization of administrative functions.[23]

He went on to say:

> Those who advocated the second theory held that the Secretariat should form, as far as was practicable, an international Civil Service, in which men and women of various nationalities might unite in preparing and presenting to the members of the League an objective and common basis of discussion. They would also be entrusted, it was proposed, with the execution of any decisions ultimately taken by the Governments. Under this scheme the Secretary-General would not only be the co-ordinating centre of the activities of the Secretariat, but its members would be

22. Lord Hankey, *Diplomacy by Conference, Studies in Public Affairs 1920–1946*, (London: Ernest Benn, 1946), p. 37.

23. Article in *The World Today*, March 1924, as quoted in C. Howard-Ellis, *The Origin, Structure and Working of the League of Nations* (London: George Allen & Unwin, 1928), p. 171.

responsible to him alone, and not to the Governments of the countries of which they were nationals, and would be remuner- ated from the general funds of the League.[24]

Lord Hankey preferred that the League Council continue the role of the Supreme War Council into the postwar period. It would, as mentioned at the beginning of this chapter, thus be- come a continuing international political conference of those states that felt they had a sufficiently strong and common basis of interests to cooperate continuously, or at least to consult together on a regularized basis.

According to Lord Riddell, even though Hankey was skeptical about how the League might achieve this goal, he nevertheless had a strong opinion about the importance of creating ma- chinery which could continue the collaboration of the victorious states:

> [Hankey] told me that he himself had drawn up a scheme for a league of nations. His idea was that the Supreme Council should be maintained in a modified form. He was opposed to the formation of a body which would have no direct connection with actualities. For that reason he declined the Secretaryship of the League which was offered to him. He fears that the League in its present form is doomed to failure. He thinks that in some way the League should now be brought into direct touch with the Supreme Council, so that gradually the League may assume some of the Council's functions and ultimately replace it as peace-maker of the world.[25]

One of the reasons, possibly, why Hankey did not favor the introduction of his demonstrably successful national admini- strative style into the League was that the influence of national delegations might have been reduced. Since the services of the British Delegation had proved effective in taking care of the

24. Ibid., pp. 171–72.
25. Riddell, op. cit., pp. 182–83. One of Lord Hankey's protéges—Lord Ismay—when he was setting up the International Staff/Secretariat of NATO, also conceived the proper function of an international secretariat in more narrow, or coordinative, terms. (See Jordan, op. cit., Chapters 3 and 11.)

work of the wartime Allied bodies and the Peace Conference, it would not be unlikely that Hankey foresaw with favor a continuation of Britain's influence if the national system were carried over into the League.

Also, it might be that the national predilection of Britain not to become too enmeshed in international organizations prevailed over the temptation to adopt the British model in the running of the various Allied councils and conferences.

Obviously, opinion went against Hankey. The powers of the League Secretary-General and the Secretariat were formulated in three specific grants in the League Covenant. A general grant of power was contained in Article II, which stated that "the action of the League under this covenant shall be effected through the instrumentality of an Assembly and of a Council, with a permanent Secretariat." The Secretariat itself was defined in Article VI as comprising "a Secretary-General and such secretaries and staff as may be required." As to the specific role of the Secretary-General, Article VI provided that "the Secretary-General shall act in that capacity at all meetings of the Assembly and of the Council."

These provisions can be seen as a reaction against the failure of international diplomacy to prevent the war. The conferees in Paris perceived that it was vitally important, when international tensions would rise in the future, that the protagonists would be able to continue to communicate with each other rather than to constrict or break off all forms of diplomatic intercourse. One way, it was thought, that this crucial international political communication could go on even as states would be maneuvering (or posturing) during a crisis, was to have in existence consultative machinery which could serve the needs of all parties, and thus be a "neutral" arena.

Beyond these rather general observations and formal provisions, the statesmen at Paris left untended questions about the structure, form, and nature of the new international Secretariat. They had had enough difficulty getting the Covenant negotiated without raising more and—politically speaking—relatively unimportant matters. As Professor Leon Gordenker has observed: "The idea and scope of the projected secretariat caused no real controversy at the peace conference, and as a result the delegates accepted a plan the implications of which had been fully explored."[26]

THE INTERNATIONAL SECRETARIAT OF THE LEAGUE OF NATIONS

An earlier expectation that the post of Secretary-General would initially be important politically proved short-lived. Originally, it had been proposed during the Peace Conference that the office be given the title of "Chancellor" and a distinguished international statesman was to have occupied the post. M. Venizelos of Greece, for whom the post was intended, turned it down, and so it was decided to give it to a civil servant. There was not complete agreement about this downgrading of the office, however. One observer at the time commented in 1945:

> All things considered, it can be stated that it was a mistake on the part of the statesmen responsible for establishing the League to choose an administrator. . . . Experience proves that it is a

26. Leon Gordenker, *The UN Secretary-General and the Maintenance of Peace* (New York: Columbia University Press, 1967), p. 5. Gordenker traces this evolution thus: "Official study groups produced textual suggestions for the League Convenant, mainly during the summer and autumn of 1918. Perhaps the earliest definite suggestion relating to a secretariat came from a French governmental commission, which showed more interest in a military staff than a civil service. The first official British draft of the Covenant, the product of the Phillimore Commission, did not even mention the subject of a secretariat. Nor did the first attempts by Colonel Edward H. House and President Woodrow Wilson. The most influential suggestion before the Versailles Conference came from General Jan Christiaan Smuts. In his seminal proposals for the League of Nations he projected a permanent secretariat, which was to keep alert to disturbances anywhere and to acquire first-hand information about them. A secretariat always appeared in subsequent drafts but not in well-defined terms" (p. 5).

statesman who must be chosen as head of a political agency. He must be an international leader. Unless he is that, no international agency can exhaust the possibilities inherent in its mission. The lesson of the League in this respect is as clear as possible, hardly open to contention, and absolutely convincing.[27]

With the change in the title also came a change in the authority of the office. For example, when M. Venizelos was in consideration as the possible head of the League Secretariat the officer was empowered to summon Council meetings on his own initiative. Afterward, along with the change in name, Articles XI and XV were slightly altered to eliminate the Secretary-General's power of initiative. He became more akin to the model of the British Cabinet secretary, even though having in addition internal responsibilities as the chief administrative officer of the international organization.

The limitation placed on the Secretary-General's political power was that he could summon a meeting of the Council only if he had been notified by a government of the existence of a dispute, and thereafter if he and the president of the Council considered that the dispute warranted such action, or if he had been requested to do so by a member state. He was responsible for making "all necessary arrangements for a full investigation and consideration thereof."

In his position as administrative head of the League Secretariat, no limitation was placed upon the Secretary-General. Decisions as to the type of staff, its composition and functions, were left to him. He was subject only to the limits imposed by the nature of the work, the position itself, and, of course, the budget. His authority for his actions was unquestioned.

With this constitutional framework, Sir Eric Drummond left his mark in two important respects: first, in the type of secretariat he established; and second, in his personal role both within the League and before the world. He justified the intro-

27. Egon F. Ranshofen-Wertheimer, *The International Secretariat* (Washington: Carnegie Endowment for International Peace, 1945), p. 49.

duction of the British secretariat method into the workings of the League in an article published in 1924:

> International conferences in the past had often suffered from the lack of any organized international preparatory work, and we felt that it was exactly in this domain that a new system was required if the League were to fulfill the purposes for which it had been founded. It seemed to us that it would be of great value if an expert and impartial organization existed which, before discussion by the national representatives took place, could draw up objective statements of the problems to be discussed, and indicate those points on which it seemed that the Governments were generally in accord. If this could be done, we held that discussion by the Government representatives would be automatically limited to matters where divergence of view really existed—and all who have had experience of international affairs know how much this increases the chances of reaching a definite and successful result. Further, we maintained that the execution of decisions should be entrusted to people who, being the servants of all the States Members of the League, could be relied upon to carry them out with complete freedom from national bias. [28]

Drummond's ideas were adopted, and he successfully created the first truly international civil service, based upon the principle of loyalty to the organization rather than to the country of national origin. [29] As a former member of the League Secretariat observed, he "ensured the Secretary-General of the League becoming a new and unprecedented institution in the history of the world." [30] The testimony of the first Secretary-General of the United Nations also paid tribute to this innovation: "His decision to create the first truly international secretariat was a decision of profound significance—surely one of the most im-

---

28. As quoted in Howard-Ellis, op. cit.

29. The material contained in the following paragraphs is paraphrased from Jordan, op. cit., pp. 6–9.

30. Howard-Ellis, op. cit., p. 172. The International Institute of Agriculture, with headquarters in Rome, in theory had an international civil service prior to the League of Nations, but in practice the staff was entirely Italian because the salaries were too low to attract other nationalities.

portant and promising political developments of the twentieth century. His place in history is secure."[31]

As a public international figure, the Secretary-General's place in history is less secure. He did not enter the debates of the Leagure organs unless it was absolutely necessary, and these occasions usually concerned personnel or budgetary matters. He did not utilize his annual report either to dramatize his own role or to forward his own views. The annual reports, however, according to a Chatham House Study Group headed by Drummond "provided the text of the chief debates in each body, and furnished delegates with all the material they required for the discussion of past and future policy."[32]

Drummond did not regard himself as an independent innovator in the political workings of the League. He was an organizer and administrator; at most, a negotiator and mediator. Having been a member of the Foreign Office and also private secretary to Lord Balfour, he was not lacking in any experience as a minute-writer. He knew full well what the secretariat system was in his own government, and was fully aware of the work of Lord Hankey. These factors undoubtedly played a part in his success as Secretary-General, which was described by one of his former personal assistants when speculating upon the first Secretary-General of the United Nations: "The new international institution will be fortunate if it secures the services of one who was as gifted a moderator, as impartial a negotiator, as trusted and well-informed a political confessor ... as Sir Eric Drummond."[33] Drummond himself has commented: "Behind-the-scenes activities suited my temperament and previous experience. I was neither a Parliamentarian nor a

31. Trygve Lie, *In the Cause of Peace* (New York: The Macmillan Co., 1954), p. 41.

32. *The International Secretariat of the Future* (London: Royal Institute of International Affairs, 1944), p. 8.

33. J. V. Wilson, "Problems of an International Secretariat," *International Affairs* (1944), Vol. XX, as quoted in Stephen M. Schwebel, *The Secretary-General of the United Nations* (Cambridge: Harvard University Press, 1952), pp. 6–7.

politician and totally unaccustomed to making speeches in public. . . ."[34]

In summary, it can be said with considerable grounds for support, that Sir Eric Drummond, as the first Secretary-General of the League of Nations, created a new kind of international machinery by which the affairs of states could be carried on, modeled on the precedent of his compatriot, Lord Hankey. Since then, this form of international administration has been incorporated, or transformed, to meet the requirements of the proliferating activities being undertaken by new multinational forms of organization. In this respect, Lord Hankey's precedent has affected and will continue to affect the development of the international system.

34. Quoted in Schwebel, ibid., p. 7. For a recent account of Drummond's successor as Secretary-General, see James Barros, *Betrayal From Within* (New Haven: Yale University Press, 1969).

2

The Evolving Concept
of the International Civil Service

ROBERT RHODES JAMES

Man is perhaps less capable as an innovator than he would wish
to believe. What are often regarded as dramatic novelties, advances, and innovations have a habit of being, on close inspec-
tion, progressions from previous arrangements or the often unappreciated results of manifold experiences. The wise dictum
of the late H. A. L. Fisher that there is nothing inevitable about
progress, and that one generation can swiftly negative the advances of its predecessor, is essentially valid. Nonetheless,
there are instances when there is a definite and clear continuity and progression of thought and experience; the fact that
these instances are rare and the progression is usually ragged
and unstructured does not mortally affect the main point.

Historians frequently miss what is an essentially simple point.
It may be subsequently convenient to divide history into eras,
periods, and stages, and to consider this event or that a "turn-
ing-point" or a "watershed"; there is a temptation—alas, too
often succumbed to—to add something to the effect that "nothing was ever the same again." Such divisions are frequently
necessary, but the men and women involved in these eras,
periods, and stages do not conveniently perish at the allotted
moment. Fifty years is a very long period in very modern history; it is a good deal shorter than the average life-span in a

modern developed country. The experiences of one generation move silently into another. "Turning-points" and "watersheds" pass by; the principals in the historical process remain.

These points are important to emphasize whenever the histories of the League of Nations and the United Nations are considered, and particularly in the case of the evolution of the concept of the international civil service. It was accordingly appropriate for Professor Herbert Nicholas to draw attention to the overwhelming impression of "the derivative, the second-hand" at San Francisco in 1945, and to emphasize that, despite the impression of novelty, the participants were in effect making a second attempt to create an international framework for peace and security.[1] Thus, although the League of Nations was being thankfully buried, one of the striking features of San Francisco Conference establishing the UN was the fact that many of the League's principal features were being carefully copied in the UN Charter. Of these, one of the most significant was the establishment of the Secretariat under Chapter XV (Articles 97-101). It is true that, although the UN Secretariat was the offspring of the League Secretariat, it differed in significant respects, which, in the main, reflected the changed concepts of the role of the Secretary-General in the two bodies. In particular, Articles 98 and 99 endowed the UN Secretary-General with a political role which had been absent both in the League Covenant itself, and particularly in the manner in which his functions were interpreted by the first Secretary-General, Sir Eric Drummond. Another difference has been well expressed by a member of the UN Secretariat, writing under a pseudonym:

> Whereas the essential quality of the League Secretariat might well be regarded as neutrality between the policies of its members, the international character of the United Nations Secre-

---

1. Herbert Nicholas, *The United Nations as a Political Institution*, 3rd ed. (New York: Oxford University Press, 1967), p. 8.

tariat must depend in large measure on its positive commitment to the Purposes and Principles which govern the Organisation itself.[2]

Nonetheless, despite several significant differences between the League and the UN, the important similarity was the preservation and re-establishment of the concept of an international civil service—and it was this concept that had been largely created by the League.

THE NOVELTY OF THE CONCEPT OF
AN INTERNATIONAL CIVIL SERVICE

The first point that requires emphasis was the essential novelty of this concept. When the League of Nations was in its birth-pangs, the post of Secretary-General was first offered to Sir Maurice Hankey. Hankey is one of the most celebrated modern administrators, and the story of how he was originally appointed to assist the Committee of Imperial Defense and then developed into the first secretary of the Cabinet affords one of those instances when a man discovers by chance where his talents truly lie.[3] The creation of the Cabinet secretariat in December 1916 is usually credited to Lloyd George. It was in practical fact the creation of Hankey, and when he came to Paris for the Peace Conference in 1919 he brought with him a very substantial British reputation. His unobtrusive professionalism at Versailles brought his name to the attention of all the delegations and their leaders. Hankey was a soldier, not a trained civil servant, and for most of his career in Downing Street he had been virtually a one-man department. With no precedents to guide him,

2. Charles Winchmore (pseud.), "The Secretariat: Retrospect and Prospect," in N. J. Padelford and L. M. Goodrich (eds.), *The United Nations in the Balance* (New York: Frederick A. Praeger, 1965), p. 264.

3. See Hankey's own account in *The Supreme Command, 1914–18* (London: George Allen and Unwin, 1961), and Volume I of Stephen Roskill's biography, *Hankey, Man of Secrets* (London: Collins, 1970).

he created them. Order emerged from chaos, organization from disorganization. The Cabinet, for the first time in its history had an agenda and minutes. Ministers charged with duties by the Cabinet found themselves under courteous but firm pressure to undertake those duties. Professional method replaced slapdash traditionalist muddling through. Ministers were amazed by this transformation, and Hankey was lavishly praised and rewarded. In bestowing these accolades few seem to have pondered the fact that all Hankey had done was to apply basic commonsense methods of work, long practiced elsewhere, to the proceedings of the Cabinet.

If Hankey had become the League's first Secretary-General he would have appointed nine national secretaries, one from each Council state, with their own staffs, and the League organization would have been based upon traditional concepts of national delegations to international conferences. There can be little doubt that this approach would have given the League Secretariat an entirely different shape from that which it in fact took. As Professor Inis Claude has commented:

> In a very significant sense, the identity of every organisation . . . is lodged in its professional staff. Members, stockholders, or citizens may control the organisation, but they cannot be it; the staff is the organisation.[4]

As it happened, the post of Secretary-General fell upon Sir Eric Drummond,[5] whose concept of the secretariat was both revolutionary and traditional. It was revolutionary in that it envisaged the establishment of a truly international body, responsible solely to the League. It was traditional in that Drummond saw the function of the secretariat in terms of British

4. Inis Claude, *Swords into Plowshares*, 3rd ed. (New York: Random House, 1964), p. 174.
5. It was perhaps a fortunate escape; Hankey wrote to Lord Halifax in 1940 that he had "never believed in either the League or Collective Security" (Roskill, op. cit., 276).

concepts of the role of the civil servant; the keystone of this edifice was efficient and unobtrusive administration.

Here we may see the significance of continuity, and the limited nature of Drummond's innovation. To a British civil servant, owing allegiance to no political party, appointed and promoted on merit alone, and the servant of a complex and well-ordered political-administrative system, the transference of that allegiance to an international body provided few traumatic changes of attitude. It was highly significant—then and later—that British officials found little real difficulty in the change from national to international administration within the framework established by Drummond. As the historian of the League has written:

> It was Drummond's deliberate policy to keep himself and the Secretariat as much as possible in the background. . . . His conduct was inspired by the traditions of the British Civil Service: by his own sense of constitutional propriety: and by a certain tendency to avoid responsibility and to mistrust enthusiasm.[6]

The extent to which the character of the Secretary-General affects the character of an organization may also be seen in the parallel work at the ILO by Albert Thomas. Here Thomas's concept of his role as providing articulate and dynamic leadership and influence was the paramount characteristic. "The Office," Thomas declared, "must be an instrument of action, not just a machine for collecting and sifting information." As E. J. Phelan has written in his delightful and penetrating *Yes and Albert Thomas,* "Albert Thomas was, indeed, much more to the International Labour Office than its successful manager. He came, in fact, to be identified with it to a degree which

---

6. F. P. Walters, *A History of the League of Nations* (London: Oxford University Press, 1952), p. 559.

made it difficult for many people to distinguish between the institution and its Director."[7]

Although it is a temptation to which many commentators have succumbed, it would be inaccurate to push the contrast between Thomas and Drummond too far. Drummond recruited some of the most able young men in Europe for the Secretariat, including Jean Monnet, Arthur Salter, and Pierre Mantoux, none of whom could be described as fearful of responsibility or lacking in dynamism. But the character of the League Secretariat was very much a reflection of Drummond's own character and background. Although it has been claimed that the League Secretariat was "from a technical standpoint at least, one of the most efficient administrations the world has ever known,"[8] the word "technical" should perhaps be emphasized. As the Committee of Thirteen emphasized in 1930, "the Secretariat does not initiate policy. It is purely an executive body," and Dr. Wilfred Jenks has commented with justice that:

> No officers of the League had an acknowledged continuing responsibility for shaping the policy of the League as a whole and for defending that policy both before the Council and Assembly of the League and before the public opinion of the whole world.[9]

From the point of view of the history of the UN Secretariat, the League's prime contribution had been the establishment, together with the ILO, of the fact that a truly international civil service could be created and could work reasonably efficiently, and went some way to contradict—although experience did not fully refute—the opinion of Lord Milner that "for all purposes of action . . . administrative internationalism may be said to lead towards the creation of administrative impotence." The

7. E. J. Phelan, *Yes and Albert Thomas* (London: Cresset Press, 1936), pp. ix–x.

8. E. Ranshofen-Wertheimer, *The International Secretariat* (Washington: Carnegie Endowment for International Peace, 1945), p. 39.

9. Wilfred Jenks, "Some Problems of an International Civil Service," *Public Administration Review* (Spring 1943), Vol. III, No. 2, p. 94.

League Secretariat, with that of the ILO, learned—although it did not solve—all the basic lessons of the international civil service, even though it was spared many of the problems, notably the size and linguistic difficulties, that subsequently assailed the UN Secretariat. Of those lessons, perhaps the most important was that well expressed by "Charles Winchmore" (pseudonym):

> In many respects the relationships within an international secretariat are diplomatic rather than administrative—diplomatic in that co-operation depends rather on persistent recourse to the arts of persuasion than on continuous exercise of the power of command.[10]

The classic view of the function of the international civil servant was put forward by Dr. Jenks in an article in 1943:

> It is no part of the duty of an international official to protect in advance the interest of his country of origin; that is the duty of the responsible representatives of that country on policy-making bodies, and of its permanent representatives accredited to the international institutions in question.[11]

It is worth emphasizing again that this concept had been almost unknown—and was certainly untried—in 1919, and yet was widely accepted by the time that the UN Charter was in course of preparation. It is also worth emphasizing again that what had happened was the transference to an international environment of an essentially British concept of the disinterested official. The concept itself was not uniquely British, but by its obvious success in a national sphere it prompted respect and emulation. In the League it cast its influence over many new officials; in the cases of many others, however, the concept was alien, incomprehensible, and mistrusted. The latter failure was less appreciated and emphasized in the preliminary discussions concerning the new world organization, and attention

10. Winchmore, op. cit., p. 260.
11. Jenks, op. cit., pp. 95–96.

was given to the more positive and hopeful aspects of the League experience. There was thus a subtle but powerful connection of thought between the Northcote-Trevelyan reforms of the 1860s—on which the modern British civil service is based—and the preparatory work on the UN in the 1940s.

CHARACTERISTICS OF THE LIFE OF AN INTERNATIONAL CIVIL SERVANT

The remnants of the League Secretariat played an important part in the formation of the new international agencies created toward the end of the war and, as Walters has written, "The last dying exertions of the League thus merged almost imperceptibly in the prehistory of the United Nations."[12]

We may, at this point, look a little more at the peculiar difficulties and features of this new personality, the international civil servant, that emerged in the years between the wars, and whose principal features remain. In the first place, there was no tradition to follow, no books to study, no degree to take, no training to be undergone, no corpus of experience on which to rely. The individual brought with him his own particular experience and national attitudes to the work of the civil service, and he was then thrown into contact with men of other nationalities, other experiences, and other attitudes.

Then, he found that he had cut himself off from the country and organization from whence he came. His fortunes were tied to those of the organization he had joined, and the act of becoming "international" had deprived him of the sense of national identity which had hitherto been the principal mainspring of public service. This "institutional loneliness," as Claude has described it—and which was considerably increased by the hostile atmosphere toward the League in Geneva —was a very real psychological and practical factor, which even now affects the decisions of individuals in the UN.

The international official found that he served no govern-

12. Walters, op. cit., p. 810.

ment, and no ministers. This vital feature of the national apparatus of government was lacking. In international organizations
such as the League and the UN there is, in a sense, a parliament
and there are departments; but there is no prime minister or
president, no cabinet, and no ministers. The international civil
servant is accordingly in a sphere of official activity that bears
no relation to any national governmental organization. He serves
an organization which services an international grouping,
and one moreover that has no executive powers—or at least
powers so limited that they can hardly be described in such
political terms.

The international civil servant, in short, found himself in an
entirely novel environment. The problems that arise from these
facts cause difficulty enough today, and we can appreciate the
achievement of Drummond and his organization better when
we take note of their complete novelty in the early years of the
League. To quote Dr. Jenks again:

> There is a legend still current among some of those, chiefly aca-
> demic thinkers, who pride themselves upon the "realism" of
> their political thought, that international public servants are
> apt to be ideologues with little grasp of practical reality. Those
> who have worked most closely with the international public
> service of the last fifty years will be the first to reject, and the
> most emphatic in rejecting, the legend. Constant exposure to the
> passions and pettiness of mankind, to craft, guile, greed, ig-
> norance and fear, no less than to broad visions and generous
> impulse, has made of us a sour breed of men, pragmatic and
> cautious rather than expansive and infectious in our enthu-
> siasms, and accustomed to appraise every proposal for a bold
> new initiative by its probable acceptance by a calculating
> world.[13]

But it should also be emphasized that this dominant concept
was very much a "Western" one. The League was essentially a
European organization, and the Secretariat—which never
totaled much more than 700 persons—was predominantly

13. Wilfred Jenks, *The World Beyond the Charter* (London: Allen &
Unwin, 1969), p. 16.

European. It was not possible to superimpose this concept upon the new organization *in toto,* and although the UN was in its inception like the League a Western organization in spirit and form, it was already apparent that the very enlarged size and scope of the UN had to affect the character and functions of the Secretariat. The Charter fully endorsed the concept of a truly international civil servant, but the declaration that "due regard shall be paid to the importance of recruiting the staff on as wide a geographical basis as possible,"[14] was a warning of trouble to come, as well as an indication of one of the essential differences between the League and the UN.

The members of the League Secretariat had also faced other problems which have become only too familiar to their successors in the United Nations. As early as 1921, a delegate from India criticized the predominance of certain nationalities in the Secretariat, and proposed a quota system. Although no action was taken, the pressures in this direction began to increase. Mr. Chester Purves has commented, with truth and with ardent feeling, that: "Recruitment is the most difficult, as it is the most important, of the functions falling to the internal administration of an international authority,"[15] and he has spelled out some of those difficulties:

> The level of administrative ability, tradition and experience varies enormously in the different countries, and sections were naturally eager to obtain recruits only from those with the highest standards, both academic and administrative. To have given way to this demand would have meant confining recruitment to a comparatively small number of countries. . . . Sections had therefore to be compelled to receive recruits from other countries; sometimes the result was an agreeable surprise, but more often an embarrassing situation arose from the difficulty of finding work commensurate in responsibility with the unwanted official's rank. . . .

14. UN Charter, Article 101.
15. Chester Purves, *The Internal Administration of an International Secretariat* (London: Royal Institute of International Affairs, 1945), p. 23.

> There were States who could not reasonably be expected to produce candidates suitable for appointment to the international civil service. . . . Other States, among them some of the most popular and important, were unable to bring forward a sufficient number of qualified recruits to fill the quota that would normally have been reserved to them. The men and women whom the Secretariat would have gladly welcomed could not be spared from the meagre cadres of the national administrations. . . .
>
> The importunities of delegates were an added complication. Some exploited their countries' national claims to try to impose upon the Secretary-General recruits of their own choice, even of their own family. Some haggled over details, such as the commencing salaries and promotion of their compatriots.[16]

Then, there were the problems of political pressures—sometimes subtle, often not—brought to bear upon international officials. These sometimes were external, but on other occasions came directly from the official's own government. As the international situation gradually deteriorated after 1932, these pressures sometimes assumed very formidable proportions, and in the conflict-of-loyalty dilemmas that arose many officials bowed to national rather than international obligations. The "pure" concept of the truly international civil servant had been, accordingly, considerably eroded long before the outbreak of World War II. It was not really assisted by Drummond himself, who, on retirement from the League, became British ambassador in Rome.

THE INTERNATIONAL CIVIL SERVICE
OF THE UNITED NATIONS

The essential reason why the UN Preparatory Commission declared that "the degree in which the objects of the Charter can be realised will be largely determined by the manner in which the Secretariat performs its task" was to endorse the

16. Ibid., pp. 23–26.

view expressed by Smuts in 1918, that the League's "peace activity must be the foundation and guarantee of its war power." The UN Secretary-General was to be a more actively political figure than his League predecessor; accordingly, his Secretariat had to be equipped appropriately to fulfill his expanded role. The theory was admirable—a dedicated group of international officials responsible only to the international community, recruited on as wide a geographical basis as possible yet with ability, with the foremost consideration being to serve mankind. It was not long before the reality began to cast a heavy shadow over this ideal.

The first setback was the speed with which staff had to be recruited in 1946. In 1946 alone, 2900 appointments were made, and it is reasonable to question whether it was really necessary to act with such precipitateness. The League experience is not comparable, but the slow build-up of the Secretariat from 182 in 1920 up to 451 in 1925 was, in principle, a more sensible course. In the first flurry, some excellent appointments were made; others were less admirable.[17] Then, some member states either refused to permit their nationals to join the Secretariat at all, or only on a short-term basis. Others went to some trouble to ensure that their most able officials were not recruited, and few could be wholly exonerated of the charge of having "dumped" unwanted officials on the United Nations—then and later. Partly because of shortage of time, but principally for practical reasons, the vast majority (some 86 per cent) of the Secretariat was recruited from Western Europe and North America, thus creating an imbalance which has not yet been fully corrected.

To the problems of adjustment to the life of an international civil servant, with which the League and ILO veterans were familiar, others were now added. Until 1952, the UN had no permanent headquarters, and the uncertainties and incon-

17. For a fair criticism, see Walter R. Crocker, "Some Notes on the United Nations Secretariat," *International Organization* (November 1950).

veniences this caused had their effects. In addition, the Charter had barely been ratified before the first icy winds of the Cold War began to blow. Throughout this period, although the first Secretary-General had his good qualities, his relations with the Secretariat were mixed, and reached a melancholy nadir in 1951–52 when, in the McCarthyite era, the issue of the status of American nationals in the Secretariat, and Lie's handling of the matter, brought him into sharp conflict with many members of the Secretariat.

The issue that faced Lie was particularly sensitive in that it involved not only the question of national and international loyalties but also the relationship between the United Nations and a host country. Regarded now, in cool hindsight, it is possible to appreciate Lie's dilemma in the heated circumstances of the time, with American suspicions about Communist infiltration into significant positions approaching a national paranoia. At the time, however, many Secretariat members were dismayed by what appeared to them to be an unheroic abandonment of the concept that an international civil servant's duty lies solely to his organization. Taken by itself, it is possible that Secretariat hostility to Lie over this matter might have been insignificant; but the episode came after a number of incidents which had aroused substantial dislike of the Secretary-General in the Secretariat. The episode also emphasized the fact that the initial period of relative tranquility which the League had enjoyed had not been vouchsafed to the UN and its first Secretary-General.

What, in retrospect, seems so remarkable was that the essential concept was still firmly adhered to, and that the Secretariat emerged at all from the first traumatic six years. The principal cause for this lay in the quality, and idealism, of some of the men and women recruited so hurriedly in 1946, and who had demonstrated their ability in this very difficult period. It was also becoming evident that the economic and social activities of the UN were assuming an importance that had not been fully anticipated. Furthermore, even in the political field, certain solid achievements could be legitimately recorded, of which the most celebrated was the mediation of Dr. Ralph Bunche in the Middle East, an episode which demonstrated the effectiveness of a man who commanded respect as a genuine international civil servant serving the international community. The concept survived, therefore, because it appeared that it had worked during a period of exceptional international tension. This was Dag Hammarskjöld's inheritance.

Hammarskjöld remains, even now, a highly enigmatic and controversial figure, whose complex personality has not yet been adequately explored and analyzed. He was responsible for some of the most striking descriptions of the pure concept of the international civil servant, yet he was basically uninterested in the Secretariat. On the subject of geographical distribution, for example, the trumpet often gave out a somewhat uncertain note, as in his Annual Report of 1960/61:

> There is no contradiction at all between a demand for a truly international secretariat and a demand found in the Charter itself for as wide a "geographical" distribution of posts within the Secretariat as possible. It is, indeed, necessary precisely in order to maintain the exclusively international character of the Secretariat that it be so composed as to achieve a balanced distribution of posts on all levels among all regions.

After his death, his period as Secretary-General tended to be elevated into a kind of UN golden age, and his statements virtually canonized. The reality was somewhat different.

Nevertheless, Hammarskjöld's reiterated faith in the pure concept had its influence. In particular, his resolute stand against Soviet pressures in 1960–61 earned him the admiration and gratitude of the Secretariat. These pressures went far beyond the proposal for the "Troika"; they concerned the entire status and independence of the Secretariat. That status and independence were already being eroded, but acquiescence to the Khrushchev proposals would have destroyed them utterly. Hammarskjöld was himself an intense admirer of the British civil service, and his own background and training fortified that faith. He can now be seen as the last major UN figure who was prepared to hazard his own position on a fundamental matter of principle. No one, before or since, has defended the concept of the international civil servant so articulately or so memorably. There are many examples, of which perhaps one may be taken from his last speech to the Secretariat, on September 8, 1961:

> What is at stake is a basic question of principle: is the Secretariat to develop as an international secretariat, with the full independence contemplated in Article 100 of the Charter, or is it to be looked upon as an inter-governmental—not international—secretariat, providing merely the necessary administrative services for a conference machinery? This is a basic question, and the answer to it affects not only the working of the Secretariat but the whole of the future of international relations.

The irony of the situation lay in the fact that the concept in practice was remorselessly disintegrating. The rapid expansion of the membership of the UN was in itself leading to increasing pressure by the new members for "equitable geographical distribution" in the Secretariat, a demand that was to become the dominant obsession of the Fifth Committee in the 1960s.

As has already been mentioned, the specter of this movement had been apparent in the League at an early stage. It had many sources and motives. One of these—that a genuinely international organization should have a genuinely international secretariat—may be accepted at once as being entirely justified. Unhappily, other motives were less worthy. The gradual establishment of a quota system and the delineation of posts "subject to requirements of geographical distribution" was one of the most marked features of the Secretariat in the 1950s and 1960s. The warning of Hammarskjöld that multinationalism is not synonymous with internationalism was unheeded, and the pressures on the Secretary-General became overwhelming. It was here that Hammarskjöld can be seriously faulted. The public statements were firm and clear; the practice was not as impressive. The erosion of the standards of the Secretariat, which became a matter of real concern in the late 1960s, originated under Hammarskjöld.

The transformation in geographical distribution which in turn reflects the question of competency was, in total numbers, very remarkable, and can perhaps be best demonstrated in tabular form:

	1948 (per cent)	1962 (per cent)	1968 (per cent)	Increase/ Decrease from 1948 to 1968 (per cent)
Africa	1.7	5.7	10.5	+ 8.8
Asia & Far East	11.3	15.6	16.1	+ 4.8
Eastern Europe	7.0	10.1	12.3	+ 5.3
Western Europe	31.3	25.6	23.3	− 8.0
Latin America	7.9	8.6	9.1	+ 1.2
Middle East	1.8	3.6	4.2	+ 2.4
North America	37.4	28.3	22.5	−14.9
Non-member States	1.6	2.5	2.0	+ .4

In this case, however—as in most—figures do not tell the full story.

The new members, despite their enthusiasm to have their nationals in the Secretariat, had their problems. Many had wholly inadequate human resources to man their own civil services, let alone to permit any of the small number of qualified personnel to go to the United Nations.[18] Several followed the Russian practice of only sending able officials on fixed-term contracts; many filled their national quotas, on which they vehemently insisted, with second-rate officials. Thus, the proportion of fixed-term to permanent appointments steadily rose,

18. There were, of course, some exceptions. One new member sent one of its only two qualified statisticians to the UN. The other was his wife, who accompanied her husband to New York.

until by 1970 it was of the order of 35 per cent to 65 per cent. [19] At the same time, the overall quality of the Secretariat declined equally steadily. It is seldom that cause and effect are so closely, and so clearly, apparent.

The conflict-of-loyalty problem, always present, was also increasing. It was particularly here that the internationalist concept had proved wanting in the League, and the same experience has befallen the United Nations. There are many areas of Secretariat activity, notably on the economic and social side, where such conflicts do not arise, but it is in the crucial area of political advice that they are dominant. It is here that the "pure" concept was quickly shown to be unrealistic. This is not to say that the new situation was wholly unfortunate, and there are those who argue that in fact it was a distinct improvement. The fact that certain key officials in the Secretariat were known to be closely connected with their national governments was, it is argued, a positive asset to a Secretary-General. Thus, if he wished to know the attitudes of such governments, all he had to do was to raise the matter with the appropriate member of his staff. This is going a very long way from the original concept, but, it is also argued, this demonstrates how unrealistic the original concept was. A group of independent international civil servants can quickly get out of touch with national political realities; the seconded official cannot. The resultant advice may not be disinterested, but it will at least be realistic.

It must be conceded at once that these arguments have considerable validity. They become dangerous if they are permitted to be taken too far, to the point where the Secretary-General does not have at his disposal at least some advice that is genuinely disinterested. It is also important that the Secretariat

19. In 1969, 91.9 per cent of the Eastern European members of the Secretariat were on fixed-term contracts; the proportion for Africans was 52.1 per cent.

should be a recipient of confidential information. National governments are unlikely to confide in Secretariat members if they believe that their comments are going to be transmitted clandestinely to other governments. If such a situation exists, the quality of the information available to the Secretary-General is bound to decline. The balance, accordingly, between avowed national representation and genuine internationalism is a very fine one, and a very important one. The UN experience has emphasized, again and again, the supreme difficulty of achieving this balance.

The erosion of the original concept was also being accelerated by serious weaknesses within the UN. It is only relatively recently that there has been a general recognition of the fact that personnel selection, promotion, and career management are highly professional matters, of crucial importance to the efficient development of an organization; it is doubtful whether this recognition has reached the UN even now. In addition to the political and other pressures acting against the improvement of Secretariat quality and efficiency, these internal structural defects assumed very substantial significance. It is no more than the truth to say that the UN has proved itself seriously deficient in the areas of staff recruitment, training, and career development.

From the very beginning, standards have been uneven, and the mounting pressure for "equitable geographical distribution" has plainly reduced them further. Political pressures are not the only cause, although they constitute the principal one. In a competitive market for talent, the United Nations must compete actively in terms of salaries, career prospects, and conditions of service. The International Civil Service Advisory Board recommended in 1949 that "the greatest need in recruitment for an international organisation is to develop an effective programme of positive research for the kinds of persons needed for international civil service." Unhappily, as with many other wise comments in that report, action did not follow the thought. Particularly in developed countries, the UN has not competed effectively, with the result that, in the main, the organization has not done as well as it ought to have done—and could have done—in these countries. There have, of course, been exceptions, but these have been the result less of calculation and skill than of good fortune.

So far as training is concerned, the UN record can only be described as dismal. "In-service training," the International Civil Service Advisory Board intoned in 1952, "properly conceived and controlled in the interests of the organisation, is an essential part of good management."[20] It is indeed, yet by 1970 only the first faltering steps had been taken toward this goal, with consequences that have been lamentable for the efficiency, effectiveness, and morale of the Secretariat.

In these circumstances, the question must be asked as to whether secondment and short-term contracts do not, after all, constitute the answer. At first glance, the attractions may seem considerable, particularly in highly technical areas, although this goes against the spirit and the letter of the UN Preparatory Commission and the Charter itself. It is perhaps significant that the most detailed attacks on the perils of a career service in the UN have come from Soviet and East European representatives, yet there are some points which are valid. Total security of tenure has its dangers, not least of which are complacency, lack of exertion, and immobility in senior positions. Certainly, the stagnation at the top of the Secretariat is highly discouraging for possible recruits, and there are many examples which underline the dangers that are involved in a fully secure career service.

It is at this point that the perils of generalization arise again. If it can be argued that a career service breeds complacency, it can also be pointed out that security can enable an official to take an independent line without fear of his contract not

20. ICSAB Report on In-Service Training in the United Nations and the Specialized Agencies, 1952, par. 36.

being renewed. The short-term official may be under heavier pressure to work harder, but is a sense of impermanence really conducive to good work? All that can be said is that the UN experience tends to demonstrate that the disadvantages of job security are more than compensated for by the advantages.

In any event, there is a real difference between the seconded official from a national government service, and an independently recruited short-service Secretariat member, particularly since the conflict-of-loyalty issue is usually less evident in the latter category. And it may also be emphasized that although seconded officials may be, as a group, more able than permanent Secretariat members, ability is not everything in an international organization if it has to be purchased at the price of total loyalty to the organization itself.

The UN Secretariat has gradually, and painfully, evolved a series of compromises with the original concept of a largely international career civil service. The dilemma is whether these compromises have not merely undermined the original concept—which was, in any event, a highly limited one—but have undermined the efficiency and value of the Secretariat to the point where it is not capable of fulfilling its tasks. The conclusion of this observer is that this nadir is perilously close, for the reasons which have been described in this chapter.

Another reason must be emphasized again, and frankly stated. The UN has never had a Secretary-General—even Hammarskjöld—who took a deep and informed interest in the Secretariat. Many failures that can be ascribed to the Office of Personnel should in reality be placed at the door of successive Secretaries-General. Some of the Specialized Agencies, and the United Nations Development Program, have fared much better, and here the influence of individuals who have devoted attention to the subject can be clearly seen. It is not really a question of theoretical concepts; it is a matter of seeking, securing, and hopefully retaining, men and women of high caliber.

It is exactly in this area that absence of leadership from the top has had such unhappy results.

Concepts cannot be static. From the starting-point of Drummond's British experience, the international civil service has evolved considerably. In some respects the changes have been good, and the results admirable; the evolution of the system of UN resident representatives may be particularly cited. Nonetheless, the evolution taken as a whole tends to justify the warning of H. A. L. Fisher, quoted at the beginning of this chapter.

The ideal conception of the international civil service was excellently described by Raymond Fosdick more than forty years ago when the League was in embryo:

> [The Secretariat] is the eyes and the ears of the League—the branch that never adjourns and that is always in session. . . . Its attitude is, and of necessity must be, wholly impersonal. Its members must be divorced from their allegiance to their respective governments. They serve only the League. . . . Of course, the Secretariat will be successful only as it commands the services of the ablest minds available, regardless of nationality. [21]

It cannot be denied that the United Nations' experience has been a very mixed one. In several of the "operational" areas— and the UN Development Program is a case in point—the concept has been substantially retained, although it is conspicuous that the rules of geographical distribution do not apply in the most successful areas. In the main—and a strong qualification must be inserted—the original "functionalist" concept of international cooperation has worked, albeit in limited areas; it is also true that an entirely novel personality, the genuine "international man," has come into being. Nonetheless, when the whole picture is examined dispassionately, the observer is

---

21. Raymond Fosdick, *Letters on the League of Nations* (Princeton: Princeton University Press, 1966), p. 23.

more struck by how considerably the original conception has been eroded.

We must accordingly return to the question of whether the concept itself was ever practicable. Certainly, experience has shown that the career of international civil service is unattractive for many highly able people; thus, if the United Nations is to attract men of such caliber, it must face the fact that many of them will stay for only relatively brief periods. This fact in itself harms the "pure concept" very severely. Then, the original concept was not only very "Western," it also contained a strong element of the British belief in the career generalist, on which the highly professional home and foreign British services are essentially based. The UN experience has tended to emphasize the importance of the professional expert rather than the generalist, with the result that the concept of a unified and planned career structure on the British pattern has not evolved. There are, furthermore, some indications that the British themselves are having doubts about the value of the generalist in modern circumstances—doubts which may result in a shift of emphasis toward the system that the UN has evolved, principally because it had no other choice.

Systems, of course, are one thing and people are another. The UN experience has been depressing less because a concept has proved largely impracticable than because the organization has in the main failed to attract and to retain men and women of the ability which the organization desperately requires if it is to survive. The UN Capacity Study of Sir Robert Jackson has emphasized this crucial aspect so far as the United Nations Development Program is concerned; it is equally crucial throughout the UN system. There is, unhappily, much truth in the comment of one of the Secretariat's most shrewd critics:

> The nature . . . of the Organization was such as to attract people of character; having attracted them, it found it could not afford them, that there was no room for personalities, and that its hope

for survival lay, like that of all organizations, in the subordination of individual gifts to general procedures.[22]

An international organization is a delicate and complex structure. It can only deserve to survive if its quality inspires confidence; the present indications are that the restoration of that confidence should be one of the major preoccupations of the next Secretary-General.

22. Shirley Hazzard, *People in Glass Houses* (New York: Alfred A. Knopf, 1967).

3

The Legacy of British
and French Colonial Rule

DAVID J. MURRAY and JOHN BALLARD

In much of Africa, international and other aid administrators have come to work in countries that were formerly British and French colonies, and the purpose of this chapter is to consider what the relevance of the administrative experience gained by the British and French is for foreign and international aid agencies. The chapter discusses first whether the experiences of colonial Powers and of international agencies makes that of the former in any way relevant to the latter; it then goes on to suggest certain aspects of the colonial experience which do have a continuing importance.

THE DIFFERENCES BETWEEN COLONIAL
AND INTERNATIONAL ADMINISTRATION

The administration conducted by colonial Powers in Africa was in many critical respects different from that undertaken by international agencies, and in a paper considering the wider relevance of the experience gained by these colonial Powers in administering colonies overseas, it is important first to stress these differences. In whatever way these colonial Powers had secured their control over territorial areas—whether by conquest or annexation, under a protectorate agreement, or under

74

mandated authority from the League of Nations—theirs was an occupation of overseas territory.

As occupiers, Britain and France, as well as other colonial Powers, acted on the conviction that they possessed an exclusive legal authority in their territories. Britain and France were sovereign Powers: they possessed an overriding authority to make law and to enforce it. The British Crown, for example, passed legislation for the colonies, legislative councils in the different territories derived their legal authority from the Crown and established laws for their particular territory, and the local customary law that continued to be applied in local courts derived its legal validity from its recognition by the colonial government. The colonial Powers were able, in other words, to establish a framework of law within which subject peoples were to act.

The colonial Powers in a similar way operated a judicial system through which they could apply the various bodies of law, and on the basis of court decisions extend and modify it. A structure of courts existed as part of the machinery of colonial government, and even where customary law was applied by native courts, their decisions were reviewed by administrative officials and superior courts who provided an important means for modifying and molding the law that was applied and enforced. Moreover, the legal authority claimed and exercised by the colonial Powers was backed by coercive power. In most of Africa the continued presence of the colonial Powers depended less on colonization by people from the metropolitan country than on the existence of effective military, police, and prison staffs. The colonial Powers always had sufficient force at their command to deal with limited outbreaks of disorder.

Beyond having the authority to make law and a coercive power to enforce it, colonial governments supplied the administrative framework for their territories—at least at the superior levels. Unlike international aid agencies which have to work alongside the national government and its established administration, the colonial governments constituted their own administration and were thus themselves the decision-makers.

Sovereign legal authority, control over the courts, the presence of troops and police, and control over the governmental administrative machine did not of course bestow on the colonial government the opportunity to exercise power in an unlimited way. Quite apart from the restrictions imposed by domestic and international public opinion, and more important the self-imposed constraints of colonial officials with a firm sense of justice, integrity, and devotion to duty, there were the practical limitations facing governments with limited resources operating in an alien environment. As Lord Hailey wrote of the legislative power in 1938:

> The chief problems of legislation in Africa still lie . . . in the provision of a law of crimes, of rules of procedure, and a simple form of procedure regulating commercial transactions, for it is common ground that at the outset anything beyond this must continue to be regulated by custom. Yet even here the law giver will have to ask himself if the law he introduces is so far alien to all the motives and associations which regulate the behaviour of the people affected as to fail to secure an instinctive respect from them. The modern conception of the function of law realizes that its process cannot be purely authoritarian; it obtains its most effective sanctions not from imposed obedience, but by evoking some answering contribution from those to whom it is applied.[1]

Hailey's argument, that a theoretically absolute power to make law was limited in practice by what acceptance and support the law would command, is given added significance when one realizes how small the colonial administration was. In Nigeria, for example, when the northern and southern halves were united into a single colony in 1914 there were only 1100 offi-

1. Lord Hailey, *An African Survey* (New York: Oxford University Press, 1938), p. 264.

cials—of all sorts, from railway officials to Secretariat officers —in an area considerably larger than modern West Germany, the Benelux countries, and France put together; and though there was a sharp increase in the civil service during the next forty years, the number of established civil service posts in 1952 (39,100) was minute compared with the 1.1 million in France, or even the 700,000 in Britain—two countries with a comparable population.[2] In practical terms this meant that there was one agricultural officer for Bornu Province, an area larger than the Netherlands. Being at the center of the governmental machine and controlling the administration put the colonial governments at an advantage as compared with latter-day aid administrators, but there were severe practical limitations on what they could do.

Similar points can be made about the limitations on the colonial governments' other powers. The period of nationalist political agitation after World War II revealed both how an effective system of courts depended on popular acceptance and how ineffectual were the limited numbers of troops and police when dissatisfaction and opposition became as widespread as it did among the Kikuyu in Kenya.

Notwithstanding these limitations on the colonial governments, their control over legislation, the courts, the instruments of force, and the whole administrative machine, placed them in a situation that was fundamentally different from that of international or foreign agencies operating in independent sovereign states. Where both were concerned with development projects each operated from a different position.

The nature of this difference is probably best brought out by considering certain specific episodes. First, take the not infrequently arising situation where foreign officials seeking to promote local development are faced with corruption, and consider the account given by Sir Bryan Sharwood Smith of

2. D. J. Murray (ed.), *Studies in Nigerian Administration* (London: Hutchinson, 1970), p. 93.

his approach as district officer at Argungu in Northern Nigeria. Determined on pushing forward a public works program in the town, he found himself confronted by an Emir, the local chief, who condoned corruption by certain followers favored by him.

> Each one of the band of favourites had his own "racket," and between them both office holders and minor officials were systematically bled until they in turn were compelled to prey upon the peasantry. . . . Drastic action was necessary. . . . A purge was the only solution, and I duly prepared a list of the ringleaders of the cabal and their principal underlings and a catalogue of their illegal activities. This I presented to the Emir at a private meeting, going on to say that if he wanted to have my co-operation in bringing progress to his emirate, then I must have full co-operation from him in cutting out the canker which was eating away all that was good in it. . . . At length, after a long silence, he sighed heavily and agreed.[3]

Many foreign aid officials would relish a position that would enable them to achieve such a radical change.

Second, to take a somewhat different example, the task of securing a slaughterhouse for the town of Ibadan in Western Nigeria has been recorded in a case study. The study shows among other things the difference in the position of the British colonial official and the American AID official in relation to the project. The British resident, as the colonial chief executive in the town, was in a position, where circumstances demanded it, to secure immediate cooperation from a variety of bodies, from the local government council to the railway corporation and a series of government ministries, and to push through an urgent decision to erect an abattoir. Ten years later after the project had first died and then been resurrected, the American AID official operated on the fringes of government, uninformed

3. Sir Bryan Sharwood Smith, *But Always as Friends: Northern Nigeria and the Cameroons 1921–1957* (Durham: Duke University Press, 1969), pp. 74–75. See also examples in Robert Heussler, *The British in Northern Nigeria* (London and New York: Oxford University Press, 1968), Chapters 5 and 6; and John Smith, *Colonial Cadet in Nigeria* (Durham: Duke University Press, 1968).

and unaware of the complexities and ramifications of the project. He worked not as a part of the machinery of government but as a separate agency with funds to dispense and the power to lay down conditions, but without any greater part in the information-gathering and decision-making processes of government.[4]

At the same time, while colonial governments had powers that do not belong to agencies operating in independent sovereign states and thus had unique opportunities, they also suffered particular disabilities. This was especially true in the period after World War II when colonial governments had to contend with anti-colonial sentiment which assumed that all government activities and policies were inspired by a colonialist motivation. Even where projects were clearly in the long-term interest of the local community, they were resisted in part because the colonial government had become wholly suspect.

One example illustrates this general point. In 1944–51 the Gold Coast government faced difficulties arising from the spread of swollen shoot disease among the cocoa plantations of the colony and in its attempt at controlling the disease by cutting out the affected trees the government came up against a deep suspicion of its true motives. Dennis Austin in his study *Politics in Ghana* reports the deep hostility to the colonial government because of that policy and quotes farmers' representations and speeches to show the general underlying distrust of the colonial government. Farmers asked, "was there, in fact, a secret motive behind government action? Did it intend the deliberate destruction of the cocoa industry, and the acquisition of land for some hidden end?"[5] And in the Ashanti Confederacy Council one member stated, "I am inclined to

4. D. J. Murray, *The Work of Administration in Nigeria* (London: Hutchinson, 1969), pp. 101–53.

5. Dennis Austin, *Politics in Ghana* (London and New York: Oxford University Press, 1964), p. 60.

infer that cocoa has been planted somewhere in Europe; otherwise Government would not persist in cutting down our cocoa trees."[6] The Gold Coast government was unable to overcome a deep-seated distrust deriving from its character as a colonial regime. As Nkrumah had expressed it:

> The colonial powers build hospitals because if the health of the colonial subjects is not taken care of it will not only jeopardise their own health but will diminish the productive power of the colonial labourer. They build schools in order to satisfy the demand for clerical activities and occupations for foreign commercial and mercantile concerns. The roads they build lead only to the mining and plantation centres. In short, any humanitarian act of any colonial power towards the "ward" is merely to enhance its primary objective: economic exploitation.[7]

In these critical respects therefore, colonial administration is to be distinguished from the sort of administrative undertakings conducted by foreign governments or international agencies in independent countries—though the latters' motives too may at times be suspect. The colonial governments exercised coercive and legal power and administrative control where foreign governments and international agencies command neither. They also suffered disabilities arising from their colonial character which international aid agencies do not suffer, at least in the same form.

SIMILARITIES BETWEEN COLONIAL AND INTERNATIONAL ADMINISTRATION

Yet within the limits of these major differences there is much to be learned from the British and French attempts at conducting administrations overseas. In spite of the number of contrasts between the administrations of the two, there are also

6. Ibid., p. 62.
7. Kwame Nkrumah, *Towards Colonial Freedom*, new ed. (London: Heinemann, 1962), p. 27.

significant similarities. First, and of overriding importance, is the fact that they had basic development objectives in common. One of the oft-recited myths about colonial rule is that it was concerned with maintaining law and order and was not interested in development—in expanding communications, improving agricultural and industrial production, and developing existing or introducing new social welfare services.

No matter what the motivations may have been, there was in fact a consistent interest in development among colonial governments. Even before World War II there was systematic spending on social and economic development services and since then, in crude budgetary terms, the proportion spent on different activities has remained relatively constant.[8]

But in some ways it is more meaningful to observe what the administrators were doing on the ground than to quote crude budgetary figures. Here, among British and French administrators there were different approaches. In all colonies there were those who saw their goal as being the preservation of what they tended to call the African way of life, and those who fatalistically believed that Africa could not be changed, but the dominant attitude was that officials had a responsibility for promoting development or, at least, that progress was desirable and should be encouraged. In practice, the majority of administrators devoted a considerable part of their time to increasing the efficiency and regularity of local administration, building roads and other public works, improving land use, promoting improved crops, and stimulating and supporting local industrial ventures. It will be recalled that it was a central concern of Rudbeck in Joyce Cary's *Mister Johnson* to push forward a road in Fada but like many others in this period of World War II—and later—he had nagging doubts about wheth-

8. As a single example, the position in Sierra Leone is described in R. Finnegan and D. Murray, "Limba Chiefs," in Michael Crowder (ed.), *West African Chiefs: Their Changing Status Under Colonial Rule and Independence* (Ile Ife: University of Ife Press, 1970), pp. 421–23.

er such development in northern Nigeria really was so desirable. Or, to take a second example, Sharwood Smith describes vividly similar road-making ventures of his own in the Cameroons and northern Nigeria between the two World Wars.

Yet the main development activity belonged to the period after World War II. Hitherto local development had been seriously hampered because funds for development had to be raised locally, but with the passage of the Colonial Development and Welfare Act of 1944 (CD&W) and the establishment of the *Fonds d'Investissement de Développement Economique et Sociale* (FIDES), the British and French governments began to make substantial contributions to development in the colonies. What this meant in the single colony of Nigeria was that, whereas the total annual revenue in the period before World War II was approximately £ 8 million, the colonial government was able to prepare a ten-year development plan in 1945 that provided for the spending of £ 55 million, £ 23 million of which was provided by Britain. The CD&W Act not only obliged the colonial governments to formulate plans, but also established social and economic development as the dominant objective. For the French colonies the planning of development was carried out on a centralized basis, but almost $700 million was spent by France in French West Africa alone between 1947 and 1956. One feature of French colonial development was its using French skills and labor very heavily rather than training Africans but, despite the fact that much development investment flowed back to France through administrative salaries and firms' profits, local production was in fact developed. [9]

Particularly, therefore, in the period after World War II colonial governments have had common objectives with international development organizations. Each has been concerned

9. For a comparison of colonial planning organizations during this period, see Barbu Niculescu, *Colonial Planning: A Comparative Study* (London: Allen and Unwin, 1958); Elliot J. Berg provides a useful comparison of the impact of postwar development in British and French West Africa in "The Economic Basis of Political Choice in French West Africa," *American Political Science Review* (1960), Vol. LIV, pp. 394–405.

with promoting economic and social development over a wide field from public works, manufacturing industry, and agriculture, to education, health, and social welfare. This common concern makes the experience of the colonial governments apposite for others.

What increases the significance of this experience is that the colonial administration had certain features which parallel those of international development agencies. Colonial administrators, like foreign aid administrators, were strangers to the society in which they worked. Many administrators learned local languages, spent their whole working lives in a single colony, and became experts on the local society, but they always remained foreigners; and in attempting to promote development, whether it was opening a new school, installing a water works, or promoting a new higher yielding crop strain, they had the disadvantages, and also the advantages, of being outsiders.

Thus, for all the differences between colonial administrators and international agency administrators, there have been two features in common: their preoccupation with development, and their position as foreigners working in a different, alien environment.

The continuing relevance of past colonial administration has been widely recognized in specialized areas. In such fields as rural development, forestry, and animal health, international aid projects have explicitly built on the prior work of colonial governments. For example, the international project for the eradication of trypanosomiasis and bovine pleuropneumonia from the savannah areas that include a large part of northern Nigeria builds on the earlier work of the Nigerian Veterinary Department in controlling, testing, and treating these diseases.[10]

A second example might be the Rural Development Program in the former eastern Nigeria. This program was operated from

10. Northern Nigeria, Veterinary Department and Veterinary Division, *Annual Reports*, 1952/53–1962/63, Kaduna.

1964 through 1967 and involved establishing cooperative community plantations in areas where there was underdeveloped land and an apparent surplus of labor, and cooperative farm settlements where there was a surfeit of underdeveloped land and a scarcity of labor. The program was drawn up and operated by the Ford Foundation acting in association with the Eastern Nigerian Ministry of Agriculture, and, in the period before the Nigerian civil war, was strikingly successful, but again it built on the earlier work of the colonial government. The Eastern Nigerian Cooperative Division had developed its experience with thrift and credit cooperatives in directing cooperative community farms, and the Ministry of Agriculture had direct experience from its ventures with capital intensive farm settlements. In addition, the program drew directly on the personal experience of former colonial administrators by involving them in the program.[11]

The basic point needs no further elaboration. Much of the specific knowledge and experience in wide areas of economic and social development in Africa was built up during the period of colonial rule, and inevitably international aid administrators in pursuing a similar goal of promoting local development have drawn on it.

Much of this knowledge and experience is particular to specialized fields and to certain areas. Understanding gained in operating a disease eradication campaign among cattle, or a soil conservation project, tends to be peculiar to these particular activities; and similarly what operates in the Kigezi district of Uganda will not necessarily apply in the Morogoro area of Tanzania—as Young and Fosbrooke show in their book *Smoke in the Hills.*[12] Different physical and social circumstances demand different approaches and remedies, and thus in Morogoro

11. The project is reported in R. Coatswith, "Establishing a Rural Development Programme in Eastern Nigeria," *Administration* (October 1968), pp. 44–58.

12. Roland Young and Henry A. Fosbrooke, *Smoke in the Hills* (Evanston: Northwestern University Press, 1960).

as elsewhere, it is essential in promoting development projects to understand the particular district and its peoples. A great deal, in other words, of the valuable knowledge and experience engendered during the period of colonial rule is relevant to specialized areas and cannot readily be expressed in terms of generalized prescriptions about the whole process of the administration of development programs.

VARIETIES OF ADMINISTRATIVE EXPERIENCE

Indeed, it is one of the more important conclusions to be drawn from past experience that the knowledge acquired both in different subject fields and in different communities is to some extent specialized. The colonial governments learned the hard way that in Africa there were no universal panaceas. What applied in one area or to one community was not necessarily appropriate in another. Indirect rule, for example, was seen as a general system of local administration which could be universally applied. It was a viable system in the emirates of northern Nigeria where it was developed, but even among the neighboring Tiv people in the Benue valley or among the peoples of eastern Nigeria it proved largely inapplicable. The image of Africa as uniform and unchanging was founded on European misconceptions; in reality there was great diversity. Administrative techniques that operated successfully among the hierarchically organized, authority-conscious people of the northern emirates in Nigeria or Ndebele in Southern Rhodesia, proved inapplicable among the egalitarian and thrustful communities of the Ibo in eastern Nigeria or the pastoral age Karamojong of Uganda; and what applied in sparsely populated rural Barotseland appeared largely irrelevant in densely populated and urbanized western Nigeria. One thing that appeared to be established by the experience of the colonial administrators was the importance of a knowledge of the area and community where development schemes were being established.

The basic point that colonial officials learned in relation

to the established peoples among whom they came to work applies also to much of the administrative superstructure which was created during the period of colonial rule. Much of the central public administration in African countries bears the imprint of the former colonial governments which is easily regarded as being both essentially foreign and something common to the different colonies belonging to one or other of the colonial powers. The administration in English-speaking Africa seems strikingly English, particularly to those who are not English, and appears much the same whether the country be Uganda or Sierra Leone. The same phenomenon occurs in the countries which were once French colonies.

There is indeed much validity in this observation about central public administrations in these countries. The administrations do derive a great deal from the former metropolitan powers, and the former British colonies in this sense resemble one another more than they do any former French colony. In the English-speaking new states, for example, the headquarters administrations are organized in ministries with permanent secretaries who occupy a position that is reminiscent of the English permanent secretary, while the ex-French colonies reflect the Parisian fashion in ministerial cabinets. What applies to organization is true also of procedures: in the English-speaking countries there is, for instance, the distinctive English practice of "minuting up" to the permanent secretary and minister. Indeed, on reading a series of case studies on Nigerian administration, Professor F. M. G. Willson recorded the judgment: "it is striking to note how even a decade after the worst traumas of the independence struggle the administrative pattern is such that a British civil servant or local government officer would fit in quite snugly."[13] Crossing the language barrier, however, can prove disconcerting. Former French colonial

13. F. M. G. Willson, "Forward," in D. J. Murray (ed.), *The Work of Administration in Nigeria* (London: Hutchinson, 1969), p. viii. See also David Brokensha, "Handeni Revisited," *African Affairs* (1971), vol. LXX, pp. 159–68.

officials serving as international aid administrators in English-speaking Africa have been perplexed and disoriented by the lack of centralized authority and other familiar administrative landmarks.

Yet there are two judgments about this administrative structure that carry dangers. First, it is easy to exaggerate the degree of conformity between one ex-colony and another. In terms of general organization and administrative style there are notable differences between countries which formerly shared a relationship with a metropolitan power. This is particularly true of the English-speaking countries, since unlike the French colonial situation there was very little attempt to establish central administrative control over British colonies.

The second danger is to make the judgment that this administrative superstructure remains essentially alien. In fact the roles, offices, organization, and procedures created during the period of colonial rule have in varying degrees become an established part of local and national societies. This has been particularly true of the longer-established roles and offices—offices in the field administration like those of district officer and *préfêt*, for instance. By now parts of what was once a colonial administration are as much integral features of the national scene as is the social structure of the Acholi in Uganda or Bemba in Zambia. It would seem therefore that it is important to understand both the local situation in which colonial administrators worked and the institutions that they helped to establish as the basis of a national government.

THE NEGLECT OF THE COLONIAL ADMINISTRATIVE LEGACY

The importance of understanding particular situations before rushing in with new development schemes has been an important lesson that colonial administrators have drawn from their experience. Yet, as a basis for further advancing our understanding of administering development, the British and French in many other ways provide poor guidance. Much scientific research was conducted during the period of colonial rule. In most British colonies agricultural research stations developed improved strains of oil palm and cocoa, bred tsetse-resistant cattle and so on;[14] and there was veterinary, forestry, and medical research. Starting between the wars, as part of the attempt to understand better the peoples among whom they worked, British and French colonial governments sponsored anthropological research, and after the passage of the Colonial Development and Welfare Act and FIDES this was broadened to include other social and economic research. Yet in all this, surprisingly little attention was given to building up systematically an understanding of the administrative process.

The British Colonial Office, after World War II, did begin the *Journal of Local Administration* as a forum for the exchange of experiences among officials, and its issues contain much interesting information about the way in which colonial officials set about introducing representative local government, organizing elections, and conducting local development projects. Indeed, in this period there was some general awareness of the potentiality for building up a body of understanding about the administration of development in the British colonies. In 1948, for instance, a House of Commons Select Committee recommended the establishment of a permanent administrative organization which would "not only be of immediate use in solving problems arising out of the impact of development plans, but would in the course of time build up a body of experience in colonial administration which would be of permanent advantage to the Service."[15] Yet this recommendation was interpreted in its execution as one simply for expanding organization and

14. For a survey of research in English-speaking West Africa, see Carl Eicher, *Research on Agricultural Development in Five English-Speaking Countries in West Africa* (New York: Rockefeller Foundation, Agricultural Development Council, 1970).

15. *Fifth Report from the Select Committee on Estimates, Session 1947–48* (London: H.M.S.O., 1948), p. xiv.

methods inquiries.[16] There was little systematic study of the way in which administration was conducted, no attempt to isolate what was peculiar to the local situation and what constituted the sort of experience which could validly be brought to play in another situation—there was no attempt in other words to build up any systematic body of knowledge, to complement the work, for instance, that had been done by the social anthropologists.

On the French side there was perhaps less sensitivity to the problems of adapting French institutions to local situations, but the need for expertise in colonial administration was explicitly recognized in the training given by the *École Nationale de la France d'Outre-Mer*. There, and at the *Centre de Hautes Etudes de l'Administration Musulmane*, administrative officers were encouraged to prepare monographs on local administrative problems and projects after one or two tours of duty overseas, and these served to enhance the development of a core of specialized knowledge available for reference. Unfortunately, however, there was no publication which served as a forum for the comparison of experience—perhaps because the monographs were treated as classified information—and the tendency to treat administration as a problem of laws and institutions restrained French social scientists from carrying out studies of comparative interest.

The first steps toward carrying out broad comparative studies were taken by international organizations established with the express purpose of comparing colonial administrative experience. One of these was the International African Institute, and another the Royal Institute of International Affairs, which sponsored Lord Hailey's African Surveys of 1938 and 1956. But Lord Hailey's surveys, though they provided very useful catalogues of colonial data, were not followed up with the analysis and interpretation of results. A similar fate befell the mountain of documents provided by colonial administrations

16. *First Report from the Select Committee on Estimates, Session 1948–49* (London: H.M.S.O., 1948), p. xvii.

to the League of Nations Mandates Commission and the UN Trusteeship Council.

The result of this lack of sustained interest among the British and French colonial governments in developing a body of knowledge about the administrative aspect of development administration—as opposed to the agricultural, public health, or educational aspects—was that much valuable knowledge has been squandered, and the opportunity for developing a systematic body of knowledge largely lost. This applies both to the general subject of the administration of development in Africa and to the more specialized aspect of the particular problems arising from the involvement of foreigners handling administration in an alien environment.

A second major lesson, then, that seems to come from the work of British and French colonial administrators in supervising local development is that their failure should not be repeated. The British and French had the opportunity of studying the way in which projects were administered, the form of organization, the staffing, the administrative techniques and styles. They could have studied the established administrative values and practices of indigenous communities and the compatibility of these with those of the colonial administration in their development work—in the way that the anthropologists had earlier investigated local political organization as an adjunct to the introduction of indirect rule and indirect administration. They were in a position to assess the observations and to compare the findings with those from elsewhere. In conducting the administration, they were for the most part understandably preoccupied with immediate and practical problems. Their concern with the immediate was reinforced by doubts about the value of social science research, hesitations over whether administration could be other than an art, as well as by the growing realization that colonial administration was likely to come to an end fairly quickly. The result was that there remains only a limited understanding of the specifically administrative dimension of development work conducted by colonial governments. It has remained to latter-day foreign aid administrators, and to such African-based institutions as the Economic Commission for Africa, and research institutes such as the Institute of Administration, University of Ife, Nigeria, or the *Centre Africain de formation et de recherche administratives pour le developpement*, Tangier, Morocco, to begin systematically to build up knowledge.

THE USEFULNESS OF THE COLONIAL EXPERIENCE OF DEVELOPMENT ADMINISTRATION

There were, however, two important exceptions to the general failure to correlate the colonial experience with development administration. One of these lay in the evolving British colonial tradition of local development through local institutions; the other lay in the limited attention given to the problems of institutional transfer. In British colonial administration one administrative approach which commanded continuing interest was that of exploiting traditional indigenous administrative structures to achieve goals formulated by the colonial governments. The earliest general formulation was the doctrine of indirect rule which Lord Lugard practiced in northern Nigeria and explained in *The Dual Mandate in British Tropical Africa.* [17] This involved the use of existing governmental structures like those of the emirates as a basis for a general system of subordinate government which, working within broad limits imposed from above, achieved general objectives of the colonial government. When the objectives of colonial government had come to include developing representative and democratic government, Sir Donald Cameron defined indirect rule as meaning indirect administration and he stimulated systematic investigation into how indigenous governmental structures could continue to be

17. Lord Lugard, *The Dual Mandate in British Tropical Africa* (London: William Blackwood, 1922).

used as a basis for carrying out local governmental activities.[18] At the same time he introduced into centralized political systems arrangements by which authoritarian rulers could be subjected to the influence of the community: the era of sole chiefs gave way to that of chiefs-in-council.[19] It is important to note that, whereas political and judicial institutions were of central concern in the formulation of indirect rule and indirect administration, the role of these institutions in promoting development was also considered. Later Lord Hailey's surveys of native administration in all British African territories examined both these aspects and the prospects for using local administrative structures as building blocks for constitutional development at the national level.

The final stage in this process of exploiting existing structures for purposes conceived by the colonial government came after World War II. At this stage, when governments were committed to promoting development on a new scale, and when in most colonies representative local government on an English model was being introduced to replace indirect administration, interest increased in using local institutions—as they were being used already in a measure in eastern Nigeria—on a piecemeal basis to act as agencies for promoting local development. Clans, welfare societies, development associations, village communities, and a multiplicity of other associations were seen to be appropriate agencies for promoting the sort of development envisaged by the Colonial Development and Welfare Act. Instead of an area government—the native administration —being the sole and all-purpose local administrative agency for promoting local development, a variety of local associations were envisaged as the partners and instruments of govern-

18. D. Cameron, *My Tanganyika Service, and Some Nigeria* (London: Frank Cass, 1939).

19. For the development of this process in Nigeria, see A. H. M. Kirk-Greene (ed.), *The Principles of Native Administration in Nigeria: Selected Documents, 1900–1947* (London: Oxford University Press, 1965).

ment. One association, for example, would build and run a school; another would concentrate on building a road. Where earlier approaches had carried the terms "indirect rule" and "indirect administration," this one was called "communal development" and an important impetus to it came with the Fifth Report of the Select Committee on Estimates, Session 1947–48.

The Select Committee's report outlined a general approach to communal development in the way that Lugard's Dual Mandate had for indirect rule. "The fact that underspending has taken place on such a scale, at a time when public expectations have passed beyond the original development plans, demands urgent and fundamental examination. . . . The emphasis in existing plans on the expansion of government departments is the natural result of planning from the top. In a democratic approach one starts with the colonial peoples themselves, their needs and their potentialities. . . ."[20]

> The existing government services are necessary and must be greatly expanded, but, if any measurable impression is to be made on the immense tasks which need to be done, there must be an upward movement of the people to meet the downward movement of Government-provided services.
>
> Communal development is no new thing in Nigeria. For many years administrative and other officers have been practicing its principles in the Eastern Provinces and elsewhere. In the main, these efforts have been confined to administrative and agricultural matters, which are a natural basis for communal development on broader lines. Elementary instruction has been given in methods of preventing soil erosion. The finance of the Native Administration has been discussed in the villages, with the result that the people have gained a very good idea of the amount of revenue collected from the taxes they pay. Thence proceeds a natural interest in the expenditure of local revenue. The people begin to think of various possible uses for local funds. Suggestions begin to be put forward for a road to be made, a dispensary to be built, a school to be started.

20. *Fifth Report from the Select Committee on Estimates, Session 1947–48* (London: H.M.S.O., 1948), p. viii.

Communal development is still experimental. Its success has been limited to small operations by villages and fractions of villages. It is, however, of the essence of the idea that it should be experimental. It has been proved in practice that it can be used to teach better methods of agriculture and domestic hygiene and to encourage village crafts; but it offers unlimited possibilities of extension beyond the village level. [21]

"Communal development" has given way as a label to "community development," and it is community development that provides an important exception to the generalization that little was done systematically to build up knowledge about the process of administration during the period of British and French colonial rule. In spite of the fundamental problems in community development as a field—notably the difficulty of whether it is concerned with developing communities or whether the interest is a particular technique where communities are agencies for development—there have been concerted attempts to draw together experience in this field, and to present the conclusions drawn largely from the British colonies so that they can be employed by other organizations concerned with promoting development. The work of du Sautoy and Batten [22] among others represents an attempt at drawing on the knowledge gained by the British colonial administrators in working indirectly—using, that is, established institutions in the society for purposes conceived in general terms by the colonial government—and making this available for others of whom international aid administrators are an important group.

The French colonial tradition of centralization, based on the metropolitan model, offers little comparable data of interest

21. Ibid., p. xx.

22. Peter du Sautoy, *Community Development in Ghana* (London: Oxford University Press, 1958); T. R. Batten, *Communities and Their Development—An Introductory Study with Special Reference to the Tropics* (London: Oxford University Press, 1965); T. R. Batten, with the collaboration of Madge Batten, *The Non-Directive Approach in Group and Community Work* (London: Oxford University Press, 1967).

concerning community development. The parallels with Lugard's indirect rule in the work of Lyautey in Morocco, van Vollenhoven in French West Africa, and Eboué in Equatorial Africa, were short-lived exceptions to the dominant practice of centralized, hierarchic control over all levels of administration.[23] During the period after World War II attempts were made to sponsor local cooperative activity, but these were so heavily controlled by the central administration that they resulted in very little development from below. Only at the end of the colonial period was there a concerted effort to organize development at the community level, and this was always on an experimental basis. There was no time left to apply findings on a territorial or inter-territorial level, but some French-speaking governments, notably that of Senegal, have consciously built local initiative into their development plans.

A second exception to the generalization made above is that there has been some limited work on the general problem of institutional transfer. This is a less significant exception, not because of the importance of the topic, but because of the limited nature of the systematic work that has been done on it. Institutional transfer is an aspect of colonial administration of importance for international administrators. It arises from the adoption of an approach to development alternative to the indirect method discussed above, that of organizing administrative institutions—particularly those of the central administration—in accordance with the ideas of the metropolitan society and the need at some point to make these a part of the local social setting. Britain and France both established, as has been already pointed out, administrations in their colonies that reflected the institutions and practices of the colonial Power and staffed them almost entirely with British and French

23. For a revealing debate on this subject, see Hubert Deschamps, "Et Maintenant, Lord Lugard?", *Africa* (Oct. 1963), Vol. XXXIII, pp. 293–306; and Michael Crowder, "Indirect Rule—French and British Style," *Africa* (July 1964), Vol. XXXIV, pp. 197–205.

officials. Because of the British predilection for an indirect approach at the local level—using established social institutions—the extent of this direct administrative structure was more limited in the British colonies than in the French, but in both there was at least a superstructure of administrative institutions which was wholly foreign in origin to the local society. A major share of the planning of decolonization was concerned with the problem of ensuring administrative continuity and development during a period of rapid constitutional and political change. This meant that the operations and values of essentially alien institutions—albeit institutions shaped to local needs—had to survive a transfusion of personnel and the super-imposition of a totally new set of political structures.

The scope and importance of institutional transfer during the period of decolonization resulted in much work being done on specific problems in individual territories. A series of reports, for example, dealt with the localization of personnel in the civil services, and others with the reorganization of headquarters and field administrations. There is in consequence a considerable amount of material available to form a basis for the study of the problem, but there has been little detailed evaluation at a comparative level.[24] This is an area of considerable significance to international agencies, and it is one where the generalization largely applies that wisdom, which could have been gained from the experience of the British and French and made more widely known, has not been distilled and made available.

The result of this general absence of systematic study of the

24. The general question is touched on in such works as Ursula Hicks, *Development from Below* (Oxford: Clarendon Press, 1961); and John M. Lee, *Colonial Development and Good Government* (London: Oxford University Press, 1967). One book that attempted to initiate a systematic approach to the question was William B. Hamilton (ed.), *The Transfer of Institutions* (Durham: Duke University Press, 1964). There is as yet no African equivalent of R. Brasbanti (ed.), *Asian Bureaucratic Systems Emergent from the British Imperial Tradition* (Durham: Duke University Press, 1966).

British and French administrative experience in promoting development in their overseas colonies is that for the most part their legacy is at no higher level than that of providing suggestive ideas. The Francophone way of organizing local government has been held out to those in English-speaking countries as something that is worth considering; likewise the system of ministerial cabinets as operating in the Ivory Coast is presented as a device that might help to solve certain of Nigeria's problems.[25]

Insofar therefore as British and French colonial administrative experience has a continuing relevance for international administrators, it is possible to suggest that it brings two major lessons: first, the importance to effective administration of a thorough knowledge of the local circumstances, and conversely, the discarding of ideas about how all Africa and Africans are the same; and secondly, the importance of analyzing the practical experience of administrators and distilling from it a wisdom that can be used later to advantage by others. The absence of such an approach in the British and French colonies has meant that with the single important exception of the field of community development, more practical yet validated generalizations have yet to be derived from the period of British and French colonial rule.

25. See J. A. Ballard, "Alternative Administrative Arrangements: the Experience of French-Speaking West Africa," in Adebayo Adedeji (ed.), *Nigerian Administration and its Political Setting* (London: Hutchinson, 1968), pp. 131–37; O. Adamolekun, "Ministerial Cabinets for Nigeria," *Administration* (Jan. 1968), Vol. II, No. 2, pp. 92–96; and O. Adamolekun, "High Level Ministerial Organization in Nigeria and the Ivory Coast," in D. J. Murray (ed.), *Studies in Nigerian Administration* (London: Hutchinson, 1970), pp. 11–42.

4

Functional Agencies
and International Administration

RICHARD SYMONDS

In 1965 when the Unilateral Declaration of Independence took place in Rhodesia, the writer of this chapter, as the regional representative of the United Nations Technical Assistance Board in the area, was instructed, in accordance with resolutions of the Security Council, to arrange for the immediate withdrawal of all experts of the UN and specialized agencies from Rhodesia. That this withdrawal was an unavoidable consequence of UDI was appreciated by most of the experts, but one of them looked up with dismay from his microscope, to complain bitterly that "some politicians in New York are interfering with science." This episode can perhaps symbolize the long and usually unsuccessful efforts of professional people and technicians to isolate the work of functional international organizations from politics in order to give that work immunity and enable it to continue at times of political strain.

The writer is representative of the United Nations Institute for Training and Research in Europe, and is also a senior research fellow at the Institute for the Study of International Organization and visiting professor at the University of Sussex. He is writing in a personal capacity, and UNITAR has no responsibility for the views expressed.

THE FUNCTIONALIST APPROACH

In this chapter "functionalism" is used in the sense in which it is most commonly associated with the writing of David Mitrany. Mitrany in 1943 described the international functionalist approach as "by linking authority to a specific activity to break away from the traditional link between authority and a definite territory"; and again as "to make changes of frontiers unnecessary by making frontiers meaningless through the continuous development of common activities and interests across them."[1] While this chapter is primarily concerned with the administrative problems of international functional agencies, in order to understand them it is necessary first to trace briefly the history of these agencies.

THE EARLY DEVELOPMENT OF FUNCTIONAL AGENCIES

The work of international functional agencies of course considerably predates this definition by Mitrany and the elaboration of the functionalist theory by his American followers.[2] Indeed, it is ironic that the great period of the development of international cooperation on a functional basis ended in the holocaust of 1914. Between 1865 and 1914, 33 intergovernmental and 182 non-governmental international organizations were created.[3] Occasionally their origins were due to the persistent enthusiasm of an individual. Thus the International Red Cross resulted from Henri Dunant's experiences at the Battle of Solferino; and the International Institute of Agriculture from

1. David Mitrany, *A Working Peace System* (Chicago: University of Chicago Press, 1966), pp. 27 and 62.

2. E.g. Ernst Haas, *Beyond the Nation State* (Stanford: Stanford University Press, 1964); and James P. Sewell, *Functionalism and World Politics* (Princeton: Princeton University Press, 1966).

3. F. S. L. Lyons, *Internationalism in Europe 1815–1914* (Leyden: A. W. Sijthoff, 1963), p. 32.

David Lubin's observation of the exploitation of farmers, because of their lack of information on world prices.

More often, the international associations in the nineteenth century emerged incidentally from international conferences held by groups of private individuals with common concerns. Their primary purpose was the exchange of information. In some cases the subjects treated could only be regulated by governments, notably in the field of communications which was developing rapidly in the mid-nineteenth century as a result of technology and the expansion of commerce. The oldest of the present specialized agencies of the United Nations, the Universal Postal Union (UPU) and the International Telecommunications Union (ITU), can trace their origins from conferences held in 1863 and 1865 respectively.

The administration of the Unions was hardly international in the sense in which the League of Nations system was to develop the concept of international administration. Although agreements and regulations were reached at intergovernmental conferences which met at intervals of a few years, the small permanent bureaus of the Unions were usually under the supervision of an individual government; thus the ITU and UPU were supervised by the Swiss government: UPU's director and most of its staff remained Swiss until the 1960s. Similarly the Bureau of Commercial Statistics and the Union for Publication of Customs Statistics were supervised by the Belgian government.

FUNCTIONAL AGENCIES AND THE LEAGUE OF NATIONS

The Covenant of the League of Nations in 1919 provided in Article 24 that "there shall be placed under the direction of the League all International Bureaux already established by general treaties, if the parties to such treaties consent. All such international bureaux and all commissions for the regulation of matters of international interest hereafter constituted shall be placed under the direction of the League."

The more important existing bureaux, however, jealously preserved their independence and were strengthened in doing so by the fact that the U.S.A. was included in their membership but not in that of the League.[4] On the other hand, within the League itself organizations grew up which were to be the predecessors of independent specialized agencies of the UN system, notably the Health Organization which, together with the International Health Office in Paris, was one of the predecessors of WHO, and the Committee on Intellectual Cooperation, which was one of the precursors of UNESCO. The International Labor Organization (ILO), which was created by the Treaty of Versailles, had a semi-independent status, with its unique tripartite structure of governments, employers, and workers, but with a budget which was incorporated in that of the League.

At the very end of the League period in 1939 a subcommittee, of which Lord Bruce was chairman, reported on "The Development of International Cooperation in Economic and Social Affairs."[5] The Bruce report proposed that a central committee for economic and social questions should be set up to "direct and supervise" the work of the committees dealing with economic and social questions. In order to involve countries which were not members of the League, it was suggested that twenty-four representatives of member states might co-opt eight members appointed in a private capacity. The committee would consider the annual draft budget relating to all economic and social activities of the League.

4. F. P. Walters, *A History of the League of Nations*, Vol. I (London: Oxford University Press, 1952), p. 60.

5. *The Development of International Cooperation in Economic and Social Affairs* (Bruce Committee Report), Special Supplement to Monthly Summary of the League of Nations, Geneva, August 1939.

FUNCTIONAL AGENCIES AND
THE UNITED NATIONS SYSTEM

The economic and social activities of the League were on the whole more centralized than those of the United Nations system which succeeded it, and the committee proposed by the Bruce report would have been considerably more powerful than the Economic and Social Council (ECOSOC) which was created by the UN Charter has proved to be.

There appear to be several reasons for the swing toward decentralization during and immediately after World War II. How far the functionalist philosophy was responsible is difficult to determine. In Britain, Leonard Woolf and H. G. Wells may be counted among its exponents. Sir Alfred Zimmern noted, as early as 1936, that "in League circles . . . it began to be believed that eventually there would be a worldwide cooperative system held together by a network of contacts between government departments (other than Foreign Offices), professional organizations and individual experts. It was indeed a curious combination of Fabianism and Cobdenism."[6]

The survival of the ILO, with its firm tripartite base, on the collapse of the League impressed a number of influential observers. The views of President Franklin D. Roosevelt were perhaps of paramount importance. In 1943, in connection with the founding of the Food and Agriculture Organization (FAO), he is recorded as favoring the establishment of entirely separate functional agencies in the economic field.[7] On a less formal occasion in 1942 a lunch-time visitor described the President as suggesting that in the postwar system "the I.L.O. would stay in Geneva; the international agricultural function in the U.S.; education in China; religion at the Taj Mahal and health at the

6. Quoted by Sewell, op. cit., p. 44.
7. Department of Sate, *Post-war Foreign Policy Preparation* (Washington, D.C.: G.P.O. 1950), p. 143.

north of Panama City; economics and finance in Russia, and art in Paris."[8]

FAO, the World Bank, and the International Monetary Fund (IMF) were established as autonomous agencies before the United Nations itself came into real existence. The Preparatory Committee of the UN, indeed, envisaged varying degrees of integration of the specialized agencies with the UN. It attached considerable importance to their location at or near UN headquarters and to the consolidation of their budgets with that of the UN. The system which emerged was, however, geographically decentralized. Of the major agency headquarters, while the UN was in New York and the World Bank and IMF in Washington, the four principal specialized agencies were established in Europe—ILO and WHO in Geneva, FAO in Rome, and UNESCO in Paris. Later at the regional level there was to be a similar dispersal. While for example the UN economic commissions were set up in Santiago, Geneva, Addis Ababa, and Bangkok, the regional offices of WHO were located in Washington, Copenhagen, Brazzaville, New Delhi, Manila, and Alexandria.

The budgets of the specialized agencies were voted independently and their memberships were different from that of the United Nations. For the first ten years after the war, while the Cold War was at its height, the membership of most of them was much more extensive than that of the United Nations. As the French delegate pointed out at the ITU conference at Atlantic City in 1947, the ITU was "technical and universal whilst the UN was political and restricted."[9] The World Bank and its complex of agencies on the other hand had an even more restricted membership than that of the United Nations

8. Elliot Roosevelt (ed.), *The Roosevelt Letters,* Vol. III (London: Harrap, 1952), p. 445.

9. Quoted in George Codding, *The International Telecommunications Union* (Leyden: A. W. Sijthoff, 1952), p. 316.

and established a procedure of weighted voting related to contributions which was very different from that of the "one nation, one vote" tradition of the UN General Assembly.

However loose, there was indeed a "UN system." Each specialized agency presented an annual report to the Economic and Social Council, usually introduced by its executive head in person. The executive heads of the specialized agencies met twice a year with the Secretary-General of the United Nations as the "Administrative Committee on Coordination." This Committee maintained a number of inter-agency subcommittees both on program and administrative questions. A common salary and pension scheme was evolved for all except the World Bank and IMF agencies.

Perhaps the high point of the decentralist period came in 1949 when, under Resolution 222 (IX), ECOSOC set up the Expanded Program of Technical Assistance—expanded because the UN and several agencies already had small technical assistance programs. Under this resolution, the bulk of the funds which were made available from voluntary contributions of governments were distributed among the agencies in fixed proportions ranging from 29 per cent for the FAO to 1 per cent for the International Civil Aviation Organization (ICAO); and management was corporately vested in a Technical Assistance Board (TAB), consisting of representatives of the agencies.

There was a school of thought in ECOSOC which would have preferred a program centrally administered by the UN in New York, using the specialized agencies as its agents. At the time, this did not prevail against the argument that such a program would be unduly slow in getting off the ground. Since 1949, however, the pendulum has gradually swung back toward centralization. First, the executive chairman of the TAB was able to withhold from the automatic allocations an increasing proportion of funds for "contingency planning." The UN Special Fund, established in 1958, gave the specialized agencies only an advisory function, with no veto such as they had enjoyed on the Technical Assistance Board. And when the Expanded Program and the Special Fund were amalgamated in 1962 as the UN Development Program (UNDP), it was the Special Fund philosophy which prevailed.

THE CAPACITY STUDY OF 1969

Until 1969, however, the specialized agencies or other UN functional agencies had always been the executing agencies of the UN technical assistance system within their field of competence. They had recruited and administered thousands of experts working in almost all economic and social fields throughout the world. Sir Robert Jackson in a remarkably comprehensive and vivid study on the capacity of the United Nations development system, published in 1969, proposed a radical change. While paying tribute to what had been achieved by the agencies in the development field over the past two decades, he described their work as hampered by the lack of any real "head piece" or central coordinating organization which could exercise effective control. A machine, he suggested, had grown up which, while theoretically under the control of thirty separate governing bodies, in effect was neither controlled by governments nor capable of intelligently controlling itself. This was not because it lacked intelligent and capable officials, but because it was so organized that managerial direction was impossible. The functional agencies, lacking any central control, had naturally advanced independent sectoral policies, often without regard to the interests either of the developing countries or the UN system. All too often, the study indicated, projects were the result of agencies' salesmanship rather than of priority needs, with a consequent "scatterization" of effort and a tendency to self-perpetuation of projects.

Jackson's proposed remedy was first to base programs of technical assistance on the needs of each country, through a periodic assessment of those needs in which all agencies concerned would collaborate jointly with the government and with the UNDP resident representative. The responsibility for programming and implementing projects would then however lie with the central body, the UNDP, using the UN specialized agencies in an advisory capacity but not always as executing agencies. While the agencies' services would continue to be used to the maximum extent possible consonant with efficiency, their previous monopoly of execution would be broken, and where necessary work would be carried out by subcontracting.

The study appeared to suggest that the major specialized agencies had in some cases over-extended themselves in technical assistance and that this had diverted them from their original and perhaps more important standard-setting function.[10] The point is of considerable importance. The study's statistics showed that by 1968 some of the specialized agencies had found themselves in a position under which the funds which they received from the UNDP exceeded their total regular budgets and that there had been increasing delays in the execution of projects. In this connection it may be noted that the joint report of the FAO Program and Finance Committees commented in 1967 that "in effect a saturation point appears to have been reached where little further absorption of additional operational, field supervisory or servicing activity by the staff concerned is feasible."[11]

THE TARGET-SETTING ROLE AND THE OPERATIONAL ROLE OF FUNCTIONAL AGENCIES

The unique function of the international specialized agencies has not been technical assistance. Sometimes technical assis-

10. A Study of the Capacity of the United Nations Development System (UN Document DP/5, 1969), but see also Comments of the Interagency Consultative Board on the Capacity Study (UN Document DP/6, 1970) for the agencies' reaction.

11. FAO Document CL/48/6, May 17, 1967, p. 12.

tance has even involved the recruitment of experts whose services could have otherwise been made available by bilateral agencies. Sometimes, as Jackson observed, the work could in any case most effectively be subcontracted to universities or even to private companies. The point should not indeed be taken too far. It was undoubtedly good for the agencies, some of whom had grown up in a very European atmosphere, to familiarize themselves through technical assistance in the fifties and sixties with the problems of Latin America, Asia, and Africa. Indeed, both WHO and FAO had the function of rendering technical assistance written into their constitutions.

The unique role of the specialized agencies however rather lay in obtaining agreements on international standards and on global strategy to reach agreed targets. The ILO's conventions in the interwar period regulating various forms of labor were its greatest source of strength. In the postwar period, WHO has made worldwide plans for the eradication of malaria and other diseases and assisted to implement them directly and indirectly through mobilizing both multilateral and bilateral aid. Similarly UNESCO, through regional meetings of educational ministers, has set targets for primary, secondary, and higher education. The World Weather Watch is an excellent example of the success of the functionalist approach. It was planned by an American and a Soviet expert under the chairmanship of the Secretary-General of WMO in order to exploit the remarkable recent technological advances which have been made in the field of meterorology over recent years. The new weather stations established under the program will not merely be of benefit to the countries in which they are located, and when these countries cannot afford to maintain them, WMO will arrange assistance either from bilateral or multilateral sources.[12]

12. For a fuller picture of the target setting role of the UN agencies see Richard Symonds (ed.), *International Targets for Development* (New York: Harper and Row, 1970).

Criticism of the functional agencies over the past ten years has been directed much more at their technical assistance activities than at their traditional role. Lord Balogh, for example, has referred to unbalanced programs in the field resulting from "single-minded technocracy,"[13] because individual specialized agencies have not taken into account the broader implications of their recommendations for economic and social development. A UN evaluation mission to Chile in 1966 found that some agencies insisted on giving quite detailed notes on experts' reports and that: "any departure from agency policy is rebuked."[14]

Here indeed was a dilemma. The agencies had traveled a long way from the days when an article on the International Telegraph Union had commented approvingly that "en raison de la sagesse de son attitude, le bureau international n'a pas d'histoire"[15]—a long way even from Loveday's description of the duties of an international official in 1956 as having "little to administer except his own office. His main task is diplomatic and, particularly in Specialized Agencies, promotive."[16] By 1965 it was estimated that three-quarters of the civilian personnel employed by the UN agencies were concerned with economic and social questions and that half of them had field duty assignments.[17] By engaging in technical assistance the agencies lost a certain aura of infallibility. How far was the executive head of the agency responsible for the recommendations of his experts? The United Nations and UNESCO tended to disclaim such responsibility; the ILO, WHO, and FAO on the other hand tended to edit their experts' reports and to

13. Thomas Balogh, *Economics of Poverty* (London: Macmillan and Co., 1966), pp. 127 and 134. See also his paper on bilateral aid at the Cambridge Overseas Conference, 1966.

14. *Report of the Chile Evaluation Team*, UN Document E/4151/Add. 2, 1966, p. 46.

15. Lyons, op. cit., p. 35.

16. Alexander Loveday, *Reflections on International Administration* (Oxford: Clarendon Press, 1956), p. 23.

17. David Owen, *Concept of an International Civil Service* (Leeds: University Convocation Address, 1966), Appendix.

present them as those of the Director-General. The delay caused by the editing process sometimes annoyed recipient governments, who believed that what they wanted urgently was the view of the expert and not that of his agency. When there were only a few dozen experts in the field, the attempt to relate their recommendations to policies and conventions of the agencies was manageable. When there were hundreds and even thousands of experts, it became unmanageable.

The rapid expansion in some cases led to a decline in the quality of the experts. The engagement of experts inexperienced in international life also often led to disappointing results because of inadequate understanding of local social, economic, and political conditions. [18]

THE EXECUTIVE HEADS OF THE FUNCTIONAL AGENCIES

The role of the executive head of a specialized agency, its Director-General or Secretary-General, is of outstanding importance, for he combines at the international level the functions which at a national level would be exercised by the Minister, the permanent secretary, and the chairman of the Civil Service Commission. Albert Thomas, the first Director-General of the ILO and a former French minister, exploited the role of the executive head in a much wider way than did his contemporary, Sir Eric Drummond, the first Secretary-General of the League, who was a seconded British civil servant. Thomas rapidly established the position by which the initiative for preparing a budget lay with the Director-General, not with the governing body; and he made his annual report to his conference a broad review of social policy. To a large degree, the executive heads of the specialized agencies have retained this kind of initiative, although in relation to the Economic and Social Council of the United Nations itself, owing to the other preoccu-

18. See R. Nairn, *International Aid to Thailand* (New Haven: Yale University Press, 1966); also Thomas Balogh, op. cit., p. 169.

pations of the Secretary-General, there has been something of a vacuum.[19]

Their position has been strengthened by the length of their service. Thus at the beginning of 1970 in the four principal specialized agencies the Director-General of ILO had held his office for 21 years; the Director-General of WHO had held the office for 17 years and had served with the organization for 20 years; the Director-General of UNESCO had held the office for 9 years and had served with the organization for 24 years; the Director-General of FAO had only served in that capacity for 3 years but had been with FAO and the World Food Program for 22 years.

Albert Thomas was also responsible for establishing a tradition of extreme centralization within the ILO. He signed all letters, saw all files, and sent for any staff member at any time regardless of administrative hierarchies.[20] Although this degree of personal control is no longer possible in the larger agencies, the extent to which all statements are issues in the name of the executive head is still a striking feature of international agencies. The career of an international official is more dependent on the favor of the executive head and less secure than that of a national civil servant in relation to his minister in most modern-style administrations.

PROBLEMS OF STAFFING THE FUNCTIONAL AGENCIES

There is one important limitation, however, on the authority of the executive head in relation to appointment of staff. The constitutions of most of the UN agencies reflect the clause in

19. See Walter Sharp, *The Economic and Social Council* (New York: Columbia University Press, 1969); and Robert Cox, "The Executive Head—An Essay on Leadership in International Organization," *International Organization* (1969), Vol. XXIII, No. 2.

20. E. J. Phelan, *Yes and Albert Thomas* (London: Cresset Press, 1936), Chapter 4.

Article 101 of the UN Charter which states that "The paramount consideration in the employment of staff shall be the necessity of securing the highest standards of efficiency, competency and integrity. Due regard shall be paid to the importance of recruiting the staff on as wide a geographical basis as possible."

In their early days most of the agencies, faced with the need to implement a wide range of resolutions and to expand technical assistance programs, tended to recruit rapidly, without much regard for geographical distribution, except in the very top posts of Assistant Director-General or Assistant Secretary-General. The British and French were over-represented in European-based agencies, and Americans in the American-based agencies. Not only the attacks of Khrushchev in the United Nations, but still more the criticisms of the new member states from Asia and Africa subsequently put heavy pressure on the executive heads to redress the balance.

Evidently the more specialized and professionalized the agency, the easier it was for the executive head to demonstrate the need for efficiency to take precedence over political considerations. Yet it cannot be said that international agencies have been as successful in dealing with the problem of geographical distribution as have some national administrations. In some cases, so many inadequately qualified people were admitted to the agencies' secretariats in middle-level positions in the sixties that there was a decline in efficiency. On the other hand, it is unrealistic for international officials to expect that the problem of geographical distribution of posts will disappear. Indeed, the strength of the organizations lies in their universality.

Some national administrations have dealt more realistically with the problem of representation of regions or races at different levels of development. Thus India in its recruitment for the central, or national, services has reserved places for scheduled castes (Harijans) within a system of competitive examination; in Pakistan, places in the central services were similarly reserved at one period for the under-represented East Pakistanis. But the success of such an approach depends on recruitment at a relatively young age, followed by intensive training.

Such training might, perhaps, be carried out within an international staff college for certain categories of personnel. There is as yet, however, as Sir Herbert Broadley has pointed out, no such thing as an international civil service.[21] The functional agencies, like some of the very small national administrations of the Caribbean and of Africa, often face the special problem of how to develop a career structure within small professionalized departments. Broadley has suggested that this problem might be met by more transfers between national and international administrations in specialized departments. This could help to improve morale and prevent staleness, yet it still must be recognized that the *international* experience of the international official is of vital importance. The headquarters specialist who is backstopping technical assistance projects can often make a valuable contribution just because he can transfer the lessons of experience from one country to another.

SOME FUTURE PROBLEMS

Looking ahead not merely through the seventies, but perhaps to the end of the century, the functional international agencies appear to face several important and interconnected problems.

First, there is that of responsibility and external control. Generally, intergovernmental conferences which meet annually or every two years, and even the smaller councils or governing bodies which meet once or twice for a few weeks each year, cannot exercise any close control over the executive heads of the agencies, who are almost irremovable between elections. A potentially dangerous situation is now present in which large

21. Sir Herbert Broadley, *Can There Be an International Civil Service?*, U.N.A. Pamphlet No. 34, London, n.d.

budget increases are sometimes voted by majorities of states which make very small contributions over the opposition of the principal contributors. A virtual donors' strike has already taken place in relation to the UN Capital Development Fund.

The challenges to the functional agencies are enormous in taking the lead in the global eradication, for example, of disease, hunger, unemployment, and illiteracy. A second problem is that there is a major question however as to whether the governments and electorates of the principal donor states have sufficient confidence in the ability of the agencies to respond to these challenges using existing procedures.

A number of ideas are in the air as to ways in which procedures might be modified and confidence increased. One suggestion is that the agencies should concentrate primarily on standard-setting and regulatory functions, and, as regards development, on planning rather than on execution; but that they should exercise a coordinating role in relation to bilateral aid programs.[22] National teams administered by their governments but coordinated by international agencies may sometimes be more effective and cheaper than internationally recruited teams. If there is less strain on international recruitment services, the quality of recruitment may be improved. Smaller staffs might be of higher quality.

The reality of "equitable geographical distribution" in recruitment has to be faced. Its application has led to a decline in standards, but member states are likely to continue to insist on its application. The most important remedy to the decline in standards is for the agencies to recruit staff from underrepresented countries when they are young, and to invest money in training them to meet high international standards.

International functional agencies need to face charges not only of inefficiency but also of taking a narrow, technocratic,

22. See Capacity Study, op. cit.; also Richard Symonds, "The Relation Between Multilateral and Bilateral Programmes of Technical Assistance," *International Development Review* (March 1968), Vol. X.

and bureaucratic approach to problems which cannot be isolated from the general social and economic context.

As regards efficiency, there is much more interest now than in the past in mid-career training of staff, but there is also a question of management, even perhaps of a critical maximum size, for the central bureaucratic machinery. WHO, partly through the historical accident of inheriting the Pan-American Sanitary Bureau, has sought to overcome this problem by decentralization of responsibility to offices within the regions. A committee of experts advising FAO on the other hand recently proposed that there should be a decentralization to regional offices which would remain at headquarters. On the whole it may be said that the agencies are aware of the need both to invest more time and money in staff training and to introduce new management techniques. As the Interagency Consultative Board (IACB) of UNDP stated in its Comments on the Capacity Study: "The world is in the midst of a revolution not only in technology but also in managerial science—a revolution of which the United Nations system must clearly take full advantage."[23]

The crisis of confidence is unlikely however to be overcome merely by training, reorganization, and improved management. The quite widespread image of the international official as a remote, one-day visitor, determined to impose irrelevant resolutions on national administrations, indicates that the specialized agencies may need to give more attention to the self-identification of governments and electorates with their work. Albert Thomas appointed in a number of countries "ILO correspondents" who were usually national officials in the ministry of labor; and the high commissioner for refugees between the wars had a similar system of representation by national officials. WMO still appoints directors of national meteorological services as its country representatives. UNESCO brings to its head-

23. *Comments of the Interagency Consultative Board on the Capacity Study,* (UN Document DP/6, February 1970), p. 5.

quarters in Paris each year the secretaries of the national UNESCO commissions for consultations. It may be that the functional agencies should give rather more attention to this kind of representation than to the appointment of expatriate country representatives of the organizations as such. The separate function of supervision of technical assistance programs in the field might be discharged by agency officials seconded to the offices of the UNDP resident representatives.

It may also be that there are lessons in the League experience for procedures by which national representatives or experts can be used more fruitfully at the headquarters and regional levels. Because the League technical organizations·were very sparsely staffed, more use appears to have been made of expert committees and rapporteurs from outside the Secretariat than has happened in the UN system. Even a brief experience of working within an international agency often produces a permanent, if not uncritical, sentiment of loyalty toward it which is quite different from the view of someone who has only been a delegate to meetings.

At the summer session of ECOSOC in 1968 the Director-General of UNESCO plaintively called for "a de-escalation of coordination." In this respect the agencies are confronted with two opposite problems. On the one hand, they are accused of sending out "traveling salesmen" who sometimes induce governments to accept programs which they do not understand, and would not want if they did understand, and which are not correlated with national development priorities. While plenty of examples can be recalled, it must also be recognized that such visits can be very valuable, when new techniques and developments are described and when governments are left genuinely free to select what they wish to adopt to suit their conditions. A day in the field, for example, with the great Swiss agronomist Dr. F. T. Wahlen, when he was director of agriculture of FAO, could prove more useful than many weeks of correspondence or many pages of documents.

The other danger is of paralysis through what has become an over-elaborate system of interagency consultation and co-ordination, a system which Sir Robert Jackson has characterized as perhaps the most complicated in the world.

There can be no going back. Perhaps the history of inter-national agencies, depicting them as small and pure, is in any case sometimes painted in too idyllic terms. Dunant, after all, was compelled to resign from the International Red Cross, which he had founded, and David Lubin, founder of the Inter-national Institute of Agriculture, was dismissed from the post of American representative to the Institute. In the interwar period the second executive head of ILO felt obliged to resign because he was unwilling to make a staff appointment desired by one of the major donors. But if functional agencies are to be entrusted with adequate responsibility on the scale required in order to meet the needs of the 1970s, they will need not only to adopt modern management techniques but to improve the standards and methods of recruitment of their staff. They have at last a chance to do so now that the flood of new member states demanding immediate representation in the secretariats has dried up.

The reaction of the executive heads of the UN agencies to the Capacity Study was not altogether happy. They criticized its historical perspective, and suggested that it underestimated the importance of the agencies' role of "substantive back-stopping which is enriched by their research and their policy-oriented activities," a role "inherent in the mandated com-mitment and continuous dedication of the United Nations organizations to assist developing countries."[24]

Yet whatever the outcome of the debate on the Capacity Study, in terms of the balance between centralization and decentralization in the UN system, nothing would ever be quite the same after the publication of an official document which

24. Comments of IACB, op. cit.

stated authoritatively, lucidly, and with a wealth of inside experience the kind of criticisms of the system which had long been circulating in national administrations and in academic circles.

One point which the Capacity Study emphasized was that the ministries in governments of developing countries which have overall responsibility for development should have the right to receive multilateral aid in the fields and in the form which most fitted their needs rather than in response to random pressures exercised by international agencies through individual ministries. Often in the 1960s, particularly in Africa in the period of decolonization, harassed ministers would protest to international officials "you are offering us everything except what we most need." The forgotten man of the fifties and sixties tended to be the local national counterpart who worked with the foreign expert. The agencies' view of needs was often formed through the eyes of the foreign expert, who sometimes had little understanding of local economic and still less of social conditions. Perhaps the heyday of the foreign expert is over. At least in the more sophisticated developing countries in the seventies, the agencies are likely to give the "counterpart" a more central role. Indeed, it may be that increasingly it will be the local official or expert who will plan projects at agency headquarters or regional offices, and that the foreign expert, sometimes personally selected on the initiative of the government, may thus become the real "counterpart."

TWO BASIC CONSIDERATIONS

Without taking a position on the issues which arise from the Capacity Study, two special considerations may be mentioned which affect functional agencies and which it may be hoped will never be lost sight of by those concerned with the work of functional international organizations. The first is the constant need to balance quality and quantity. In the writer's view, for example, a specialized agency of the UN should never send an expert into the field unless the quality of his expertise can be guaranteed. Amid strong pressures to expand programs it may be hard to hold to such a principle, but once the agency's hallmark of quality becomes questioned, its prestige is impaired.

The second consideration is that the vitality of the functional agencies depends on the strength of their roots at the national and professional level—the support of doctors and nurses for WHO, of farmers and nutritionists for FAO, of trades unions and employers for ILO, of teachers and scientists for UNESCO, and so on. Any reorganization which cut the agencies off from these roots and made them mere departments of the United Nations could turn them into withered bureaucracies.

SCIENCE AND POLITICS

A frequent and sometimes rather pathetic preoccupation of the functionalist agencies has been "to keep out of politics." In the early days of ITU it was seriously proposed that telegraphs should be neutralized in wartime; and when UPU was asked to expel Franco's Spain shortly after World War II there were protesting cries in the conference of "but we are Postmen." It cannot be concluded that this desire has often been rewarded. It is true that the Cold War was somewhat muted in the specialized agencies and that ECE maintained fruitful relations throughout it. When racial questions arose, however, the functionalist approach got short shrift. For years WHO's regional committee for Africa had to meet in Europe because no African country would issue visas to all the representatives of the member states; and as we have seen, when unilateral independence was declared in Rhodesia, the experts of all the specialized agencies were withdrawn even though most of them were working for African education. In the two cases in which governments as a political gesture have asked for the withdrawal of international experts—in Guinea and in Indonesia— no distinction was made between those of the United Nations and those of the specialized agencies.

Yet science is seldom neutral. The discoveries which are promoted by and the innovations which are introduced by international functional agencies often contain a concealed and unappreciated element of political dynamite. Technical assistance has not infrequently contributed to an increasing gap between rich and poor within nation states; it has sometimes increased unemployment; it has certainly assisted to increase educated unemployment. It has been an element in precipitating revolution.

This is not an argument for diminishing the aid role of international functional agencies. But those who work for them should not be surprised, as was the expert quoted at the beginning of this chapter, if "some politicians in New York" continue "to interfere with science."

PART TWO

The Application of International Administration

"The most vital political problems today are perhaps those that relate to institutional evolution. Prescribed constitutional procedures alone cannot always ensure the successful adaptation of existing institutions to needs and circumstances. Even revolution, the most violent and radical type of political change, fails in its effect unless it subsequently finds the means to transform the institutional structure which it finds already established."

Evan Luard

5

International Administration
of Peace-keeping Operations

LARRY L. FABIAN

The word "peace-keeping" appears nowhere in the index to Alexander Loveday's *Reflections on International Administration*. Nor does the body of his study examine peace-keeping as a significant task for an international civil service. To the book's audience at the time of its publication in 1956, these omissions were in all likelihood not regarded as particularly surprising. The reputation of the United Nations as a peace-keeper was still embryonic. Indeed, the UN Charter itself does not even refer explicitly to peace-keeping either as a general purpose of the organization or as a responsibility for the Secretariat or the Secretary-General. Furthermore, Loveday's exclusion of peace-keeping from the ambit of international administration would have seemed perfectly consistent with the experience of the League of Nations, which he served as a departmental director; a standard scholarly work on the Geneva Secretariat[1] also conveys the impression that peace-keeping was not an especially noteworthy concern of international administrators during the interwar years.

But for the present-day observer of international organization, who has watched the UN enter its second quarter-century, the

1. Egon F. Ranshofen-Wertheimer, *The International Secretariat* (New York: Carnegie Endowment for International Peace, 1945).

123

gap in *Reflections* seems conspicuous and glaring. It needs to be understood, not primarily as an oversight of the author's, but rather as a reflection of historical circumstances in the mid-1950s and then-prevailing assumptions about the UN's political and security role. Ironically, the very year that Loveday went to press has since been christened as the opening—to borrow Lincoln Bloomfield's label—of the Age of Peace-keeping. [2]

Even though the frequency of international conflict during the past fifteen years belies such an inflated description, this label nevertheless pinpoints accurately the substantial shift of UN priorities and self-conceptions that occurred after the General Assembly dispatched the first large-scale peace-keeping force to the Middle East in the wake of the 1956 Suez War. No longer would it be possible to write comprehensively and thoughtfully about international administration without exploring the implications of peace-keeping, some of which Dag Hammarskjöld began elaborating shortly after the Suez experiment. In his Oxford address, the operations in the Middle East and in the Congo were said to have grafted new responsibilities for political decision-making and administrative implementation onto the agenda of the Secretary-General as head of an independent, international staff. [3] A few years later a major study of the international civil service devoted prominent attention to peace-keeping-related questions. [4] In 1965, writing under a pseudonym, a member of the UN Secretariat argued that "perhaps the most novel extension of the concept of the international secretariat in the past decade has been the involvement of the military profession in peacekeeping activities under the direction of the Secretary General." He then described peace-

2. Lincoln P. Bloomfield, *The United Nations and U.S. Foreign Policy*, rev. ed. (Boston: Little, Brown and Co., 1967), p. 70.

3. See the Epilogue of this book for the Oxford Address of Dag Hammarskjöld.

4. Georges Langrod, *The International Civil Service* (Dobbs Ferry: Oceana, 1963), esp. Chapters 10 and 11.

keeping forces as "an outgrowth of the Secretariat."[5] Not only has the office of Secretary-General been entrusted with broader assignments because of the UN's peace-keeping career, it also has gained new influence and prestige as a result, perhaps more than from any other sector of activity.[6] And as the organization approached its twenty-fifth anniversary, one experienced commentator concluded that the evolution of an independent Secretariat, especially in peace-keeping matters, ranks among the most significant political developments in the life of the UN.[7]

HAMMARSKJÖLD'S FUSION OF OLD AND NEW

To document the explosion of attention since the mid-1950s to the relationship between peace-keeping and the functioning of the UN Secretariat is a relatively straightforward exercise. To uncover and to trace the roots of the phenomenon, however, require a much larger historical canvas, one that stretches back even beyond 1945. Underlying historical trends, patterns of attitudinal and institutional evolution, and the overall maturation of international organization all stubbornly resist compression into phases that are neat multiples of five or ten. Similarly, in an organization's history, seemingly decisive turning points may ratify or dramatize the direction of change but they do not always illuminate its sources.

In this category belongs the constellation of events and human actors that produced the UN Emergency Force (UNEF) in 1956. This clearly deserves to be called a genuine milestone

5. Charles Winchmore (pseud.), "The Secretariat: Retrospect and Prospect," in Norman J. Padelford and Leland M. Goodrich (eds.), *The United Nations in the Balance* (New York: Frederick A. Praeger, 1955), pp. 265 and 269.

6. This is one of the principal conclusions developed in a study by Leon Gordenker, *The UN Secretary General and the Maintenance of Peace* (New York: Columbia University Press, 1967), esp. Chapters 10–13.

7. Andrew Boyd, "The Role of the Great Powers in the United Nations System" *International Journal* (Spring 1970), Vol. XXV, No. 2, pp. 356–69.

in UN annals. All of the ingredients were there: a local confrontation that could have sparked potentially nuclear and
global escalation; a relatively new Secretary-General trusted
by both Cold War giants after his predecessor had been rendered totally ineffective by a boycott by Moscow; a UN membership recently enlarged by the 1955 "package deal" and
searching for an international security role that would fill
Cold War vacuums rather than (as happened in Korea) align
the organization with one half of the bipolar world. Mixing
with these situational factors were the Soviet Union's softened
attitude toward the UN after Stalin's death, a strong desire on
the part of the U.S. to rely on UN intervention in this case, and
the imaginative leadership of Dag Hammarskjöld, Lester Pearson, and the handful of other key statesmen eager to find an
intermediary role for the UN as a face-saver and a buffer. For
a brief time, the UN was able to emerge from the doldrums into
which it had slipped during the worst years of the early Cold
War and to occupy the center stage of international crisis
management.

If all this sounds too grandly heroic, it is worth remembering
that there was a dash of heroism at work. But correctives for
overstatement are available, and few are as crisply revealing
of the mundane improvisation, the groping, and the guesswork
of November 1956 as the brief recollections of one senior
Canadian diplomat who was deeply involved: "I recall being
called out of the Assembly in the early hours of one morning
with a fierce headache by a member of Mr. Hammarskjöld's
staff, carrying a small notebook, who asked just what concrete
ideas we Canadians had for this force we were proposing. The
truth was that we hadn't gone that far. We retreated to the
Delegates' Lounge to concoct a force on a few sheets of note-
paper. . . ."[8]

Whatever the dynamics of the immediate diplomatic situation

8. John W. Holmes, "Geneva: 1954," *International Journal* (Summer 1967),
Vol. XXII, No. 3, p. 458.

in 1956, the more important thing, from the standpoint of the larger history of internationally administered peace-keeping operations, is that UNEF was a blend of discontinuities and continuities, of the unique and the cumulative.

This peace-keeping force, composed initially of some 6000 troops from 10 of the 24 UN member states that volunteered contingents, stands as the first multinational peace-keeping force to be commanded and controlled by an international secretariat in the twentieth century. But it is not the first multinational peace-keeping operation to be conducted nominally on behalf of a modern international organization. The Council of the League of Nations sent a 4-nation, 3300-man force to the Saar in 1935 and designed and planned, but did not deploy, another in 1921 during a dispute over the territory of Vilna.

UNEF was the UN's first major peace-keeping force consisting of traditional military-type formations. But it was not the first peace-keeping mission using military personnel to be authorized by the Security Council or the General Assembly. Blue-helmeted UN officers performed a variety of peace-keeping fuctions in Greece (UNSCOB), Palestine (UNTSO), Indonesia (UNCI), and Kashmir (UNMOGIP)—all of which were dispatched between 1946 and 1949, and two of which, UNTSO and UNMOGIP, were still operational when UNEF was launched in 1956.

UNEF was the first UN peace-keeping operation to be directed from the outset by the Secretary-General rather than under the umbrella of a special *ad hoc* political commission composed of UN member states specially designated for the job by a UN political organ. But UNEF was not entirely novel in this respect either, for the observer corps in Kashmir and Palestine, though originally established under political commissions, subsequently were transformed into missions controlled directly by the Secretariat along lines later adopted by UNEF.

UNEF was the first UN peace-keeping operation for which various operating agencies within the Secretariat undertook substantial administrative and servicing responsibilities. But here too it was quantity rather than quality that distinguished the Secretariat's administrative involvement in peace-keeping before and after 1956. As Hammarskjöld himself was later to point out, UNEF burdened the Secretariat administrators with demands of greater magnitude, but the contours were nonetheless familiar on the basis of experience in supporting missions during the UN's early years.

UNEF was the UN's first full-blown laboratory for discovering how best to prepare the organization for future peace-keeping responsibilities, a challenge that Hammarskjöld took up, with some success, almost as soon as UNEF settled down into a post-crisis routine. But, once again, his efforts echoed those of an earlier day. Trygve Lie had also attempted to institutionalize some of the early *ad hoc* arrangements in ways that seemed to him to be insurance on the future, but his bold designs and aggressive advocacy proved far too ambitious for his time and circumstance. By contrast, Hammarskjöld was able at least to lay down a general, if still imperfect, corpus of political and administrative principles, called "preventive diplomacy," that guided the conduct of operations after UNEF—in Lebanon (UNOGIL), 1958; in the Congo (ONUC), 1960; in West Irian (UNTEA), 1962; in Yemen (UNYOM), 1963; in Cyprus (UNFICYP), 1964; on the India-Pakistan border (UNIPOM), 1965; and at the Suez Canal (UNTSO, expanded), 1967.[9]

Finally, it is true that, more than any preceding case in the

9. League and UN peace-keeping structures and their performance are surveyed in David W. Wainhouse, and others, *International Peace Observation* (Baltimore: Johns Hopkins Press, 1966); and are analysed in detail in Alan James, *The Politics of Peacekeeping* (New York: Frederick A. Praeger, 1969); D. W. Bowett, *United Nations Forces* (New York: Frederick A. Praeger, 1964); and Ruth B. Russell, *United Nations Experience with Military Forces: Political and Legal Aspects* (Washington, D.C.: Brookings Institution, 1964). The political and technical dimensions of building institutional capabilities for peace-keeping are assessed in Larry L. Fabian, *Soldiers Without Enemies: Preparing the United Nations for Peacekeeping* (Washington, D.C.: Brookings Institution, 1971).

UN's record, UNEF brought about a distinctive marriage between the practice of international administration and the local conflict-reduction services that now customarily go by the name of peace-keeping. But it is also true that the marriage would have been far less likely to endure had not the traditions, habits, and experiences of an international civil service been crystallizing for more than a generation. Without the background and foundation of the League years, without the potentially expansive stature given to the Secretariat and the office of Secretary-General by the constitution-makers of 1945, and without the legacy of political activism left by the UN's first incumbent on the 38th floor, Hammarskjöld's performance as a political administrator in charge of peace-keeping operations may well have been — literally — inconceivable.

TRANSFORMATION OF PURPOSE IN TWENTIETH-CENTURY INTERNATIONAL ORGANIZATION: FROM COLLECTIVE SECURITY TO SELECTIVE PEACE-KEEPING

The "death" of collective security as a prospective method of peace-maintenance has variously been lamented, chronicled, confirmed, or applauded, depending on the point of view of the obituary writer. Few argue that the concept ever had much operational viability in the modern international system. Fewer still are willing to deny that the death is real, however much they continue to differ in diagnosing its causes. Inis Claude, who has consistently exposed the illusions and fallacies of the collective security idea with special clarity and persuasiveness,[10] reflected recently on its demise since 1945:

10. See, especially, Inis L. Claude, Jr., *Swords into Plowshares*, 3rd ed., rev. (New York: Random House, 1964), Chapter 12; *Power and International Relations* (New York: Random House, 1962), Chapters 4 and 5; *The Changing United Nations* (New York: Random House, 1967), Chapters 1 and 2; and "The Collectivist Theme in International Relations," *International Journal* (Autumn 1969), Vol. XXIV, No. 4, pp. 639–56.

Perhaps the most significant development in the thinking of scholars and statesmen about international organization in the postwar period has been their gradual emancipation from the collective security fixation, their breaking out of the intellectual rut in which it was taken for granted that the suppression of aggression was so crucial a function of general international organizations that if this function could not be exercised, the only issue worth thinking about was how to make its exercise possible. Dag Hammarskjöld gave dramatic and forceful expression to the new and less constricted approach to international organization when he put the question of how the United Nations could contribute directly to keeping the peace when it could not enforce the peace and answered the question by formulating the theory of preventive diplomacy, now generally known as peacekeeping.[11]

This metamorphosis, and its pre-Hammarskjöldian origins, are significant for international administration because—briefly put—they have altered the purpose, conception, and structure of military forces arrayed under the auspices of international organization. The administration of peace-keeping forces and the administration of collective security forces are essentially different subjects because peace-keeping and collective security are conceptually and operationally distinct modes of international action, each with its own administrative assumptions and functional requirements.

The consequences of these dissimilarities have been paradoxical for modern international organization. In theory, both the League and the UN were supposed to have been prepared to administer collective security armies, although the drafters of the Charter drew a more detailed blueprint in this respect than did their predecessors at Versailles. In practice, neither organization ever employed collective security armies in ways contemplated by their founders. In theory, neither the Covenant

11. Inis L. Claude, Jr., "The United Nations, the United States, and the Maintenance of Peace," in Lawrence S. Finkelstein (ed.), *The United States and International Organization: The Changing Setting* (Boston: M.I.T. Press, 1969), p. 73.

nor the Charter made provision for anything called peace-keeping by military forces. In practice both organizations deployed military formations for this purpose, with the UN refining the practice into a fairly sophisticated politico-military art.

A CAPSULE COMPARISON OF COLLECTIVE SECURITY AND PEACE-KEEPING

Both the notion of collective security and the awareness of its internal contradictions long pre-date the present century. Nearly all manifestations of collective security thinking fall within the boundaries sketched in the following sentence: "The scheme is collective in the fullest sense; it purports to provide security *for* all states, *by* the action of all states, *against* all states which might challenge the existing order by the arbitrary unleashing of their power."[12] Wrongdoers are to be confronted with a credible deterrent threat from the community at large; or if deterrence fails, a collective response, in military dimensions if need be, is to be brought to bear against the aggressor.

History affords many examples—both in what men wrote and in what they tried to do—of efforts to translate this idea of collective security into a working system of community order. The underlying rationale of mutual and universal protection was even stated in Plato's *Republic*, which argued that if unity and peace are not preserved among the ruling class of guardians by the force of mutual respect, then harmony would be assured by "fear of all those others who as sons or brothers or fathers would come to the rescue."[13] Greece of antiquity had been experimenting in practice with collective security before Plato's birth, most prominently in the Peloponnesian Confederation and the Delian League of the early fifth century B.C. Modern

12. Claude, *Power and International Relations*, op. cit., p. 110.
13. *The Republic of Plato*, translated with introduction and notes by Francis M. Cornford (London: Oxford University Press, 1967), p. 166.

critics of collective security who fear the concentration of power that a collective security organization gives to its strongest members can take some comfort from the fact that both these city-state systems gradually succumbed to the hegemonies, respectively, of Sparta and Athens.[14]

Approximately two millennia later a succession of collective security proposals accompanied the protracted and fitful emergence of a Western states system from the disintegrating feudal structures of medieval Europe. Some were thinly disguised plans to cement the political or military predominance of one continental ruler; others were in effect alliances constituted for defensive or aggrandizing purposes, or for waging the prevailing version of a "just war"; others were more or less utopian schemes for war prevention, usually on an intra-European scale.[15] It was a plan in the last category that prompted a devastating, much-quoted gibe from Frederick the Great: "the thing is most practicable; for its success all that is lacking is the consent of Europe and a few similar trifles."[16] It also was this spate of peace plans, which spread over several centuries, that served to call attention to one of the principal dilemmas of collective security as a way of organizing interstate relations: in the extreme, to secure a collective peace may entail first waging a collective war. The condition of peace becomes indivisible in a critically real sense for every member of the community; each must be willing, in the abstract, to go to war on behalf of community purposes, irrespective of who the agressor might be; each must be willing to merge his own interests with, and perhaps even to sacrifice them to an overriding goal of protecting the status quo.

In another context, James Madison and Alexander Hamilton

14. Adda B. Bozeman, *Politics and Culture in International History* (Princeton: Princeton University Press, 1960), pp. 80–81, 87.

15. Consult F. H. Hinsley, *Power and the Pursuit of Peace* (London: Cambridge University Press, 1967), esp. Chapters 1–7.

16. Frederick was referring, in a letter to Voltaire, to the celebrated plan entitled *Perpetual Peace*, first circulated by Saint-Pierre in 1712. The quote is recorded in ibid., p. 45.

warned the American Constitutional Convention of 1787 that collective sanctions or collective enforcement against deviant states in a federal union would, in essential respects, be tantamount to war. This same awareness on the international plane has been one of the main contributors to the reluctance and inability of twentieth-century international organizations to equip themselves with sanctions weapons that could be effective among sovereign states. Even larger did the obstacles loom in the post-1945 environment dominated by nuclear and ideological rivalries.

In the practice of both the League and the UN, member states turned to peace-keeping as a workable, constructive alternative to classical collective security. This alternative has rested on a qualitatively different set of assumptions and expectations about what is to be accomplished by an international organization, what methods are to be used, and what types of conflict situations are to be regarded as appropriate for internationally concerted action. The international organization as peace-keeper makes no collective judgment of aggression, assigns no guilt for violating community standards, and applies no coercive measures against wrongdoers. Instead, it acts as an intermediary rather than adversary, adopts the mantle of pacifier rather than enforcer, uses persuasion rather than punishment, aims at minimizing violence rather than repelling aggression, and relies on the consent of parties to a dispute rather than on a mandate to compel them into compliance by force of arms or economic sanctions.

These roles cast an international organization essentially as a third party in regard to the contestants and interests involved in a particular conflict situation.[17] Peace-keepers have employed a rich repertory of techniques to help lessen local tensions, to reduce risks of escalation and outside military intervention, to encourage local negotiation, and to limit the parties'

17. For an excellent theoretical analysis of third-party attributes and methods see Oran R. Young, *The Intermediaries: Third Parties in International Crises* (Princeton: Princeton University Press, 1967), esp. Chapters 1–3.

resort to military measures. Functionally, peace-keeping has involved monitoring agreed cease-fires, supervising plebiscites, patrolling borders, guaranteeing demilitarization and troop withdrawal arrangements, assisting in maintenance of internal security, and helping to preserve essential governmental or administrative services in strife-torn areas. Organizationally, peace-keeping chores have been entrusted to mechanisms ranging from observer corps staff by a handful of officers to much larger military forces consisting of as many as 20,000 men, as was the UN's most ambitious peace-keeping force in the Congo. In all of its variations peace-keeping has been a mixed politico-military form of conflict control, entailing not only the usually more visible military presences at scenes of confrontation but also diplomacy at local levels and in international political councils. And in a few cases, international military personnel have been paralleled by civilian policemen and by other civilians performing operational tasks in rehabilitation, reconstruction, and other ancillary services.

The responsibilities of international secretariats for managing and supporting operations such as these have expanded markedly during the past several decades as peace-keeping has become a more regular function of international organization. It became progressively clearer that a brand of peace-keeping purporting to be politically impartial in intent required an independent and likewise impartial administrative setup for implementing political mandates, particularly as Secretaries-General have come to be widely accepted as chief executives in the peace-keeping sphere. The kind and scope of material demands in field operations generated an obvious need for centrally coordinated decision-making, resource control financing and procurement, civilian as well as military logistics systems, communications facilities, and a host of other indispensible backup services. Finally, greater involvement of international administrators in peace-keeping mirrored the broader trend—discernible even during the League era—that found international secretariats taking on increasing numbers of external, operational assignments, that found them moving beyond the restrictive housekeeping or technical functions characteristic of early secretariats and accepting more dynamic and somewhat more autonomous policy-making and execution responsibilities. This broadened secretariat role is by now a standard component of many UN economic, social, and political activities.[18]

ANTECEDENTS TO UNITED NATIONS ADMINISTRATION OF PEACE-KEEPING

Except in a rather narrow functional sense, the nineteenth and early twentieth centuries were barren of significant precedents for the essentially non-coercive, order-maintenance activities subsequently brought under the rubric of peace-keeping. Perhaps faint resemblances are to be seen in the policing methods concocted by great powers to supervise certain of their mutually agreed upon measures concerning international navigation and sanitation. These governments sent representatives to constitute on-the-spot commissions with authority to call upon local officials and police as supplemental supervisory agents. On this model, sanitary police operated in Constantinople, Alexandria, and Tangiers; and navigation police monitored the Danzig and Memel harbors. Still more complex and far-reaching were the joint multinational administrations set up by Europeans over important territories to forestall unilateral appropriation or competive intervention. Special mechanisms were thus given responsibility for Cracow, Crete, Shanghai, and Tangiers, the latter two involving combinations of local gendarmerie, imported policemen, and military units in reserve to keep order.[19]

18. On changing conceptions of international secretariats see Ranshofen-Wertheimer, *The International Secretariat,* op. cit.; and Langrod, *The International Civil Service,* op. cit.

19. Case studies of these pre-League of Nations arrangements can be found in Meir Ydit, *International Territories* (Leiden: A. W. Sijthoff, 1961), pp. 95–184; also Hans Wehberg, *Theory and Practice of International Policing* (London: Constable & Co., 1935) pp. 11–14.

From the standpoint of contemporary peace-keeping, the most interesting cases under the auspices of the League were two: the Vilna dispute of 1920 in which the dispatch of an international peace-keeping force was aborted after the operation had been planned in some detail; and supervision of the Saar plebiscite in 1934–35, which is rightly regarded as the century's first successful experiment with international peace-keeping on a major scale, involving multinational military units mandated by an international organization to carry out politically impartial tasks with non-fighting techniques. Both cases point up significantly not only the modest progress that had been made in developing genuinely international forms of peace-keeping but also how much remained to be done by the League's successor. Both instances demonstrate the minimalist assumptions under which the League Secretary-General and Secretariat operated. Both highlight the pervasiveness of the League's principal great powers, France and Great Britain, in the organization's work generally and in its peace-keeping missions in particular. Both contain evidence of growing awareness on the part of League members that, once it is acknowledged that parties to a dispute who consent to a peace-keeping presence expect any international force to perform impartially, the question of national composition of these forces becomes a central one.

VILNA AND THE SAAR: THE LEAGUE OF NATIONS AS AN ADMINISTRATOR OF PEACE-KEEPING

Today's student of UN peace-keeping has little trouble establishing the intimate and multiple connections between the Secretary-General, plus his staff, and the workings of peace-keeping forces in the field, both in terms of overall policy and day-to-day miscellany. Select a representative series of published records from the major UN missions, and they will somewhere contain references to: explicit grants of peace-keeping authority from the Security Council or General Assembly to the

Secretary-General; special advisory committees of national representatives to assist the Secretary-General in making and implementing peace-keeping policies; the activities of various technical-administrative branches of the Secretariat responsible for providing support—sometimes massive and complex, other times trivial and routine—to peace-keeping forces in the field; reports over the signature of the Secretary-General dealing with an unexpected political crisis in some mission, or merely conveying periodic information to UN members or to the authorizing body; proposals by the Secretary-General or his representatives for changes in structure or performance of field operations; copies of instructions from the Secretary-General to peace-keeping commanders or to special UN political negotiators at peace-keeping sites; and so on, through a list that could be extended for pages.

Not quite ten months after the Saar plebescite had been completed, the supreme military commander of the League's peace-keeping force filed a comprehensive official report to Geneva on his recent assignment; and during this same period, a colonel who had occupied a responsible slot in the Saar force joined with other military and scholarly experts to analyse the Saar experiment in a published pamphlet. Both documents, though with somewhat more detail in the supreme commander's report, review the organization of the four-nation force, its performance, the principal problems it faced, the reasons for its success, and the lessons that this venture contained for the future conduct of peace-keeping operations by the League. One of the first things a reader of these documents notices is that in neither is there any mention whatsoever of the League Secretary-General, the Secretariat, or activities by them that might have been somehow related to the functioning of the force. [20] In-

20. The two documents are, respectively, J. Brind, "League of Nations. Report by the Commander-in-Chief, International Force in the Saar," October 26, 1935, reprinted as "International Information Center on Peacekeeping Operations," *Documentation*, Paris (February 1968), No. 29; and Capt. B. H. Liddell Hart, Col. A. H. Burne, and Miss Sarah Wambaugh, "Policing the Saar," *The New Commonwealth*, London (April 1936), Series A, Pamphlet No. 8.

deed, from the reports themselves, one would infer that the League Secretariat did not even exist.

These were not errors or distortions. In truth the Secretariat seems to have played no significant part in managing or supporting the Saar force. It seems instead to have been adhering to a precept, which throughout the League years embodied the style of a mostly non-operational international civil service, dictating that once policy is determined an international organization will be content to "leave actual implementation of decisions to cooperating national administrations."[21] It is possible to characterize the evolution of international administration of peace-keeping as a gradual movement away from this exclusive reliance on a principle of delegation and toward a more extensive, shared role for an international secretariat.

To date, with sovereign states still the central if no longer the only important actors in the international system, this shift has remained limited in scope. The UN is accordingly denied the trappings of a fully, or even a largely, internationalized peace-keeping apparatus. It has no military forces independent of those offered by member states for peace-keeping. It has no carte blanche to use these forces unless the supplier government agrees in each particular case. Its Secretary-General may deploy these forces only after receiving a formal mandate from a UN organ and then only with the consent of host states. The UN has no sources of revenue to pay for peace-keeping missions independent of the contributions of member states. It has no choice but to continue to rely on certain members for material goods and services that are too sophisticated, too massive, or too expensive to be provided independently by the Secretariat. Nonetheless the UN Secretariat has carved out for itself a much more active and influential place than was ever conceived by its predecessor in the "actual implementation" of peace-keeping

21. Royal Institute of International Affairs, *The International Secretariat of the Future* (London: Oxford University Press, 1944), p. 21, quoted in Wertheimer, op. cit., p. 240.

decisions, a role that has entailed both wider policy-making responsibilities and substantial direct administration and control by international civil servants following international rather than national instructions.

But in the earlier realm of League peace-keeping—at least when fairly sizable military resources were involved—this principle of delegation entailed in practice giving special administrative responsibilities to the militarily advanced great powers, France and Great Britain. Peace-keeping structures represented, in microcosm, the overall political complexion of the League, which was a largely Europe-centered organization with a Franco-British core. These two governments supplied the League with one Secretary-General apiece, with most of its senior professionals for the Geneva bureaucracy, with the bulk of its revenue, with its standard working languages, and with the two civil service systems that were adapted successively in the Secretariat. The linchpin of the proposed Vilna force was to have been France, while Britain played the key role in the Saar arrangements, though in both cases other nationalities were engaged as well.

When, under the League's auspices, a plebiscite was agreed on in order to resolve issues in dispute over the territory of Vilna, which was contested by Poland and Lithuania in the immediate postwar period, French influence touched all phases of the dispute. French nationals occupied positions of central diplomatic importance. One of the outstanding French men of the Left and long-time internationalist, Leon Bourgeois, was then president of the League Council and active in its activities on this question. The Council was meeting in Paris; a preliminary cease-fire in Vilna had been monitored by a five-man military commission headed by a French colonel, also diplomatically active and scheduled to become commander of the larger peace-keeping force that was to have supervised the voting; and detailed military preparations were being undertaken by the French general staff of Marshal Ferdinand Foch, which took charge of planning transporation and all basic logistical support for the proposed nine-nation peace-keeping force. Most of the necessary arrangements were completed when the plebiscite was canceled for lack of agreement between the local parties and because of disunity among the great powers over the issue. Throughout this preparatory period Secretary-General Drummond, in office only about a year, remained in the background. He drafted some of the Council's formal communications, such as requests to League members for peace-keeping units, but beyond this, most execution tasks were assigned to France as the Council's specifically appointed national agent.

Britain's no less central role as the League's agent in the Saar case also had both diplomatic and military dimensions. The Versailles peace-makers had decided that, for an interim, pre-plebiscite period of fifteen years, the economically and politically important Saar territory would be governed by a five-man international commission established by the League Council. As the time approached in the mid-thirties for the plebiscite that would determine whether the Saarlanders would opt to join Germany, or France, or to remain under League control, the accession of Hitler to power raised some doubts about how a majority of the territory's inhabitants would vote. Their natural inclinations as Germans were now counterbalanced by the prospect of threats to their Catholicism under Nazi rule. During a turbulent year of bitter political agitation preceding the 1935 vote, the League Council instructed the governing commission—not the Secretary-General—to recruit a peace-keeping force that could ensure an orderly and fair vote. At the time the commission's chief was British, Britain's Anthony Eden was a key figure in the Council's diplomacy, a British major general was appointed commander of the Saar force, Britain's contribution to the force was the largest of the four supplying nations, the force's headquarters was staffed entirely by British military personnel, and the planning and operation of the force were conducted according to standard British military procedures.

As the UN was to do later, notably in the Congo, West Irian, and Cyprus cases, the League supplemented the military peace-keepers in the Saar with a variety of non-military specialists to handle related functions, in this instance mainly technical supervision of the complicated plebiscite. Here too, operating authority rested less with permanent international civil servants than with national agents or specially constituted commissions of national experts. A little-noticed element in the League's impressive Saar machinery was a small contingent of international civilian policemen to assist in the maintenance of local law and order. They were required because of factors strikingly similar to those that nearly thirty years later prompted the UN to use its first corps of ordinary civilian policemen in Cyprus, where the local police also wielded great power and were too divided in political loyalties to enforce laws fairly and impartially. Beyond this, the League presence in the Saar included nearly a thousand civilians of more than two dozen nationalities serving as plebiscite staff officials, tribunal judges, and presidents of each of the voting bureaus in the territory. To ensure a free vote, every one of the more than 500,000 ballots cast—90 per cent of them for return to Germany—was handed directly to an international official, and remained constantly under international surveillance until counted and eventually transported to Geneva for destruction. For their part, the military peace-keepers were able to ensure tranquillity without serious incident.

In both Vilna and the Saar, the League Council's instructions and the stated expectations of national representatives on the Council made it clear that the proposed forces were to conform to the norms of non-coercion and political impartiality— both regarded as essential conditions for receiving the consent of the Poles and Lithuanians, and the French and Germans. In these instances, the League began to grapple with the question that still plagues contemporary peace-keeping policy-makers: how can political impartiality be assured and reinforced to the satisfaction of the parties involved?

One part of the answer is to provide peace-keepers who are managed and administered under impartial auspices. But impartiality is not an objectively ascertainable quality, and each situation tends to generate its own conclusions about what frameworks are or are not likely to be impartial—hence in 1964 Archbishop Makarios of Cyprus rejected NATO-sponsored peace-keeping in favor of the UN; whereas in 1954 Communist negotiators at the Geneva Indochina Conference rejected truce supervision by the UN, which they saw as dominated by Western powers, in favor of an *ad hoc* organizational arrangement that produced the infamous and immobilizing troika of the International Control Commission. In a similar vein, it might be added that in the Saar case Hitler at one point briefly considered rejecting any solution that involved military peace-keepers from the League (from which he had already withdrawn) in favor of a plebiscite policed entirely by the Swiss not acting on behalf of the League.

Another part of the answer is to choose, under whatever organizational umbrella is decided upon, national participants in peace-keeping forces who are politically disinterested in local outcomes of the dispute, or whose political leanings somehow "balance" the composition of the force. The League did both. One of the stumbling blocks of the Vilna episode—though not the decisive one—was the predominance of the French, whose public opinion and official sympathies were quite correctly regarded by the Lithuanians as pro-Polish. Some of the potential suppliers of troops for the operation seem to have been sensitive to this problem, for at least one of them made its offer conditional on explicit assurances that the force would function impartially and be broadly based in composition. In an evident effort to enlist politically unexceptionable states, the League Council, after initially tendering an open invitation to all League members to participate, shifted its approach by specifically asking the Danish, Norwegian, and Dutch governments to take part, each of them an acknowledged neutral.[22] A decade and a half later, two great power Saar units, British and Italian, were coupled with two neutrals, Sweden and the Netherlands. To give emphasis to impartial intent, the Dutch offered troops on a condition that was subsequently to reappear in UN experience, namely that another neutral must also be designated a participant. As regards the daily operations of the force, the commander made special efforts to maintain scrupulous impartiality toward the dispute and to communicate this posture to all contingents as well as to the parties themselves.

Very shortly after the Saar force and its civilian counterparts were disbanded, having prevented a Franco-German conflict that everyone wished to avoid, the Italian attack on Ethiopia laid bare the League's impotence as a collective security organization and sealed firmly its irrelevance as an agency for turning back Nazi and fascist expansionism. It was to be nearly twenty years before the peace-keeping model fashioned for the Saar was resurrected and considerably modified for Suez, but an international organization markedly different from the League, having a Secretariat that reflected many of the most important of these differences.

PEACE-KEEPING ADMINISTRATION SINCE 1945

The historical genealogy of internationally administered peace-keeping passed through several important detours before reaching Hammarskjöld and the Middle East in 1956. The UN's first decade was the period of its most intense, if sporadic, preoccupation with implementing the Charter's collective security,

---

22. Countries initially slated to be contributors of troops to the Vilna force were Belgium, Britain, Denmark, France, Greece, the Netherlands, Norway, Spain, and Sweden.

or collective enforcement, provisions. Peace-keeping—although the word itself was not yet in vogue—occupied a distinct second place until the organization managed to trim its pretensions. Yet the UN's formal, constitutional priorities and its actual practices were by no means identical, and while most attention focused on institution-building for collective security, the Secretariat was beginning to involve itself more and more centrally in early peace-keeping missions, those observer corps that had been established in rapid succession during the late 1940s. It did so in ways that moved appreciably beyond the limited role of its League forerunner, gradually transforming these missions into more genuinely international endeavors controlled progressively more by UN civil servants rather than by national agents acting under a transparent UN cover.

Administration of Collective Enforcement: Military Staff Committee and Uniting for Peace

In order to impose some manageable form on the varied UN experience with international military forces, it is necessary to distinguish the administration of collective enforcement from the administration of peace-keeping.[23] This makes it somewhat easier to clarify the significantly different institutional assumptions underlying each system. It helps in sorting out the origins of each, their important interconnections, and their separate relevance for the future of UN military capabilities and attendant administrative structures. Perhaps most importantly, the distinction is instructive for understanding the political currents that during the past quarter-century have shaped the issue of how a UN military arm should be created, used, and sustained.

23. A careful historical study that separates the two is Ruth B. Russell, *The United Nations and United States Security Policy* (Washington, D.C.: Brookings Institution, 1968), Chapters 5 and 6; compare with James, *The Politics of Peacekeeping*, which employs a concept of peace-keeping that comprises collective enforcement as well as lesser forms of conflict control.

That the Charter of the UN, like most constitutive documents, was written to deal with a known past rather than a vaguely perceived future is particularly evident in matters of international security. The military provisions written into Chapter VII of the Charter were designed to prevent another war like the one drawing to a close in the summer of 1945, and they were intended to remedy the defects that riddled the collective security machinery of the League of Nations. The result was a limited collective security scheme—limited in that mandatory sanctions could not be imposed against the wishes of a veto-wielding permanent member of the Security Council—that its framers hoped would project into the postwar world the security concept embodied in Roosevelt's vision of wartime great powers, their unity preserved after defeat of the Axis enemies, continuing to act in concert as the world's "Four Policemen."

The drafters of the Charter at San Francisco substituted five for four, but the essence of this idea was translated into the Charter's Security Council-centered collective enforcement apparatus. It was supposed to give the UN the military "teeth" never possessed by the League, although insistently urged upon it by France and some other members who felt that a militarily powerful League could be used to contain Germany. Dismayed, therefore, at the Covenant's reliance on economic more than on military sanctions, the French repeatedly sought to give the Geneva organization a standing, permanent, and comprehensive military capability: at Versailles, then in the early 1920s, and again at the disarmament conference in 1932, French initiatives toward this end were rejected, which was consistent with the generally dominant counter-emphasis in the League, evident also in the early 1920s, on diluting the Covenant's collective sanctions provisions.

In military terms, the core of the UN approach is outlined in Articles 43 and 47 of the Charter, which made clear how completely the new collective security system was to be managed and manned by a presumably unanimous Big Five. These articles governed the raising of military forces in accordance with special agreements to be negotiated with the Security Council. Although the language does not explicitly say so, there was a universal understanding—written, it has been said, into the Charter with invisible ink—that the overwhelming bulk of these forces would be supplied by the Big Five. They themselves would also exercise jointly supreme command authority over these and any supplementary forces offered by other member states once the great powers agreed on their own contributions. For this purpose the Charter provided the Security Council with a Military Staff Committee patterned consciously on the Combined Chiefs of Staff that served the Anglo-American Allies during World War II. In a sense, the Military Staff Committee was to be to the Council what the Combined Chiefs had been to Roosevelt and Churchill. Now each permanent member's chief of staff, or representative thereof, would sit on the Committee, which was empowered to exercise "strategic direction" of UN armies and to provide military advice for the Security Council.

The subsequent history of these provisions is well known.[24] Fifteen months of negotiations in the Military Staff Committee merely confirmed that the Cold War antagonists viewed each other as the world's lawbreaker rather than as a co-guarantor of global collective security. Deadlock in the Committee, which has remained moribund since 1947, was cloaked in disagreements over technical matters concerning the nature of projected contributions from the Big Five, but the real impediments were the political suspicions and mistrust on all sides. In the increasingly polarized world of the immediate postwar years, neither adversary was willing to give an international organization any military capabilities that could be employed against its own interests. Just as the onset of the Cold War rapidly disfigured the grand edifice produced at San Francisco, the continued waging of that Cold War inside the UN during its first

24. Claude, *Power and International Relations*, op. cit., pp. 173–90.

decade prevented creation of a substitute collective security framework.

Much that can be said in retrospect about how the Charter-based system would have operated is necessarily speculative. However, some aspects are worth mentioning in the context of international administration. While the Big Five were content to incorporate into the Charter (Articles 100 and 101) the essential principles of an independent civil service, these same great powers apparently felt it necessary to ignore, perhaps even to violate, those principles in regard to the administration of any UN collective security operations. Originally, the Military Staff Committee was not to be mainly serviced by the regular UN Secretariat but rather by a separate secretariat appointed by and primarily responsible to the Committee, operating under regulations never approved by the normal UN political channels, and composed equally of Big Five nationals who would, it seems, first have had to be granted security clearances by their respective governments. Only in the latter half of the 1950s, after the question of administering collective enforcement armies had become moot, was this separate unit integrated into the regular Secretariat, a step intended to establish conformity with Charter principles.[25]

The existence of this special secretariat was merely one manifestation of how the Big Five were determined to keep in their own hands, as far as possible, all important levers over the collective security system, resisting intrusion of international civil servants in all but marginal capacities. As early as the 1944 Dumbarton Oaks Planning Conference, the option of an internationally controlled, fully internationalized sanctions force was unanimously rejected. From then on, each great power hewed strictly to the notion that if there was to be a Chapter VII military sanctions capability it would have to be constructed on the basis of jointly made and jointly executed sovereign deci-

25. Langrod, The International Civil Service, op. cit., p. 58, n. 8; and p. 206, n. 14.

sions that would go no further than the minimum common denominator of Big Five agreement. It was the later, definite shift in UN purposes away from collective enforcement and toward peace-keeping that opened the way to more extensive and significant involvement by international civil servants in the functioning of UN military forces. Even the slight degree of partial and temporary internationalization that has been achieved in peace-keeping operations—for instance the latitude of a Secretary-General's authority to appoint and instruct military commanders-in-chief of UN forces, or the expectation that in most circumstances the participating national units follow international rather than national orders—would have been dismissed as preposterous by negotiators on the Military Staff Committee.

But these developments in doctrine did not take clear shape until after the search for a UN collective security system passed through its second, and terminal, phase. For shorthand purposes this might be labeled the Uniting for Peace phase, referring to the title of the General Assembly's 1950 resolution. One of the overriding purposes of this document was to establish a functional substitute for the methods of mobilizing collective sanctions resources laid out in Chapter VII of the Charter and relegated to limbo by disagreement in the Military Staff Committee.[26] Procedurally, the new framework was designed to buttress the authority of the General Assembly to recommend and apply collective sanctions when the Security Council was stymied by a great power veto. Militarily, the 1950 resolution envisaged UN call-up of national units held on standby, a panel of military experts to advise participants, and a special committee to study problems of imposing collective measures— all to do what the Charter had intended in Articles 43–47. Politically, the new framework was a Western, largely American, effort to transform the UN into an agency capable of wield-

26. Claude, *Swords Into Plowshares,* op. cit., pp. 245–48.

ing the power of collective enforcement against the will of the Soviet Union; it was an attempt to anticipate the "next Korea," when the Soviets might not so obligingly be absent from the Security Council as they were in the summer of 1950; it was, in effect, a proposal that would have enlisted the UN as another ingredient in the strategy of containment being pursued by the Western powers who for the most part dominated the UN organization. Historically, Uniting for Peace was both an offspring as well as a casualty of the Cold War. It was born in the autumn of 1950 amidst a good deal of UN euphoria over the novel collective enforcement experiment in Korea, but disowned as Washington itself soured over continued use of the UN for such purposes, as significant portions of the UN membership came to share this conviction for various reasons, and as it became more evident that the UN's most constructive contribution to peace would be in ameliorating the impact of superpower competition rather than in serving as a weapon for one of the contestants.

Only scant interest was shown in implementing the resolution's military provisions, and the fact that what little there was came from U.S. allies simply confirmed the accuracy of Nehru's observation that the arrangement would have remade the UN "into a larger edition of the Atlantic Pact." [27] Or, as a scholarly analyst later put it: the resolution "represents a stage in the alignment of United Nations members in hostile military camps," and "it 'divides for war' even as it 'unites for peace.'" [28] With these implications in prospect, the military components of the revolution languished quickly, and the collective measures committee authorized by it closed its doors for good in

27. Quoted in David Cox, "Canada's Interest in Peacekeeping: Some Political and Military Considerations," in the Canadian Institute of International Affairs, *Peacekeeping: International Challenge and Canadian Response* (Toronto: CIIA, 1968), p. 44.

28. Julius Stone, *Legal Controls of International Conflict*, rev. ed. (London: Stevens and Sons, 1959), p. 275.

1954—an event that symbolized the abandonment of collective security institution-building under the aegis of the UN.

PEACE-KEEPING: THE EARLY YEARS

In a number of important respects the UN's first decade, during which it began its peace-keeping career with the four early observer or fact-finding missions in Greece, Palestine, Indonesia, and Kashmir, was a kind of bridge between the practices of the League and those of the more mature UN. Viewing the period in this way, however, is a luxury of the historian. At the time, the Secretariat officials who were taking these first uncertain steps were consciously neither looking over their shoulders at the League nor thinking very systematically about the precedents they were setting for the future. Instead, as one Secretariat member long associated with peace-keeping matters recounted many years afterwards, early practices developed "almost by accident."[29]

Material demands for field administration varied greatly from mission to mission, in some instances reaching quite pressing proportions for so untested an organization. In manpower terms the smallest observer corps never exceeded 75 military officers; the largest, about 700. Support items of civilian and military natures ranged from routine personal equipment, through standard logistical hardware and services, to the more complex requirements such as special communications and transport systems, including naval and air elements on few occasions.

Carry-overs from the approaches seen first in the League experience were evident in the incidental role of the UN Secretariat, in the patterns of national composition, and in the decision-making structures at field levels. Peace observation under UN auspices was initially carried out by commissions of national representatives, diplomatic and military, acting under a general

---

29. Brian E. Urquhart, "A UN Perspective," in Lincoln P. Bloomfield (ed.), *International Military Forces* (Boston: Little, Brown, and Co., 1964), p. 129.

mandate from a UN political body but responsible operationally to their own governments. Inexperience and incapacity combined with a still-prevalent, passive conception of an international civil service to reduce the Secretariat's early responsibility to minor servicing of these essentially nationally administered missions.

They were not only nationally administered at first; they were also selectively staffed, with national composition often restricted to governments with consular representatives already active in the troubled area. The motivation for using this criterion was less a striving for efficiency than a Western desire to manipulate participation so as to exclude Soviet involvement in these regions, a tactic found especially useful in the cases of Palestine and Indonesia. It is worth keeping in mind that the origins of persistent Russian antipathy towards UN peace-keeping go all the way back to this early practice of Western-controlled majorities on the Council or in the Assembly. This antipathy of course increased drastically when the organization was mobilized against Soviet interests in the Korean case, which triggered Moscow's first breakdown of relations with the UN, and by the controversial Congo episode, which triggered the second and led to the personal vendetta against Hammarskjöld, the unsuccessful troika gambit, and eventually the constitutional and financial crisis of the mid-1960s over non-payment of peace-keeping assessments by the Soviet Union, France, and others.

Like the League, the UN relied in its early operations on the great powers of the day for peace-keeping expertise. As the British and French during the League years were prominent peace-keepers, so too were the Americans and other Western powers central to the missions authorized during the late 1940s. From them, and particularly from the U.S., came most of the logistical and financial support as well as substantial numbers of actual operating personnel. The contrast with subsequent practice is sharp. While the UN continued to depend heavily on American material assistance throughout its later peace-keeping activities, the requirements for impartial peace-keeping after 1956 and the intent to use peace-keeping as a device for circumscribing great power involvement in local conflicts meant that all permanent members of the Security Council were ineligible as front-line participants. Only in the case of British participation in the UN force in Cyprus did special circumstances dictate a departure from this normal policy.

Slowly these early patterns underwent significant modifications, visible most clearly in the Kashmir case, which was the last of the four early missions to be set up, and in the partial restaffing of the Middle East observers in the early 1950s. The Secretariat acquired broader responsibilities in all spheres: unified control under the Secretary-General replaced the use of national commissions; the Secretariat challenged and eventually altered the original practice of relying on nationally instructed military officers; progressively wider functions in supporting observers in the field were taken over by permanent international civil servants or by officials seconded to the UN by member states; and the Secretariat began accepting broader overall financial responsibilities, purchasing its own equipment, or reimbursing national agents for goods and services rendered. Also, the bases of national composition of these missions became less restrictive, permitting greater emphasis on selection of impartial states, consultation with host governments, and a more active role for the Secretary-General in negotiating membership questions.

PEACE-KEEPING AFTER 1956: NEW MAGNITUDE OF CHALLENGES FOR THE SECRETARIAT

On the eve of the so-called Age of Peace-keeping, international administrators had at their disposal not only the collected experience of the early observer missions but also several constitutional and political buttresses for more comprehensive peace-keeping involvement by the Secretary-General and his staff. Relevant provisions of the Charter had been fleshed out by a decade of interpretation and application. The Secretariat, granted in 1945 a co-equal status with the political bodies as a principal UN organ, had steadily extended itself, beginning in the late 1940s, as an operating agency with field programs in economic, social, and humanitarian activities—paralleling the still modest Secretariat role in support of the observer corps and assorted other special purpose political commissions sponsored by the UN. Secretary-General Lie had vigorously pursued opportunities to make use of the potentially expansive political role given to his office in the Charter, and he exercised his authority as chief administrative officer of the organization in molding an independent and unified civil service, a goal threatened gravely by the McCarthyite assault on the Secretariat late in Lie's tenure.

Each of these strands became vitally important during the stewardship of Hammarskjöld and U Thant as political administrators of peace-keeping operations.[30] Between 1956 and 1967, the most recent year that the UN set up a new peace-keeping presence (at the Suez Canal), the Council or the Assembly entrusted the Secretary-General with peace-keeping mandates on the average of about one every year and a half. The total number of soldiers to serve under the UN flag rose from the meager levels of the first decade to somewhere between 200,000 and 250,000 men, while the tally of contributing countries grew from a handful to more than 50. Assignments undertaken by military peace-keepers and the civilian administrators supporting them comprised, at one extreme, relatively simple cease-fire monitoring by a hundred or so military observers plus a smaller complement of UN civilians; and, at the other, the operational nightmare that was the Congo mission, with its military force peaking at 20,000 men from more than 30 states, with its military logis-

30. See Gordenker, *The UN Secretary General and the Maintenance of Peace*, op. cit., esp. Chapters 9–12.

tics requirements for a territory more than four times the size of France in which normal transport and communications had been heavily disrupted, and with its unprecedented UN Civilian Operations Component, staffed at one point by more than 1000 technical experts and backup personnel responsible for emergency relief, for maintaining essential governmental and administrative services, and for training and educating Congolese nationals.

Enormous variations in structure and detail are found in the administrative machinery that has been set up to manage peace-keeping operations in the field. Each mission's unique problems have led to differences in the chains of command linking the Secretary-General and his military or civilian subordinates, and in overall UN headquarters-field relations. Also the division of labor between participating national governments and the Secretariat has differed greatly; for example, proportionally fewer Secretariat civilians are involved in the logistics of the Cyprus force than has been the case in the other larger forces, mainly because existing British facilities and logisticians on the island have made the support job much less burdensome for the Secretariat. And there have been differences in the extent to which the Secretariat has been obliged to call on special outside, non-military resources, whether an *ad hoc* multilateral salvage team to clear the Suez Canal as one did in 1957, a loose consortium of specialized agencies to help with expert services as they did in the Congo, or civilian policemen with the skills to monitor local law enforcement agencies as is done in Cyprus.

Yet underneath these and a myriad of other distinguishing characteristics a fairly constant and so far enduring bureaucratic pattern has been evolved in the Secretariat's basic organization for handling peace-keeping chores. There are two pillars supporting the system, one responsible for overall politico-military policy and implementation, the other for the range of administrative tasks at the headquarters and field levels. Both overlap a good deal; both establish numerous connections with troop-supply countries; both are formally under the unified authority of the Secretary-General.

The politico-military apparatus is simply one part of those sections of the Secretariat into which political affairs have been progressively concentrated as the political responsibilities of Secretaries-General have expanded over the years.[31] Principally this means that basic peace-keeping decisions have involved the chief executive personally and the staffs of his executive office and of the two Under Secretaries for Special Political Affairs. The last are twin posts without portfolio that have been used very flexibly since their creation early in Hammarskjöld's first term. One of the occupants, Dr. Ralph Bunche, has ever since then been delegated the main burden of managing peace-keeping missions from headquarters. It was Bunche whom Hammarskjöld once dubbed wryly his "minister of defence." In reality his "ministry" has never been more than a skeleton staff of political officers, and in the best of times, a few military experts who were usually attached formally to the executive office.

The Secretariat's administrative hub for supporting peace-keeping is in the Office of General Services, headed by an Assistant Secretary-General with vast administrative and housekeeping responsibilities for UN activities, in New York and the world at large. For the most part, the UN structure for servicing peace-keeping is bureaucratically undifferentiated; most administrative units involved deal with more than just peace-keeping. This practice of integrating peace-keeping support into the regular channels of the Secretariat originated in the late 1940s, and today a peace-keeping operation is likely to be assisted at one time or another by virtually all Secretariat departments. Various sections of General Services would take charge of matters such as procurement, transportation, and communications between the mission and headquarters.

31. An especially helpful analysis of internal Secretariat organization and its complex evolution since 1945 is ibid., Chapter 5.

Within General Services, the Field Operations Service that Secretary-General Lie created in 1949 to consolidate lower level support functions for peace-keeping, would be concentrated responsibility for providing technical personnel ranging from radio operators and mechanics to office managers and secretaries. And, finally, other major departments of the Secretariat, such as legal or public information offices, would be expected to help as needed in their areas of specialization.

Those who have observed the performance of the Secretariat bureaucracy as a manager of peace-keeping operations during the past fifteen years tend to find themselves in broad agreement on at least one point: the Secretariat has been unprepared for meeting most of the demands placed on it, and it is still unprepared for major peace-keeping responsibilities in the future. While the Secretariat has been something of a miracle-worker in accomplishing what it has, given the constraints under which it has had to function, its shortcomings have been undeniable. As regards peace-keeping-related capabilities, it is under-financed, under-manned, under-equipped, under-skilled, under-planned, under-standardized, and under-informed.[32] Institutional, material, and manpower inadequacies of the Secretariat must certainly be included in a diagnosis made by U Thant in 1967: "While it seems to be agreed that the United Nations must have some capacity to act effectively in time of danger, it has not so far been possible to agree on methods by which that capacity would be increased and made more reliable."[33]

32. Detailed examinations of Secretariat readiness for peace-keeping support can be found in Washington Center of Foreign Policy Reasearch, School of Advanced International Studies, Johns Hopkins University, National Support of International Peacekeeping and Peace Observation Operations, prepared for the U.S. Arms Control and Disarmanent Agency, ACDA/12–161, February 1970, Vols. I–V passim; also Edward H. Bowman and James E. Fanning, "Logistics—Experience and Requirements," in Lincoln Bloomfield (ed), International Military Forces (Boston: Little, Brown, 1964), pp. 145–71.

33. "Introduction to the Annual Report of the Secretary General on the Work of the Organization," UN Monthly Chronicle (October 1967), Vol. IV, No. 9, p. 101.

THE SECRETARIAT AND REFORM OF
PEACE-KEEPING INSTITUTIONS

The impasse cited by the Secretary-General, as well as the consequent improvisations and uncertainties that plague most UN peace-keeping missions, are by-products of long-standing and acute political controversy, primarily but not only among the great powers on the Security Council. Its repercussions have been widely felt, in the stunted growth of peace-keeping capacities within the Secretariat, in the persistent absence of a truly effective aggregate of national standby forces for peace-keeping call-up, in the once-bitter though now rather muted feuding over how peace-keeping forces ought to be authorized and financed, and in the continuing inability of the UN to reform itself in line with a large number of practical recommendations that have been circulating in expert circles for many years.

None of these improvements and refinements can be treated, in the UN political framework, as mainly technical questions. The governing criteria have far less to do with efficiency than with political acceptability, for there exists vastly more technical know-how than diplomatic consensus about putting it to use. Just as the inglorious and demoralizing Article 19 confrontation between the U.S. and the U.S.S.R. in the mid-1960s over peace-keeping arrearages was not really a dispute about money *per se,* so too arguments about whether the Secretariat ought to contain effective in-house military staffing and planning are not going to be resolved on the basis of the suggestions' instrumental merits. Disagreements on such pragmatic proposals—and they have been haggled over since the era of Trygve Lie—hinge ultimately on member states' differences of purposes and interests regarding the UN as an agent of international security. Involved here are diverse and often incompatible national judgments about what kinds of peace-maintenance responsibilities ought to be entrusted to the organization, what types of attendant military institutions are likely to be both operationally adequate and politically responsive, what built-in controls over their performance are desirable, and generally what comprehensive ground rules should be established to determine how peace-keeping operations should be prepared for and conducted.

Because a working consensus on these fundamentals has been either imperfect or absent entirely, [34] the Secretariat has been exposed continuously to the severest of political cross-pressures. Its position has been especially vulnerable because it has had to be, simultaneously, one of the many actors bargaining over peace-keeping issues and one of the objects or stakes in that bargaining process. In this dual identity, for example, the Secretary-General has frequently been a prime source of initiatives designed to bolster the organization's readiness for peace-keeping, while at the same time his right to do so was being challenged, or his political powers and executive authority to direct ongoing peace-keeping missions without being harnessed to the Security Council were being disputed.

With the post-1956 expansion of peace-keeping activities and the resultant controversies, the dilemmas facing the Secretary-General and the Secretariat became progressively more troublesome and debilitating. In contrast to the preceding era's emphasis on collective enforcement, with it corresponding focus on the Chapter VII machinery and the great powers, this new period found the Secretary-General thrust into the vortex of affairs concerning UN military institutions. He began to provide a doctrinal foundation for their use in ways not contemplated in the Charter. He began to elaborate concepts of what he called UN "executive action" by "a Secretariat so organized and developed as to be able to serve as a neutral instrument for the Organization" in carrying out the broad decisions of political bodies. This he saw as one embodiment of the UN as the "dynamic instrument of governments" that he juxtaposed, in his famous, final *Introduction to the Annual Report 1960–1961*,

34. The broad outlines of the continuing debate up to 1968 over peace-keeping issues are traced in Russell, *The United Nations and United States Security Policy*, op. cit., Chapter 6.

with the regressive notion of the organization as "static conference machinery."[35]

Because peace-keeping was, for Hammarskjöld, an important category of executive action, he was determined not only to concentrate on directing existing operations but also to spur those institutional reforms that would place the UN on sounder footing for future peace-keeping assignments. During the years just after UNEF was created, he proposed a number of guiding principles for such reform, stressing the need for new Secretariat capabilities at an appropriate time and for new measures by member states to prepare portions of their national military establishments for peace-keeping service under international command. In locating the Secretariat at the center of the network of readiness arrangements he was outlining, Hammarskjöld gave to it much of the responsibility that was supposed to have been exercised by the specially established Collective Measures Committee under Uniting for Peace and by the Military Staff Committee under Chapter VII of the Charter. In this and other ways he underlined the changing institutional relationships and the growing centricity of an independent Secretariat that accompanied the UN's transition from collective security to peace-keeping concerns. He also, during the years before the Congo episode, developed increasingly close relations with what might be called the new peace-keeping "constituency" within the organization, that is, the cluster of middle-ranking and small powers who politically supported peacekeeping and were most interested in active participation as military suppliers of peace-keeping personnel. With these states, notably Canada and the nations of northern Europe, Hammarskjöld entered into a tacit alliance aimed at securing wider political support for institutional reform and at encouraging national initiatives such as the creation of standby forces,

35. The quoted passages are all from this Introduction, reprinted in Wilder Foote (ed.), *Servant of Peace* (New York: Harper and Row, 1962), pp. 354, 367–68.

a step that by 1960 had been strongly advocated by Hammar-skjöld and Lester Pearson of Canada, implemented by the Ottawa government, and actively discussed by Nordic planners.

Much of Hammarskjöld's reformism eventually took less ambitious shapes than he at first had envisaged. Measures that he formally proposed had to be pursued quietly in more informal channels when political organs of the UN, for various reasons, declined to give their imprimatur, or when other factors compelled caution. It is also clear with hindsight that, in the mild afterglow of the UNEF success, the Secretary-General tended to underestimate how much reform was needed. Nevertheless, the basic momentum toward reform had been triggered, a key role had been played by the Secretariat, and the concept of genuine internationally administered peace-keeping had been given clearer direction and meaning.

The operational demands of the unprecedented Congo operation shattered whatever complacency there was about the adequacy of Secretariat support capabilities for major peace-keeping efforts, and the crisis's political shock waves undermined early assumptions about how much freedom the Secretariat might enjoy in institution-building for future peace-keeping. The Soviet attitude was, of course, a decisive factor. The virulence of Moscow's challenge to Hammarskjöld and his office, and the depth of the hostility toward that brand of UN presence which helped to undercut Soviet designs in central Africa threatened the viability of the peace-keeping idea.

Soviet attitudes toward peace-keeping had always been ambivalent. Even during the years of the initial observer missions, rhetorical condemnations alternated with indifferent or reluctant toleration, even when political guidelines were set by Western-dominated parliamentary majorities able to outmaneuver Communist bloc resistance, when the Western great powers were prominent in the field missions, and when Soviet nationals were nevertheless excluded from participating. (Russian observers had been volunteered for the original Palestine

Corps.) But whatever its views on this or that specific mission, the Soviet government was unrelentingly opposed to efforts to create institutionalized military capabilities except under Article 43 and the Military Staff Committee. Opposition stemmed in part from ideological conviction that no military or quasi-military powers be available to any international agency —it was Soviet Foreign Minister Vishinsky who once remarked contemptuously that the Secretariat did not need soldiers to run its mimeograph machines. Or it stemmed from the more pragmatic conviction that UN military capabilities would be controlled by Western powers; hence the opposition to the military provisions of Uniting for Peace and to a special unit in the Secretariat that Lie, who roundly supported the resoution, set up to administer those provisions.

Although in the latter half of the 1950s the Soviets displayed no willingness to support Hammarskjöld's reform proposals, there may well have been some prospect of partial acquiescence on the part of Moscow. The post-Stalin shifts in Soviet foreign policy had brought about improved relations with the UN generally, overall satisfaction with Hammarskjöld's peace-keeping initiatives in the Middle East, cordial and respectful dealings with the new Secretary-General whom Moscow supported for a second term in 1957, and friendlier dispositions toward some of the states in Hammarskjöld's emerging peace-keeping constituency. In any event, even if it is correct to say that Hammarskjöld was probing for the limits of an ambiguous consensus in the pre-Congo period, there is little doubt that the ensuing confrontation over peace-keeping abruptly undercut hopes for significant institutional reform.

The Congo affair and its aftermath did not entirely squelch the spirit of reform, but they did compel some short-lived changes in tactics. Inside the organization the impasse on peace-keeping questions, especially on the constitutional and financial aspects that were under increasingly active discussion in the early 1960s, remained unbroken, although the membership refused to accept the notorious troika restructuring of the Secretariat proposed by the Soviets, and although the great powers agreed on a mutually acceptable successor to Hammarskjöld after his death. The new tactics, inspired mostly by then-Prime Minister Lester Pearson of Canada, seemed at first deceptively simple: the peace-keeping constituency that had begun to jell in the late 1950s was now being urged by Pearson to sidestep the obstacles clogging formal UN channels, and concentrate instead on banding together *outside* the organization to strengthen their collective military capacity to respond to requests from the UN for peace-keeping services. This proposal—particularly in the initially ambitious form it took in 1963, with outside-the-UN consultative machinery, a military staff for coordination, and the like—would have substantially altered the Secretariat-centered institutional system that Hammarskjöld had begun to develop but which had recently stagnated. Also, the proposal was intended to coincide with the completion of the planning for the national standby forces for the UN, which was in the first stages of implementation, mainly in Nordic states, in 1963–64.

The Pearson design ended essentially in failure, although a watered-down version did result in a minor technical conference at Ottawa in 1964, attended by some two dozen states with experience in peace-keeping. It may well have failed even under the most propitious circumstances, for it would have created serious political problems for participating governments and the Secretariat. It was in fact presented under the worst of diplomatic circumstances, coinciding almost exactly with the unfolding Article 19 crisis that touched everything to do with peace-keeping, whether inside or outside the UN. Soviet objections, again, were an important impediment to Pearson's plan. In Moscow's view, it and the Article 19 dispute were each fractions of the same whole: the former was an attempt to institutionalize UN military capabilities in ways that could avoid Soviet influence and formal controls, while the latter was an American-led attempt to force the Soviet Union and others to pay for peace-keeping operations which they opposed politically. Moscow reacted by threatening to leave and thereby wreck the organization. That Pearson compromised his original plan, and that the U.S. eventually backed away from its initially tenacious insistence on disenfranchising non-payers of their Assembly votes as provided in Article 19 were both signals of the important shifts that were occurring in UN approaches to peace-keeping questions.

Perhaps the central implication of these two events, as well as of the failure of a reform proposal at the 1966 Assembly mainly because of Soviet resistance, is that peace-keeping institutions stand no chance of being substantially strengthened without an identifiable consensus between the superpowers as a minimum permissive condition. In the practical application of peace-keeping during the 1960s, the so-called "return to the Security Council" as the authorizing body was unmistakably in evidence, notably in the Cyprus, India-Pakistan, and Suez cases. From the proposition that peace-keeping forces be used only for purposes that are jointly approved by the superpowers, it is a logical step to the conclusion that longer-range peace-keeping institutions and procedures will likewise have to be mutually acceptable. Attention shifts, therefore, from the question of how a Secretary-General or a particularly concerned national statesman can maneuver around the Soviet-American standoff that has customarily characterized deliberations over peace-keeping institutions, to the question of whether the superpowers can directly reach the necessary understandings. They themselves have acknowledged this shift during the recent course of their negotiations within the UN Special Committee on Peace-keeping Operations. After several years of futile rehashing of stale doctrinal controversies, they began a new tack in 1968—a serious effort to formulate mutually agreed upon guidelines for conducting future peace-keeping missions. Whether one takes a skeptical or an optimistic view of the likelihood that these negotiations can eventually produce worthwhile results—and either view is arguable—it cannot be denied that even these tentative steps constitute a sharp break from the usual dialogue of the deaf between the superpowers on peace-keeping matters, for this is the first time in UN annals they have engaged in genuine bargaining over the shape of future peace-keeping institutions. [36]

The detailed implications for the Secretariat and international administration of peace-keeping are still uncertain, but these recent activities, coupled with some of the broader historical trends, do seem to support five final observations:

1. The concept of internationally administered peace-keeping appears to be solidly established in UN doctrine and practice. The independent and unified Secretariat has gradually taken over more responsibilities for the functioning of nationally offered peace-keeping forces placed temporarily under international command by member states. The result, as one former Secretariat official put it, is that the "regulations for the forces which defined their international character have been derived, *mutatis mutandis*, from the Staff Regulations which govern the Secretariat," and "the position of the United Nations forces may be considered as at least analagous to that of the Secretariat." [37] In large part, this development was facilitated by the transformation of UN purposes from collective security to peace-keeping, which generated a clear need for impartial peace-keepers and administrators, and which placed the Secretary-General in a pivotal position as chief political executive and chief administrator.

2. The role of the Secretary-General as reformer of peace-

36. For status reports on these negotiations, see UN Doc. A/7742, November 3, 1969; and a report to the U.S. Congress by the American ambassador who is the principal negotiator, found in *25th Anniversary of the United Nations*, Hearings before a Subcommittee of the House Committee on Foreign Affairs, 91st Cong., 2nd Sess. (1970), pp. 72–79.

37. Charles Winchmore (pseud.), "The Secretariat: Retrospect and Prospect," op. cit., pp. 269–70.

keeping institutional structures was relegated, perhaps only temporarily, to a secondary place during the 1960s, at first because of the intensity of the peace-keeping-related controversies early in the decade, and later because of the growing awareness that major reforms would have to await a more effective superpower consensus. Even though U Thant and his political advisors may well have been overly cautious in some matters, there is little question that the Secretariat's comparative passivity is the assertion that ultimate responsibility for building viable peace-keeping institutions now rests squarely on the shoulders of the superpowers. To the extent that this once again becomes the operating premise, it constitutes a reversion to the charter-based assumptions about how UN military capabilities are to be created, except that now the target is peace-keeping, not collective enforcement, and the burden of active military participation falls on lesser powers, not on the permanent members of the council.

3. The tacit but partially fruitful alliance between the Secretariat and the middle-ranking and smaller powers most actively committed to peace-keeping has been strained during the past decade. The peace-keeping constituency has been particularly dismayed at the peace-keeping malaise and at the Secretariat's impotence to ameliorate it. For example, they have regretted the Secretary-General's inability to do more than take official note of the standby forces offered to the UN in 1964–65—the further development of which has since lost a good deal of momentum. They were unhappy at his decision in 1968 to abolish the office of military advisor in the Secretariat, although it had been largely inactive for some time. They, and others as well, shared in the disillusionment that followed the Secretary-General's withdrawal of UNEF at the request of Nasser just before the third round of the Arab-Israeli conflict. But the peace-keeping constituency, too, has become increasingly conscious of the need for a fundamental consensus about peace-keeping, and they are able to anticipate that if superpower un-

derstandings can be thrashed out middle-ranking powers must once again be principal suppliers in peace-keeping missions and proponents of a durable readiness system in conjunction with the Secretariat.

4. The Secretariat continues to be a stake in the diplomatic bargaining over peace-keeping, and in some ways it has become even more important in this respect than it was in the past. The main battlegrounds in the superpower debate today are no longer whether the Security Council versus the Assembly has the constitutional power to launch peace-keeping, or whether mandatory assessments for peace-keeping budgets are legitimate and enforceable. Instead, the incessant constitutional bickering has been set aside, and the hope of imposing mandatory dues has been quashed, for the time being at least, in favor of some essentially voluntary financing system. The crucial point in the superpower dialogue is now the question of how to divide responsibility between the Secretary-General and the Security Council in peace-keeping decision-making and implementation. The Soviets, French, and others argue for more comprehensive Security Council authority; while the U.S., the peace-keeping constituency, and the bulk of UN members opt for a continuation of the Secretary-General's independent role within the framework of enabling resolutions, and for minimum intrusion by the Council. In practice the positions are more blurred, especially in the demonstrated willingness, during the 1960s, of the Soviet Union to allow a generally satisfactory degree of elbow room for the Secretary-General and Secretariat (whose purely administrative role is not being challenged) once the Security Council has been able to enact the initial grants of authority and terms of reference.

5. Re-emphasis on the indispensability of great power, and especially superpower, consensus as a basis for peace-keeping institution-building and performance may affect the Secretariat negatively as well as constructively. A more solid consensus, if it emerges, is likely to reflect broader changes in superpower

relations outside the UN that reinforce their desire to rely upon mutually acceptable conflict-control devices; and such a consensus may well strengthen the foundations for a more active and relatively independent Secretariat. On the other hand, as the permanent members of the Council seek to make peace-keeping institutions more politically responsive to themselves jointly—a need that is now recognized "in principle" if rather abstractly by both superpowers—the effect may be to constrict the leeway available to the Secretary-General and the Secretariat. If one lesson of the past twenty-five years' experiences with both collective enforcement and peace-keeping is that effective military capabilities for the UN are likely to follow rather than precede political understandings about their intended uses, another is that cross-purposes among the membership over peace-keeping have tainted the acceptability of institutions associated with it. The Secretariat has been especially so affected, having alienated primarily the Soviet Union, but also on occasion France and Great Britain as well. Nor is it necessary to stretch credibility too far to imagine "futures" in which Secretariat behavior as a peace-keeper could seriously antagonize the United States, traditionally the Secretariat's most attentive great power supporter and material provider. Finally, speculation about the potential obstructiveness of a mainland China that cannot for long be excluded from the Council can generate even more cautious prognoses for the Secretariat. The dilemma is plain: a system of peace-keeping procedures and institutions including a vitally essential and independent Secretariat and active middle-ranking powers willing to exert major efforts can be constructed only if satisfactorily embraced by great powers who trust it, but it can be smothered and enfeebled if that same embrace is too close or too lengthy. The balance will be a delicate one, and its desirable proportions are still far from certain.

6

Political-Military Regionalism and International Administration

FRANCIS A. BEER

One of the most striking innovations of the system of international relations which developed following World War II was the multidimensional growth of international institutions. Geographically, the semi-universal United Nations, with its various suborgans and specialized agencies, came to include a far weightier proportion of the world's sovereign states than had the League of Nations which preceded it. More limited groupings flourished in various regions and subregions of the world. Functionally, such institutions concentrated not only on economic, social, cultural, and scientific activities, but also on political and military problems.

Political-military regional organizations were largely epiphenomena of the Cold War. As the United States and the Soviet Union moved toward dominant and competing positions of power, each side constructed a series of alliances, seeking to define its sphere of major security interest. The United States, on its side, entered into agreements which did not irrevocably bind it

This essay develops themes introduced in two earlier volumes: *Integration and Disintegration in NATO: Processes of Alliance Cohesion and Prospects for Atlantic Community* (Columbus: Ohio State University Press, 1969) and *Alliances: Latent War Communities in the Contemporary World* (New York: Holt, Rinehart and Winston, 1970).

to fight for its allies, but which indicated that American decision-makers, nevertheless, viewed this as a realistic possibility. In 1947, on the basis of a historical tradition of involvement in Latin America for over a century, it signed the Inter-American Treaty of Reciprocal Assistance (Rio Pact), undertaking to "assist in meeting [an] attack" against one of the other American states. Two years later it joined the North Atlantic Treaty Organization, which stated that it would take, "individually and in concert with the other Parties, such action as it deems necessary, including the use of armed force, to restore and maintain the security of the North Atlantic area." The United States was a party to the Australia-New Zealand-United States Security Treaty (ANZUS) in 1951; the Southeast Asia Collective Defense Treaty (SEATO) in 1954; and was a signatory of bilateral agreements with Iran, Pakistan, and Turkey in 1959 which brought it into relationship with the Central Treaty Organization (CENTO).

During this period the Soviet Union acted similarly. In 1950 it concluded a Treaty of Friendship, Alliance, and Mutual Assistance with the Chinese People's Republic; and in 1955 it joined with seven other Eastern European states in establishing the Warsaw Treaty Organization.

At the same time, the nations of the third world attempted to cope with outside military intervention in their affairs by establishing regional organizations with political-military aspects. While security activities tended to be only one facet of these multipurpose institutions, and while the nations which composed them could not begin to match the sophistication in weapons technology of either of the superpowers, they yet remained significant as expressions of solidarity. They included the League of Arab States, which assumed security responsibilities through the Joint Defense and Economic Cooperation Treaty of 1950, and the Organization of African Unity, established in 1963.

NATO AND INTERNATIONAL ADMINISTRATION

The most significant political-military regional group was probably the North Atlantic Treaty Organization, which was unique
in membership, breadth of activity, and scale of construction.
Including the heavily industrialized nations of North America
and Western Europe, it formed a substantial link in the chain
of organizations which criss-crossed the area—including the
OECD, the Council of Europe, the WEU, the Communities of
the Six, EFTA, and the Nordic Council.

NATO itself elaborated an impressive array of activities, involving both military and non-military cooperation. The Western
Allies worked together not only in areas directly related to defense, but also in broader economic and social activities. Article
2 of the North Atlantic Treaty had stated that the parties "will
seek to eliminate conflict in their international economic policies and will encourage economic collaboration between any or
all of them," and the report of NATO's Three Wise Men in 1956
re-emphasized this point, and the necessity for providing the
alliance with a broader base.

In addition to NATO's military force program, the Allies
worked together in consultation on politics, armaments, infrastructure, and science. They also collaborated in general
economic affairs, air traffic control, civil emergency planning,
cultural affairs, and information.

To service NATO's activities, permanent administrative
machinery was created, an accomplishment to which a generation of commentators have pointed as an important innovation.
While previous alliances had included structural machinery
for cooperation, NATO was the first to enter wholeheartedly
into the age of organization.

A plethora of permanent committees flourished, composed
principally of representatives from the member nations and
overseeing Allied activity in a variety of areas. The well-known
infrastructure cost-sharing formula was an important adminis-

trative innovation. Under this procedure, nations agreed to contribute a fixed amount for a period of several years, leaving for later settlement the exact selection and nature of expenditures.

Perhaps most importantly, two sizable bodies of international administrators sprang up. On the military side, a complex and wide-ranging international structure was established, the most significant command being the Supreme Allied Headquarters, Europe (SHAPE), which was originally located just outside Paris in 1951 and shifted to Casteau, Belgium, in 1967. The civilian bureaucracy, NATO's International Staff/Secretariat, was given a home in Paris in 1952, where it stayed until June 1967, when it moved to Brussels.

The formal chiefs of these bureaucracies provided dynamic institutionalized leadership. Successive Secretaries-General and SACEUR's consistently worked for alliance expansion and change. The first Secretary-General was Lord Ismay, a British soldier who had made his early career in the outposts of the British Empire and who had served closely with Winston Churchill during World War II. Lord Ismay was the guiding hand behind the establishment of much of NATO's civilian administrative machinery. Those who succeeded Lord Ismay— Paul-Henri Spaak, Dirk Stikker, Manlio Brosio—came from political rather than military backgrounds. In different ways, however, they helped to maintain what had already been built and added to the administrative foundation.

The most important military leaders were those American generals who assumed the role of Supreme Allied Commander, Europe (SACEUR). General Eisenhower, in transition between the presidencies of Columbia University and the United States, played much the same military role which Lord Ismay had performed on the civilian side, overseeing the operating of a mixed-manned international military headquarters and the creation of an international army composed of national elements up to the division level. His successors—Generals Ridgway, Norstad,

Gruenther, Lemnitzer, and Goodpaster—together with other Allied commanders, made their own contributions in the years that followed.

INSTITUTIONAL STRAINS

After some time, however, the foundations of the Alliance began to appear strained. To be sure, there were a variety of institutional changes and innovations. Budgets grew in a number of sectors, and new programs were created. But overall gains were relatively slim, and there was some retrenchment. NATO's Lisbon force goals of 1952, which had looked forward to 96 divisions by 1954, gave way to more modest military projections. The NATO infrastructure program, which had included average annual budgets of approximately £117 million during 1951–56, declined to about £45.6 million for the years 1965–69. The French military withdrawal which culminated in 1966–67 not only removed further forces and territory from the Allies; it also threw the infrastructure program back to a state of project-by-project distribution of cost-sharing.

NATO leaders grew cautious. "The unity of the alliance was no longer what it had been at the beginning," Dirk Stikker felt, and "new disagreements both in political and military affairs, some of them acute, were to arise. As I saw it, my first responsibility was to ensure that NATO continued to function. . . . My second was obviously to narrow the areas of disagreement to workable dimensions."[1]

In spite of its accomplishments, the North Atlantic Treaty Organization remained largely an alliance of separate nation-states. While there was substantial institutional innovation and growth, the authority of such institutions—their ability to produce coordinated action in accordance with common decisions—remained highly limited. In spite of a program of

1. Dirk U. Stikker, *Men of Responsibility: A Memoir* (New York: Harper & Row, 1966), p. 336.

NATO political consultation, there was little joint decision-making or action on matters of primary importance; NATO's military plans and annual reviews did not obviously lead to national compliance with common objectives or standards; in spite of NATO's armaments programs, almost all weapons systems continued to be produced independently outside the structures of the Alliance; NATO's infrastructure and science programs represented only a small portion of national activity in these areas.

The failure of NATO to become more integrated was probably the result of two major factors: a change in the nature of the crises confronting it and a change in the ratio of benefits to costs. The main impetus not only for the creation of the Atlantic Alliance, but also for the early development of the greater Atlantic international system, had come from the deepening confrontation between East and West following World War II, which culminated in the Czechoslovakian coup and Berlin blockade of 1948 and the attack on South Korea in 1950. "The real clincher," Dean Acheson had said, "was the attack on Korea. Korea was the first time that the Russians had clearly used power to change a situation in which we were vitally interested. After that everybody said, 'You had better watch yourselves, this is very dangerous.'"[2]

Later external crises provided second-stage boosts, but were of a more minor nature: during 1956–58, the Soviet intervention in Hungary, the launching of Sputnik, and Khrushchev's Berlin proposal; in 1961–62, the erection of the Berlin wall, the resumption of Soviet nuclear testing, and the Cuban missile crisis; and in 1968, the Soviet intervention in Czechoslovakia.

During later years, there were also crises of Allied internal dissension. Among such situations were Suez in 1956, which found the British and the French on one side and the United

2. U.S. Congress, House of Representatives, Committee on Foreign Affairs, Subcommittee on Europe, *Hearings, The Crisis in NATO*, 89th Cong., 2nd Sess. (1966), p. 188.

States aligned with the Soviet Union against them; the Nassau meeting of 1962 between President Kennedy and Prime Minister Macmillan, at which the Skybolt missile program was canceled; and the completion of President de Gaulle's military withdrawal from NATO in 1966–67.

The declining salience of the external threat—in both absolute and relative terms—devalued the Alliance's major presumed benefit. During NATO's early years, Lord Ismay had been able to say that it provided "insurance against measureless catastrophe," and General Eisenhower could refer to it as a "wall of security for the free world," in the face of a "godless tyranny that would stamp out freedom with machine-like efficiency."[3] After thirty years of relative regional peace, however, the Communist invasion increasingly appeared to be a non-event with limited persuasive appeal as a call to continued constructive action.

More specific NATO benefits were limited and to some extent indeterminate, but the costs they engendered were concrete. NATO's military force program both represented a demonstration of Allied intentions and resulted in some improvement of Allied capabilities, at least in terms of coordination. Some Allied units could be jointly deployed in accordance with the concept of forward defense, and special units such as the ACE Mobile Force and the Standing Naval Force, Atlantic (STANAVFORLANT) were created. The range and scope of air defense could be increased. American nuclear weapons could be "engaged"[4] in Allied units and stockpiles, though still remaining under ultimate American control. NATO's various attempts at force planning—the Annual Review, the Force Planning Exercise, and the Five-Year Rolling Defense Program —probably had some effect on divisional strengths, combat

3. Lord Ismay, "Rules for NATO Conduct," Address to English-Speaking Union, London, June 4, 1957, pp. 5–6; Supreme Allied Commander of Europe, *First Annual Report* (Paris: SHAPE, April 1, 1952), p. 11.

4. General Lauris Norstad, Speech to the Western European Union Assembly, 7th Ordinary Session, December 13, 1961 (mimeo.), p. 34.

readiness, ammunition and supply levels, training, and the availability of support troops and reserves.

NATO's program of political consultation resulted in the exchange of information, but much of this was already available through bilateral contacts. While there was some joint political action, it occurred mostly in areas of low significance, such as the issue of Maltese independence and the issuance of East German travel documents. On issues of major importance—Algeria and Tunisia, Cyprus, Berlin, the Congo, Cuba, arms control, and Vietnam—there was no authoritative decision-making or implementation. NATO's armaments program offered the hypothetical possibility of economies of scale for larger production runs, shared costs of research and development, and fitting military strategy and weaponry. NATO's infrastructure program aimed at the construction of a wartime chain of command and logistics and the provision of a base for peacetime military planning. It included some new allied capabilities and the possibility of relatively free territorial transit. In addition, fixed facilities provided further evidence of Allied resolve. NATO science programs offered some assistance for scientific development among the members.

The concrete costs for such advantages came in a number of forms. Not only were there the annual military budget—which had risen to $81 million by 1967—a variety of other budgets, and the military and civilian personnel required to staff the international bureaucracies. There were also the expenses and foreign exchange losses of stationing national troops in other countries. In the late 1960s, the foreign exchange costs of United States defense expenditures in Western Europe averaged approximately $500 million per year, and Britain's 51,000 man army on the Rhine contributed to an annual drain of over £90 million. In the event of war, which might represent a situation of undesired involvement due to rash action by another ally, one could be drawn into a conflict that could result in extensive military and civilian casualties.

Other NATO activities implied a variety of additional costs:

losses to national employment and balances of payments from multinational efforts, loss of independence and prestige for non-national production of important items, annoying restrictions on use and transfer of material, dispersal of scientific and industrial secrets.

The ultimate benefit-cost question still concerned NATO's intangible contribution to peace. NATO's advocates had traditionally cited the pre-existence of a Soviet threat and the necessity for military containment—and they had drawn on the postwar European peace to balance NATO's account. Nevertheless, an increasingly vocal group of Western revisionists began to argue that this benefit was mythical. The very existence of NATO, they said, aggravated regional tensions. NATO formed the lynchpin of an interlocking and mutually self-reenforcing system of social conflict which could only be defused by the Alliance's elimination.[5]

INSTITUTIONAL FUTURES

NATO's difficulties suggested that the 1970s might well see it dissolve into a less formal Atlantic Alliance. While this might bring the danger of fragmentation to a regional system of relatively atomistic nation-states, it could also carry the possibility of the emergence of a greater European regional community.

The loosening of the Atlantic Alliance in the 1970s might be heralded by a substantial weakening of American participation, transforming NATO into a primarily European group. Institutionally, this might mean the establishment of an Atlantic Summit in Washington, where Europe might be collectively represented, to supervise the Alliance's civil and military affairs in

5. A revisionist review of the literature is presented by Christopher Lasch, "The Cold War, Revisited and Re-Visioned," *New York Times Magazine*, January 14, 1968, pp. 26 ff. Arthur Schlesinger, Jr. presents a "traditionalist" reply in "Origins of the Cold War," *Foreign Affairs* (October 1967), Vol. LIV, No. 1, pp. 22–52.

a general way. Direct oversight of the European Command, however, would be exercised from a European capital by Europeans, and the International Staff/Secretariat would be close by. American participation in Allied headquarters would be progressively reduced, except perhaps in nuclear affairs, until United States officers performed mainly liaison and observer functions. Should a European Nuclear Force come into existence, there might be close ties with the United States and Canada, but the ENF would still be autonomously controlled.

Subsequently one could envision the gradual disappearance of NATO into a web of special relationships. The Alliance would be composed of several categories of members, acting together and pooling resources in varying degrees, depending on interest in the activity involved. At an advanced stage one would see diminishing participation or individual withdrawal of NATO's peripheral members: Canada, Portugal, Greece, Turkey, and Iceland. In addition there would occur the reduction or elimination of meetings of government delegates, from the Council downward, and the abolition of the International Staff/Secretariat and NATO's military headquarters.

France might continue half in and half out of NATO. Although no longer an active member in many Alliance programs, France might still participate in early warning and air defense activities, as well as retain its seat on the NATO Council or at the NATO Summit.

In any case, NATO authority would continue to be conspicuous by its absence, and NATO legitimacy would decline. Should Western European unification recapture the political tide, the Europeans might decide to travel increasingly outside NATO, without American help or interference. With or without European unification, the United States and Britain would leave military forces on the continent for some time, but gradually cut their number in response to mounting domestic pressure. The German army would be reduced, perhaps to eight divisions, and turned into a largely professional body.

The decline of NATO might coincide with an East-West settlement of European differences. NATO might have a role in achieving a general security treaty and could even serve in a reduced capacity as one supercomponent of a new European system. Nevertheless, individual national governments would still sign the document, with the United States, Britain, France, and the Soviet Union perhaps serving as guarantors.

Such an agreement might include mutual and balanced force reductions by both East and West involving: the substantial dismantling of command structures on both sides, withdrawal of American and Soviet troops from Central and perhaps Western and Eastern Europe, agreement on force ceilings within a specified area, denuclearization of Germany and perhaps other Central European nations.

From NATO's ashes might arise a much more comprehensive institutionalized regional system. An East-West settlement might include not only non-aggression provisions, agreement on the legitimacy of current German borders, and provision for all-German institutions, if not for complete or immediate reunification. It might also involve creation of a European Security Commission, responsible for surveillance and supervision of European security arrangements and troop configurations. In addition an East-West Political Assembly and an East-West Economic Assembly might be established, possibly incorporating existing regional organizations in each half of Europe.

Nevertheless, the road to a general European settlement could remain under construction for some time. Most obviously, the creation of the greater European security community would rely on the willingness of the Soviet Union. The military intervention in Czechoslovakia during August 1968 indicated that it might be premature to assume that either the Soviet Union or the other states of the Warsaw Treaty Organization were ready to move quickly and decisively along the highway of détente.

Soviet caution in response to NATO proposals for mutual and

balanced force reductions in June 1970 showed not only a skepticism about Western designs on Eastern Europe, but also the realization that it might be both possible and prudent to allow the West to move first.

In this perspective, the heavy American commitment of resources in Southeast Asia and concomitant strains in NATO might contribute to serial rather than simultaneous military disengagement from Europe. Thus a gradual unilateral withdrawal of American forces from Western Europe and dissolution of NATO might pave the way for analogous Soviet action in Eastern Europe and loosening of the Warsaw Pact. Soviet fears of losing control in areas such as Czechoslovakia and Rumania might diminish if American troops were all across the Atlantic. A Soviet temptation to exploit the situation in Western Europe militarily would presumably be tempered by the capabilities of Western strategic airlift.

The attitudes of the major Western European Allies would also be crucial. The building of bridges would seem an obvious first step, with calculated promotion of cultural, social, scientific, and economic links between East and West Germany and between other states of Eastern and Western Europe. At later stages, it is possible to imagine the signature of bilateral treaties of friendship and non-aggression with the Eastern European states and the Soviet Union. Included in such treaties could be provisions for political cooperation in Europe, Asia, Latin America, and Africa; military cooperation in the preparation of plans to counter possible third-party threats; armaments cooperation in research, development, and procurement; infrastructure cooperation in building a satellite communications system linking Eastern and Western Europe; and scientific cooperation in the exploration of space.

Wider political-military regional institutions, including both Western and Eastern Europe, might then be the capstone rather than the cornerstone of détente.

On the other hand, new political-military crises might provide an impetus for a rejuvenated Atlantic Partnership or Atlantic Community. The ultimate external crisis would be World War III, a situation presenting a wide range of violent options, some of which might be particularly difficult for NATO: Soviet nuclear strikes on European targets, but not American ones; Soviet nuclear strikes on American targets, but not European ones; post-strike Communist advances into Western Europe; pre-strike Communist advances into Western Europe.

At a lower or pre-violent level, external crises might include escalation of East-West conflict in Asia to the extent that European governments feel themselves in serious and immediate danger; new Soviet ultimata demanding permanent settlement of the status of the two Germanies and Berlin; blockades of land and air access routes to Berlin, possibly leading to armed conflict; unintended escalation of incidents at the Berlin wall; substantial Communist military assistance to revolutionaries in Greece or Turkey; border incidents in Denmark or Norway; Soviet breakthroughs in offensive missilery, in anti-ballistic missile defense, or in anti-submarine warfare, neutralizing all or part of Western long-range nuclear capability.

Proponents of NATO's continued utility might seize on some of these crises as opportunities to construct a more solid Atlantic Partnership. Relying on the inspiration of the Kennedy administration's "grand design," but taking account of the institutional strains of the 1960s, they might work for a structure in which the United States could play a reduced role, but in which the Western Europeans would increasingly take up the political-military slack. Should the pace of Western European unification accelerate, deepened Western European political cooperation might take form around a European Political Community. The European Defense Community might also be revived and Western European Union strengthened. There might be a significant movement toward a European Nuclear Force based on British and French capabilities, and consideration of a European Technological Community to coordinate defense research and development.

In this situation, there would be provisions to represent the new entity of Western Europe in NATO and to regroup the other Allies congruently. NATO institutions might be altered to represent corporately the North Americans—Canada and the United States; the Western Europeans—Belgium, France, Germany, Italy, Luxembourg, the Netherlands, and perhaps the United Kingdom; and the Border States—Greece, Denmark, Iceland, Norway, Portugal, and Turkey. The new EDC, ENF, and ETC would be housed either directly under the NATO roof or linked with NATO through WEU.

If Western European reunification remained in the doldrums for some time, Europeans might still make gains within NATO. Thus the position of SACEUR could change from American to European hands, although nuclear planning and control would remain under an American deputy. Within NATO's military organization, command positions would be reapportioned to give Europeans a much larger representation.

In the event of more extreme crises, NATO's supporters might go further to advocate the systematic and symmetrical upgrading of common structures and tasks; the aim would be the construction of a homogeneous, integrated Atlantic Community. Under this roof they might hope that provision would be made for the NATO Council to meet regularly at the level of heads of government and at the level of deputy foreign ministers. An Atlantic Commission or permanent Committee of Three—similar to NATO's previous experiments with the Three Wise Men of 1952 and 1956—would be established. A NATO Policy Planning Council would be set up for long-range planning, and under it would be created committees dealing with particular geographical areas and restricted in membership to those nations with immediately relevant interests. In addition a NATO War Cabinet system would be organized for crisis, with one minister from each country on permanent standby.

The unofficial North Atlantic Assembly would attain formal sponsorship as an advisory body. Its secretariat would be greatly strengthened and it would receive regular access to NATO official information.

While the MLF would probably continue to sleep, an Executive Committee, consisting of the United States, United Kingdom, France, West Germany, Italy, and one smaller rotating member, would be established for nuclear decision-making, with authorization to act in emergencies for the Alliance as a whole. The chairman of the Military Committee would be given the title of NATO chief of staff and undertake to oversee and coordinate the activities of the regional military commanders. A NATO Payments Union would be created in order to redistribute the economic burdens involved in the stationing of foreign troops on Allied soil.

The Assistant Secretary-General for Defense Support would begin to receive an annual budget for a limited number of feasibility and design studies; and a NATO satellite organization would be created under the Secretary-General to supervise a joint telecommunication and reconnaisance satellite program. In scientific and cultural affairs, a NATO university would provide facilities for cooperative study and research in all areas of learning.

Binding institutional procedures might be strengthened by provisions for majority voting in all NATO committees, though votes would be weighted. Each ally would maintain the right of appeal to the Council, which could render its verdict by a two-thirds majority.

NATO authority would be increased by granting the international civilian and military bureaucracies greater scope for direct administration. NATO ambassadors, subordinate to the Secretary-General, would be accredited to the capitals of non-NATO nations. NATO major military commanders would have command authority in such areas as logistics, deployment of forces, air defense, and possibly the firing of nuclear weapons in certain clearly defined situations. In matters of armaments, infrastructure, and science, the military and civilian staffs would increasingly assume responsibility for new programs.

NATO legitimacy would also grow. France would resume full cooperation in all areas of NATO activity. National permanent representatives to NATO would be given formal national Cabinet rank and would be national political figures of the highest importance. National contributions of money and personnel would mount; and nations contributing nuclear capabilities to NATO would remove physical and electronic controls which formerly prevented independent NATO use. At the domestic level, political opposition to NATO would remain isolated in splinter groups of the right and left, while stable NATO associations of industrial, labor, and scientific representatives might appear.

During crisis situations the primary exponents of the Atlantic Partnership or Atlantic Community might be expected to be NATO's international administrators. At a general level, they might emphasize the common danger, using variations on the domino theme, in which no piece falls alone. In situations of external crisis, they could point out that the threat was relevant to all Allies, not only to that Ally immediately under attack; in situations of internal crisis, NATO leaders might show that defection from the ranks not only would increase the dangers to the remaining members but also to the defector. At the specific level, institutional leaders could call for particular structures and tasks of the Atlantic Community or Atlantic Partnership. As for clients, nations under immediate external threat might agree to leadership suggestions which seemed to make more certain the commitments of their Allies. In situations of internal strain the possibility of mass defections might persuade core members to support leadership platforms promising to maintain cohesion.

Such combinations of crisis and leadership might produce some of the structures and tasks of the Atlantic Partnership or the Atlantic Community, but it is less likely that stable patterns of binding institutional procedures, authority, and legitimacy will appear. There is no evidence that innovations in NATO's institutions are likely to generate this kind of development. Conflict has outweighed consensus not only in NATO areas like political consultation and military planning, but also in more usually technical sectors such as armaments, infrastructure, and science. There are no indications that conditions have been different in other areas of NATO activity: general economic cooperation, coordination of air traffic, civil emergency planning, cultural cooperation, or even information activities. In some sectors—trade, aid, money, manpower, investment—the Organization for Economic Cooperation and Development has seemed to be a more appropriate organ. The attempt to use NATO, and simultaneously infuse it with new life, in connection with currently popular causes—for example, environmental control—is not likely to fare better.

It appears visionary in most circumstances to expect such components of the Atlantic Community or Atlantic Partnership to come into existence as majority voting; corporate representation of Western Europe; greater direct administration by civilian and military bureaucracies—NATO ambassadors subordinate to the Secretary-General, NATO military commanders with substantial command authority, armaments, infrastructure, and scientific program control; permanent representatives of Cabinet rank; steadily increasing contributions of money and personnel; the removal of national nuclear controls; and stable NATO-centered subnational groupings.

While the political and administrative leaders of NATO may ardently wish a more integrated future, they have available no important coercive or utilitarian sanctions. They are unable to compel actors to follow directives which they prefer to ignore or to undertake actions which they are reluctant to implement. They control no significant budget which they can use to reward the faithful and punish the wayward. Ultimately, the leader's only major tool is the normative power of his ideology, through which he can appeal to the common perceptions and aspirations of the Allies.

Attempts to use NATO as an implement for crisis management may lead to relatively empty versions of either the Atlantic Partnership or the Atlantic Community. On the other hand, an assiduous policy of crisis avoidance by NATO's leaders seems likely to make the Atlantic Alliance the mold for NATO in the 1970s. In this situation, the maintenance of orderly processes of liquidation and the encouragement of broader European regional institutions may offer the most promising course for future action.

POLITICAL-MILITARY REGIONALISM AND INTERNATIONAL INTEGRATION

NATO in particular, and political-military regional organizations in general, appear to be fragile and inherently limited coalitions, unlikely to advance toward deeper and more permanent forms of community. Not only NATO, but many of its brothers, have shown signs of tension and deterioration over the years. Military cooperation between the Soviet Union and Communist China began to decline during the late 1950s, and the Albanian government had ceased full participation in the Warsaw Treaty Organization by 1961. During 1959 Iraq withdrew from the Baghdad Pact, which was subsequently renamed CENTO. In 1965 the French began a military withdrawal from SEATO, and they did the same in NATO the following year. In 1967 Pakistan started a progressive disengagement from SEATO; and in 1968 Prime Minister Wilson stated that Great Britain would withdraw all military forces east of Suez by 1971.

In spite of the best efforts of formal international political and administrative leadership, the limited and uncertain benefits of such associations will continue to be challenged by their costs. Changes in Communist military posture and policy, together with the vast Western resources required by a policy of permanent and exhaustive response in Europe, Asia, the Middle East, and Latin America, can be expected increasingly to affect not only NATO, but the whole ring of remaining Western security arrangements, including SEATO, ANZUS, CENTO, and the OAS. Similar dynamics in connection with mirror specters—the Western threat and the neo-colonialist danger—may have parallel effects, sooner or later, on the political-military activities of such bodies as the Warsaw Pact, the OAU, and the Arab League.

The uncertain future of particular political-military regional groupings is matched by their paradoxical implication for international administration in general. The very existence of such associations is testimony to a skepticism about the possibilities of successful international administration at the universal level of the United Nations. Alliances are supposed to be necessary because the only effective safeguard against the inherent aggressiveness of certain national elites is perceived to be military force. Since such force can not be coordinated in the form of universal collective security arrangements, it must be organized as regional, collective self-defense.

Nevertheless, the very existence of political-military regional associations demonstrates the ability of national elites to cooperate in common international enterprises. The strains induced by changing perceptions of benefits and costs may thus suggest not a necessary return to the pseudo-autonomous nation-state, but movement to a broader market. In this context it may be time for new and more synthetic institutions of international administration with lower military content. For such organizations there are self-evident economies of scale which can be realized by overcoming currently perceived contradictions between opposed regional groupings.

7

Economic Regionalism
and International Administration:
The European Communities Experience

LAWRENCE SCHEINMAN

In his review of the fifth General Report on the activities of
the European Community, the rapporteur for the European
Parliament, Arvid Deringer, critically singled out certain aspects of the Commission's style in developing Community
policy: the allegedly excessive importance it seemed to place on
proposing only solutions which had the strongest chance of being adopted by the Council of Ministers instead of maximizing
the potentiality of its power of initiative; and, as a corollary, the
tendency toward increased infusion and influence of national
administrations in the policy orientations and decisions of the
European Economic Community (EEC).[1]

Several years later, the French government made the following claim in a ten-point *aide-mémoire* designed to serve as a
negotiating basis for the resolution of the crisis of June 1965—a
crisis that emanated from a French assault on the institutional
system and operational norms of the EEC:

---

1. *Agence Europe*, October 16, 1963.

Parts of this chapter have been adapted from an article by the author
which earlier appeared in *International Organization* under the title, "Preliminary Notes on Bureaucratic Relationships in the EEC." The author would
like to thank *International Organization* for permission to use the relevant
parts of this article.

> Cooperation between the Council and the Commission constitutes the driving force of the Community. This cooperation must occur at all stages. Consequently, before finally adopting a proposal of special importance to the states, the Commission must consult the governments at the appropriate level. . . .[2]

Granted the ambiguity of the phrase "at the appropriate level," i.e. whether it was intended to mean the ministerial or some inferior level of administration, these two critiques imply diametrically opposed conceptions of what ought to be the nature of the relationship between the Commission of the EEC and the member states of the Community. Such relationships can take any number of forms and assert themselves at many levels, from meetings between ministers and commissioners, through interadministrative contact, to contacts between interest groups and the various representatives of the Commission. We are here concerned with one particular level of relationship —that which obtains between the national administrations of the member states and the bureaucracy of the EEC Commission. Our purpose will be to investigate, in a preliminary and schematic fashion, the nature and scope of this relationship and to evaluate it tentatively in terms of the impact of bureaucratic interpenetration on the development of economic and political regional integration and the impact of such integration on the nature of bureaucratic power. As a consequence

---

2. *Agence Europe,* January 18, 1966. This point, as drafted, was not acceptable to France's partners and was modified considerably in the agreement reached at Luxembourg at the end of the month. The text finally accepted stresses the importance of close collaboration between the Council and the Commission and provides that, "Before adopting a proposal of particular importance it is desirable that the Commission make the appropriate contacts with the Governments of the Member States *through the Permanent Representatives.* This procedure however, in no way impairs the right of initiative the Commission holds under the Treaty" (*Agence Europe,* January 31, 1966; emphasis supplied). It is still unclear whether the permanent representatives are the sole medium or merely apprised of contacts which may occur at any of several levels. Experience seems to sustain a liberal interpretation of this provision.

of this investigation we also hope to reach some tentative conclusions about the nature of interaction between regional integration and the evolving nature of international administration. Most of what follows is based on the experience of the EEC between 1958 and 1966. Generally speaking the pattern described below has not altered in any significant manner since that time, but where changes have occurred they have been taken into account. The first section deals with definitional questions and the matter of limiting factors which inhere in this study. The next four sections spell out and treat analytically the interaction between national and regional administration in the context of policy-making. The final section summarizes this experience and introduces the ongoing problem for regional administration of the relationship between the bureaucratization of policy-making and the politicization of regional integration.[3]

BUREAUCRATIC INTERPENETRATION

For the purposes of our discussion bureaucratic interpenetration is defined both formally and conceptually. In its formal, mechanistic sense, bureaucratic interpenetration is the intermingling of national and international bureaucrats in the various working groups and committees in the policy-making context of the EEC. The intermingling of bureaucrats *per se* is not peculiar to the EEC and is found in other regional international organizations such as the North Atlantic Treaty Organization (NATO) (e.g. in the Committee of Economic Advisors or the

3. Much of what follows is based on documentary and interview research in several Community sectors—competition (cartels and ententes, state aid, harmonization of legislation), the right of establishment, transport, and certain dimensions of commerical policy (development of the list of exceptions in the Kennedy Round of General Agreement on Tariffs and Trade [GATT] negotiations, development of a common commerical policy). The national administrations referred to are the French, West German, Dutch, Italian, and Belgian, which have been studied in roughly that order of priority.

Committee of Political Advisors) and the Organization for Economic Cooperation and Development (OECD) (e.g. in the Economic Policy Committee or the Energy Committee). Although the tasks of these various committees do not differ radically, at least on paper, the situation in the EEC must be distinguished from that of other organizations in terms of the nature and impact of the interpenetration of bureaucratic organizations.

The source of this difference can be found principally in the institutional and environmental contexts in which interpenetration occurs. The members of the EEC have undertaken certain commitments and obligations which extend beyond simple cooperation or agreements to agree. Furthermore, they have developed an institutional framework within which these commitments are to be carried out. The commitment is to develop a customs union (now completed) and eventually an economic union (still only in its incipient stages). The institutional framework is the system of authoritative decision-making lodged in extranational organs: the Commission and the Council of Ministers. These factors create an environment which gives added meaning and impulse to the mingling of national and international administrators.

Bureaucratic interpenetration also may be considered as a conceptual tool with which to analyze the growth pattern of integration. If we accept Ernst Haas's definition of integration as "the process of *increasing* the interaction and the mingling [of actors] so as to obscure the boundaries between the system of international organizations and the environment provided by their nation-state members,"[4] then we may find bureaucratic interpenetration useful as an indicator of system transformation. Thus, we may postulate that to the degree that the level of decision-making rests on the bureaucratic plane or is conducted in the bureaucratic style, to that degree integration has progressed; when the normative pattern of decision-making is ad-

4. Ernst B. Haas, *Beyond the Nation-State: Functionalism and International Organization* (Stanford, Calif: Stanford University Press, 1964), p. 29.

ministrative problem-solving (gradual, incremental, and un-
burdened by symbolic or emotional considerations) rather than
classic diplomatic negotiation, we can speak in terms of sys-
temic change and adaptation.

Thus, using the degree of bureaucratic decision-making as
a variable, we may be able to make certain judgments about the
intensity of integration. This approach assumes that, normally,
"high policy issues," dealt with on a multinational basis, will
not be left in the hands of public administrators but rather will
be resolved at the level of politically responsible ministers
operating in a more or less classic diplomatic context.[5] We
do not, for example, assume that the question of nuclear diplomacy will be left to politically unaccountable administrative
decision-makers. If issues are found to be resolved at the bureaucratic level (even granted the need of a final formal imprimatur on the level of political responsibility), then we may
be able to conclude that the issues in question and the policy
sector they represent have become internalized, i.e. shifted
from a classic diplomatic to an integrated or Community level
of resolution.

Our emphasis is less on the character of the decision-maker
involved (i.e. bureaucrat, technocrat, or politician) than on the
style and context in which decisions are made. This flows from
the assumption that the question of *how* decisions are reached
is more relevant than the question of *who* makes them. It takes
us away from the simple dichotomy between political and non-
political actors as defined by the sources of their authority
and influence, and from distinctions between "technical" and

5. On levels of decision-making and styles of negotiation see Ernst B.
Haas, "International Integration: The European and the Universal Process,"
International Organization (Summer 1961), Vol. XV, No. 3, pp. 366–92; and
Ernst B. Haas and Philippe C. Schmitter, "Economics and Differential Patterns
of Political Integration: Projections About Unity in Latin America," *Internation-
al Organization* (Autumn 1964), Vol. XVIII, No. 4, pp. 705–37. See also Leon
Lindberg and Stuart Scheingold, *Europe's Would-be Polity* (Englewood Cliffs,
N.J.: Prentice-Hall, 1970), passim.

"political" questions. The traditional dichotomies offer a static, time-circumscribed definition of how particular problems are viewed; the emphasis on style and context gives us a more dynamic perspective. At the same time we are sensitive to the possibility, indeed probability, that the style is susceptible to its broader political surroundings and to its immediate institutional context either or both of which can alter prevailing patterns of interaction at any given time. We are not, therefore ready to conclude "diplomacy yesterday, administration tomorrow."

To approach bureaucratic interpenetration in this manner would require its measurement. Although this task lies beyond the pale of our present concern it may be suggested that such an undertaking would entail the analysis of at least three factors: the question of the level of authority at which decisions are made both within the member states and within the organizational context of the Community itself; the style of dialogue in the negotiating process; and the kinds of circumstances and conditions under which decision-making and negotiation shift from one level of operation to another.

Before turning to the subject matter itself one caveat is in order: in the realm of interadministrative activity and its relationship to integration, generalization often may be not only inopportune but even misleading. Spatial and temporal considerations intrude. In terms of the former, differentiation occurs not merely from general directorate to general directorate of the Commission but from service to service and even from problem to problem within a given service. Bureaucratic interpenetration has been conspicuously high, for example, in the sector concerned with right of establishment[6] where a frame-

6. Right of establishment is governed by Title III, Chapter 2, of the Treaty Establishing the European Economic Community (Treaty of Rome) and refers to the free movement of non-wage-earners between the member states. These persons are to be allowed to establish themselves for business or commercial purposes in any member country on the same conditions as nationals of the state in question.

work program, largely the handwork of experts, slowly has been filled out by still other experts. Even in this relatively narrow sphere of activity, however, the results of penetration have been found to vary from subsector to subsector often depending upon the composition of, or spokesman for, a particular national delegation or the political clout that affected vested interests were able to give. In other words within a fairly generalized structural and institutional framework of bureaucratic relationships the basic human factor or the intrusion of external factors may be crucial. Many of the generalizations which might be offered should therefore be taken with caution. Similar considerations apply to temporal factors. Thus, the concept of socialization which summarizes the processes of learning and the growth of a kind of corporate identity among bureaucratic actors in integrating contexts is a powerful explanatory force for understanding bureaucratic conduct. Nevertheless, countervailing forces such as changes in the political environment, or in the attitudes and policies of national political leaders, or the growth of real or perceived inequities in the distribution of the benefits resulting from integration (phenomena not infrequently encountered in less-developed regions of the world but exemplified in part in Western Europe in the case of EURATOM) must also be taken into account. Very often it is these external factors which account for breaks or disparities in the pattern of interadministrative activity.

THE SCOPE OF BUREAUCRATIC INTERPENETRATION

Let us now return to the problem raised at the outset—the scope and effect of bureaucratic interpenetration. If it were not for the qualifying phrase "at the appropriate level" and the political context in which the French aide-mémoire, noted above, was submitted (a condition of Community crisis). France's insistence on close consultation between the Commission and the national governments would appear paradoxical in view of the operational code of the Commission. For it is indeed a central characteristic of the Commission's style, subject to variations in distribution, frequency, and utility, that there exist a large number of expert and consultative working groups composed of national administrators sent to Brussels at the request of the Commission and its services.[7] There are, furthermore, many personal contacts between Commission personnel and national administrators and among national administrators themselves which fall outside the formal framework of interaction.

What is even more paradoxical in the French *aide-mémoire* is that at the same time that it called for closer liaison and consultation, Paris was making an effort to control what the French regarded as a burgeoning problem of working-group proliferation.[8] Taken from a political perspective the two apparently contradictory goals can be reconciled: closer liaison meant the opportunity to exercise a priori control by national governments over the initiatives of the Commission, hence over the tempo and direction of regional integration. Control

7. There were, at the end of 1966, over 260 such groups which met periodically in Brussels. More than one-third of these groups were clustered in two Directorates-General: Internal Market and Agriculture. About 55 per cent of these groups consisted of governmental bureaucrats only. Of the remainder, approximately 25 per cent were mixed groups of governmental and private experts. The balance (about 20 per cent) consisted of private experts exclusively.

8. In the first half of 1966 the French government refused to send administrative experts to Brussels to participate in working groups on three separate occasions. Two of these refusals pertained to the social field where, France insists, the Community lacks authority to act under the Rome Treaty except in a limited number of cases. The third refusal concerned the establishment of a working group to study the harmonization of penal law for the breach of Community regulations and directives.

Under any circumstances, however, manageability would appear to be a growing problem for the national governments. It is reported that in 1964, for example, close to 1200 meetings of expert groups took place. These groups generally consist of medium- or high-level *fonctionnaires*, the delegations from each state varying from two to six members, so that including Commission personnel the average meeting consists of some twenty to twenty-five persons.

over the proliferation of interadministrative contact ensured against the risk that national bureaucrats might escape the surveillance of national political authorities and move in directions contrary to those desired by the political leadership. Thus the attempt to limit and control the working groups should be read not simply as a concern for administrative efficiency but as an integral part of the political campaign the French government was waging against the activities and prerogatives of the Commission.

From the inception of the Community the great majority of Eurocrats (i.e. EEC administrative-class level personnel) have considered the need to cultivate close relations with the national bureaucracies not simply important but virtually axiomatic. There is less uniformity of view on the purposes to which such relationships could most efficaciously be put and on whether or not they are more fruitful in the conceptualization, negotiation, or execution phase of policy development. In the final analysis the perception of the use of bureaucratic interpenetration appears to turn on three principal variables: the specificity of the Treaty of Rome regarding the subject matter in question; the psychological orientation of Community *fonctionnaires*; and the constellation of political forces around the policy area in issue.

It might at first appear that there would be a close and direct relationship between the perception of the utility and timing of administrative penetration and the strength of the juridical foundations upon which the Commission happens to be operating. In other words, we might expect that as the commitments undertaken by the states in the Rome Treaty became more vague, and the need for political as distinguished from juridical resources to sustain policy action grew, the importance of bureaucratic interpenetration would become correspondingly greater. Although the general tendency is in this direction, the pattern does not hold uniformly true. Variations occur all along the authority distribution continuum. They are more noticeable at the extreme where the Commission has the most authority than at the other extreme where it has the least ability to act independently. By way of example let us look briefly at several cases in point.

The Commission is vested with considerable legal authority in the cartel and in the state aid sectors. In both instances treaty provisions are self-executing and binding on the member states. In the former case the Commission service more or less shunned or minimized bureaucratic relations, bringing in its wake a considerable amount of ill will.[9] In the state aid sector, on the other hand, the Commission service assiduously sought to develop close relations with national administrations for the completion of this chapter of the Treaty of Rome. Admittedly, there are particular difficulties in the state aid sector which render it more susceptible to and reliant on national administrative action.[10] The distinctions between the operational codes of these two services, however, appear to rest less on the solidity of the juridical foundations than on the combination of personal attitudes and the conceptualization of tasks confronting the bureaucratic service in question.

Further along the Treaty power spectrum, where the position of the Commission is more tenuous, as in transport or harmonization of legislation, use of bureaucratic interpenetration in the conceptualization and proposition-building phase

9. Bureaucratic interpenetration in the cartel sector is relatively weak both in the conceptualization and executory stages. In the latter instance there is a Consultative Committee of national administrators. This committee was established under Regulation 17 (1962) to assist the Commission in the application of cartel provisions, but the Commission has sought to minimize its role by interpreting the provisions which govern it in a very restrictive fashion. The members of the committee, on the other hand, have sought to expand its role. For a partial justification of the low level of interpenetration in this field, see below, footnote 15.

10. Unlike the cartel sector in which information can be gleaned from investigations of cartels and from other members of the industrial community, in the state aid sector information often may be exclusively in the hands of the national administrations responsible for the management of this aid.

also has markedly differed. In the case of transport policy (or, rather, the lack thereof) the interpretation of certain Treaty articles probably would sustain the argument that unanimity will be necessary for adopting regulations on basic policy issues even as voting patterns in the Council of Ministers shift more toward majority rule. Consensus is high both in and out of the Commission that the general directorate of transport did not make adequate and effective use of the national administrations in developing transport policy proposals. [11] While it would be quite erroneous to argue that "transport failures" have derived solely or even principally from this fact, it does remain probable that a certain amount of progress would have been made on some issues if the Commission had used more effectively the potential of bureaucratic interpenetration. [12] Harmonization of legislation, on the other hand, another area where unanimity

11. In order to keep the analysis in perspective it should be noted that transport differed from agriculture in several respects including the constellation of political forces operating in the respective sectors and the nature of Commission leadership. Thus, no member state pressed for policy decisions in the transport sector and no transport lobby emerged at the level of user or supplier associations. As for Commission leadership in transport, it was distinguished more for its capacity to alienate the one country with substantial interests in transport (the Netherlands) than for its ability to compromise divergent interests. The Commission aimed less at consensus politics than at isolating a country which it may have assumed would not be capable of withstanding the pressures thus created. In some respects transport was like cartels with the difference that it lacked the latter's strong juridical base. Our point, however, is that transport theoretically offered possibilities for common policy development but that it did not, at the level of bureaucratic interpenetration and coalition-building, marshal the available resources.

12. Article 83 of the Rome Treaty provides for a Transport Committee. This committee is composed of independent experts designated by the governments of the member states, and among these experts are high-ranking civil servants from the ministries of transport. The Commission made poor use of the potential of this committee and thus increased certain tensions which already existed between the Commission bureaucracy and the national administrations. For example, the Commission would often submit to this committee problems which presupposed a non-existent common transport policy, but questions basic to a common policy itself were rarely discussed with this committee.

usually is required in the Council, represents what even may be an excess in the reverse direction—the *overestimation* of the potentiality of administrative decision-making. This is one of several sectors in which working-group proliferation has been most noticeable and the proliferation is in part tied to the weight attributed to bureaucratic interpenetration by the responsible Commission authorities in this area.[13]

The relative importance of the specificity of Treaty provisions to bureaucratic interpenetration becomes more clear when one considers the second variable noted above—the psychological orientation of the Community administrators responsible for the sector in question. At the risk of slight distortion it appears that many of the Community's civil servants fall into one of two camps—ideologists or pragmatists.[14] An ideological orientation may derive from either or both of two sources. Many ideologists may be militant "Europeans" whose total energies are devoted to the building of a united Europe, although it must be pointed out that many a committed "European" approaches his tasks from a highly empirical point of view. The ideological approach also may be the result of self-identification with the Treaty of

13. There is another side to this coin: the desire of the national administrations to institutionalize working groups which have been set up to prepare proposals by turning these groups into continuing consultative or surveillance committees. While a number of such committees already exist, their proliferation is not looked upon very favorably by the Council of Ministers (and especially France) largely because of the financial costs involved and also because of a concern over the deconcentration of authority.

14. The terms "pragmatic" and "ideological" are employed here in a methodological sense. We are not referring to the degree of commitment of Community administrators to their organization and its goals but rather to the procedural code by which they operate.

Community administrators also might be categorized according to whether they are activists who seek to integrate or non-activist "pencil pushers" who passively fulfill their assigned tasks. Indeed, there is a problem of non-activism in the Commission and it is due essentially to the minimal direction or instruction by the Commissioners to their administrative staffs. Lack of direction also accounts for the glaring problem of overlapping jurisdictions and competition among various Commission services. The term "legalist" could be substituted for "ideologist" without doing violence to the distinction in question.

Rome—in other words, an intense and personal devotion to the successful and complete fulfillment of the Treaty unrelated to any ideological commitment to supernational Europe. To the extent that any generalization can be formulated, one can sense that the tendency toward this way of thinking is greater among those with a legal than with an economic background and greater among West German and Dutch than among French or Italian administrators. When the ideological approach converges with a provision upon which the Treaty is very specific, then the provision takes on a great importance and bureaucratic relationships may be given correspondingly less weight. The cartel sector appears to fall somewhat in this category. [15] Those who are more pragmatic in their approach, on the other hand, tend to turn to and utilize bureaucratic interpenetration to an equal extent whether they are working in the context of very specific or very vague Treaty provisions.

Finally, there is the question of the political environment of the policy sector at issue. Bureaucratic interpenetration may be responsive to this factor rather than to legal or psychological conditions. Indeed, in the last analysis, the political factor is paramount. In the field of agriculture, for example, the tendency of the Commission service was to minimize the importance of administrative penetration at the conceptual stage without,

15. It should be pointed out that under any circumstances the development of an effective dialogue on cartel problems in the Community would have been difficult. At the time the Rome Treaty went into effect Belgium, Italy, and Luxembourg lacked legislation on restrictive practices and even longer time lapsed before Italy and Luxembourg passed the necessary legislation. The absence of a body of law on the subject meant the absence of qualified individuals capable of intensively discussing cartel issues. On the other side, the Commission had to deal with the highly organized and influential West German *Bundeskartelamt* which sought to impose its cartel philosophy on the entire Community. Caught in this dilemma, even more pragmatic administrators might have sought to work in relative isolation rather than run the risk of becoming the prisoners of the West German cartel office or of losing valuable time in nugatory discussion. There does exist a *Conference des Ententes* which serves as a meeting ground for national Community experts, but this organ has never been turned into a consensus-building body for cartel policy.

however, discounting it and to sharply upgrade the importance of this level of operation in the executory phases of policy. The most striking example of administrative interpenetration occurs in the agricultural management committees *(comités de gestion)* which also probably represent the most advanced form of technocratic decision-making the Community has yet developed. As Leon Lindberg's studies on the evolution of agricultural policy in the EEC attest, the hard decisions have been the result of vigorous political bargaining which extends byond the pale of technocratic activity.[16]

Several factors may account for the agricultural policy developments which are not easily reproduced in other policy contexts. The unusually cohesive and effective team developed under Sicco L. Mansholt's auspices, coupled with a political constellation of forces which put a major Community member, France, squarely behind the bid for a common agricultural policy as a *quid pro quo* for further development in industrial policy, and a common starting point of agricultural protectionism in the six member states, all provided certain advantages unlikely to be repeated in the near future in the EEC.[17] The

16. Leon N. Lindberg, *The Political Dynamics of European Economic Integration* (Stanford, Calif: Stanford University Press, 1963); and Leon N. Lindberg, "Decision Making and Integration in the European Community," *International Organization* (Winter 1965), Vol. XIX, No. 1, pp. 56–80.

17. It seems likely that progress in other fields will require a stimulus equal to that which France provided in agriculture, especially given the less "Communitarian" attitude which has prevailed since France vetoed British entry into the EEC in 1963. It is open to question whether such a stimulus might not have to await the entry of new members, such as the United Kingdom, to the Community. Under conditions of extended membership, however, there arises the problem of the extent to which the Community style will remain the same.

The summit conference of the member states of the EEC held in December 1969 at The Hague gave the Community a psychological boost and helped in the restoration of an atmosphere of increased mutual confidence. Coupled with European sensitivity to the trans-Atlantic technology gap and a heightened awareness of the need for closer monetary cooperation, the Hague summit may prove to be the catalytic agent for a move to a higher plateau of integration.

development of a common agricultural policy did *not* rest initially on administrative consensus, and the winning of national administrative support came not at the inception but only at a later stage in the process of policy development. We should also note that in agriculture the crucial initial decision was to construct a new system, i.e. a single managed market, rather than to seek to coordinate or harmonize existing agricultural systems. By definition, such a decision would necessitate different tactics than would be required in a sector where the Commission chose to operate through existing systems and structures entailing less radical change.

Experience may sustain the contention that bureaucratic interpenetration was less important at the developmental stage than at the management or executory stage in the agricultural sector. This probably would not hold true, however, for many other sectors such as monetary, cyclical, or medium-term policy where minimal Treaty provisions, coupled with the problem of stimulating any great public interest—hence, of mobilizing mass support—and a certain esoteric quality of the subject matter at issue proportionately increase the potentialities of administrative decision-making and the importance of technical knowledge. But even in other less specialized sectors, such as transport, social, commercial, or energy policy, it does not seem likely that the Commission can avoid seeking accommodation through administrative media; for in these areas the probability of marshaling a team and public opinion as was done in agriculture is fairly remote. It will unquestionably take a political decision to reap any major success in these areas, but we submit that the achievement of success will follow a somewhat different path than that followed in agriculture.

THE PURPOSES OF INTERPENETRATION

Perhaps the basic question which first must be answered is: what is the purpose and utility of bureaucratic interpenetration? A principal purpose is to secure *information*. An essential source of bureaucratic power is expertise, and a Community bureaucracy largely composed of former national civil servants is not likely to overlook this vital fact. Quite aside from the question of presenting proposals likely to win Council approval there is the matter of developing proposals which are technically and economically in accordance with the facts of economic life in the member states. Such information as will contribute to this end is most likely to come from the competent national authorities. Generally speaking, EEC *fonctionnaires* feel that more objective and complete information will come from national administrations than from the *milieux intéressés* although this latter source of information is frequently resorted to as well, either to complete Community information or to serve as a cross-check. [18]

A second equally if not more important factor in bureaucratic interpenetration is the generation of administrative *support* for Commission proposals. The EEC is not yet an autonomous political actor and in its present stage of development has a fairly limited clientele capable of sustaining it. The existence of a "European class" in the member states is still rudimentary and insufficient to serve alone as a social support for the Commission. [19] Also, the EEC bureaucracy is less effectively related

18. There is a danger in overemphasizing information and the expert knowledge it brings in its wake. Where sensitive political and economic interests are involved, expertise alone is insufficient to carry major policy proposals. It may be argued that in overemphasizing expertise in the transport sector, the Commission lost sight of certain important economic and political interests, a loss which eventually cost the Commission its leadership role.

We should also bear in mind that both national and Community administrators could use the information medium to achieve particular ends and thus distort the objective flow of information. This is, in fact, a not uncommon practice of national administrations when they first learn of Commission interest in a specific sector.

19. For some evidence that European youth represent an incipient form of broad-based support for the European system and Community integration see Ronald Inglehart, "An End To European Integration?" *American Political Science Review* (1967), Vol. LXI, No. 1, pp. 91–105.

to national pressure groups than are the national administrations with whom national pressure groups still maintain their principal dialogue. While transnational interest groups capable of rendering effective support for Commission policies do exist, e.g. COPA and UNICE, their quality of organization is uneven, their representative capacity is highly disparate, and their overall impact is still often only nominal. In part this reflects the conviction of many associational interest groups that the nation-state is still the principal source of power and the place where their limited resources can best be used. As a consequence, national administrations emerge as potentially the most effective source of support for Community policies and often serve as the major clientele groups of the Commission. Not infrequently, Commission members and *fonctionnaires* have remarked that "you cannot integrate against the national administrations."

There are two closely related aspects to the *support* function of national administrations—a negative and a more positive one. On the one hand, there is the expectation that the acquiescence of national administrators in "Community" solutions will minimize resistance to Commission proposals at the Council level and in the discussions of the permanent representatives' working groups which review Commission proposals and prepare the Council meetings. The frequently heavy reliance of ministers on their experts, the immediate access of the technician to the minister, and the highly complex nature of much of the EEC's work support this expectation. This is especially true when one considers that the expert who negotiates on behalf of his government in the context of the permanent representatives' working groups may be the same expert who participated in the working groups presided over by the Commission which discussed or elaborated the proposal at issue. Despite the inevitable limitations imposed on the national administrator (interadministrative competition within his own government, the countervailing activity of interest groups), as a rule he carries considerable weight with his minister. To ignore the national expert until the moment he appears across a negotiating table where some of his vested interests may be at stake is to court great danger of failure unnecessarily.

On the other hand, there is the hope that the Commission-presided-over working group can lead to a positive consensus on the policy orientation embodied in the proposal and that the spillover effect of this consensus will either induce the national participants to lobby actively for the Commission proposals or, more subtly, to avoid suggesting other equally valid policy alternatives. Given the tendency of most civil servants to avoid running unnecessary risks and to disengage themselves from political controversy, the latter alternative appears to be the medium more frequently resorted to by the national administrators interested in supporting the Commission's proposals.

One further point should be made at this juncture. There is a certain penchant for technocratic decision-making among Community administrators which is frequently given tacit support by their national counterparts, and this serves as yet another factor in bureaucratic interpenetration. National administrators who are competent in given fields of activity may, and sometimes do, find quite inviting the temptations of asserting greater authority in their national context through the medium of Community policies.[20] Commission administrators, themselves marked by what might be described as administrative imperialism and operating in the same substantive channels, nourish this temptation by joining forces with the responsible national civil servants in elaborating minutely detailed proposals. The expectation is that the economic and technical logic of the proposed solution will leave little if any room for dis-

20. The planning sector would seem to be particularly amenable to such tactics. The Community policy context gives national administrators a means of escaping the influence of their clientele groups and of reshaping and reorienting national policies.

cussion at higher policy-making levels and consequently will be given almost routine approval in the Council of Ministers.

The success of such gambits is highly erratic. Occasionally, proposals which are presented in such an unimpeachable manner are so constructed as to give complete satisfaction to all the negotiating partners and in doing so really give satisfaction to none, i.e. lowest common denominator solutions. The real problems, rather than being tackled, simply have been pushed ahead. Furthermore, it is not uncommon for highly detailed propositions to be laced with ambiguous phrases and *malentendus* allowing open season on interpretation, although the parties may also choose not to raise many uncomfortable questions. This is especially likely where the proposal is part of a larger package deal. [21] Finally, even where such qualifying factors are not present, there is still the problem of threading the proposal through the difficult political maze which awaits it in the meetings of the permanent representatives and the Council of Ministers.

The preceding commentary has dealt with only the question of institutionalized bureaucratic relations. Interpenetration is also fostered through the myraid personal contacts between national and Community administrators and contacts between national administrators themselves. These relationships derive not only from the personal friendships which develop as a result of frequent contact in the multilateral meetings discussed above

---

21. Problems of this nature tend to cluster in the harmonization field. A typical example may be found in the second *projet de directive* for the harmonization of pharmaceutical legislation where the provisions for the selection of experts to pass judgment on the marketability of pharmaceutical products was sufficiently broad to accommodate the rather liberal West German and rather restrictive French systems. The result of so broad a provision was to gain the accord of all the national delegations but at the same time to leave the considerably different national systems in very much the the same state that they were before the directive was drafted. In other words, harmonization was terminological only, not substantive.

but also from the fact that many Community administrators come from national administrations either on a permanent or temporary (seconded) basis. Fairly close contact is maintained with the home bureaucracy for the most part although this is more true for nationals of some states (France, West Germany, and Italy) than for those of others (the Netherlands and Belgium).[22] Despite these many individual and bilateral contacts there is a strong conviction among both Community and national administrators that whatever benefits are to be derived from bureaucratic interpenetration are more likely to be achieved in multilateral contexts. Bilateral meetings serve to clarify certain specific problems of a given state or to allow national civil servants to discuss more frankly the reasons for objections they may have raised in the multilateral reunions. Intimate knowledge of the mechanism of a national administration may permit an international administrator, familiar with the system and in contact with its personnel, to sense the advantages and dangers of particular courses of action. But, for the purposes of building bureaucratic consensus and for maximizing the potentialities of bureaucratic interpenetration, the multilateral medium appears to be the most fruitful.[23]

In sum, there is an intensive pattern of bureaucratic relationships in the European Economic Community, developed in vary-

22. One of the problems the EEC must cope with is the lack of a real administrative training ground. There is a long-standing debate on whether a fully independent career administration or a seconded (but independent) administration is best suited to the needs of the EEC, and there are compelling arguments on both sides.

23. One aspect of bilateral relationships which is deserving of special note is the relationship of the Commissioners and their cabinets to the national governments. Both the commissioners and their cabinets operate at the political level in the countries of which they are nationals (and elsewhere as well). Often, Commission *fonctionnaires* report to the cabinets in order to seek a means to neutralize or eliminate national bureaucratic resistance. Conversely, the cabinets can and do keep an eye on what the Commission services are doing in terms of national interests. As in the case of the Commission bureaucracy, however, not all the cabinets function equally effectively or efficiently, nor are all used for the same purpose by the commissioners in charge.

ing degrees and utilized with greater or lesser effectiveness by the Commission bureaucracy. These relationships are generally formalized in Commission-presided-over consultative and working groups in which national administrators participate with a view to protecting vested interests but often also with a view to participating effectively in the process of economic integration. From the vantage point of the Commission the principal benefits to be derived from such relations are first, the garnering of information and securing of expertise, an essential requisite of bureaucratic power, and secondly, the minimizing of national resistance by appealing for the support of a principal national economic power-wielder in the modern welfare state—the public administrator.

INTERPENETRATION AND INTEGRATION

Granted the extensiveness of these transnational bureaucratic relationships, how do they relate to the process of integration? What sort of impact does bureaucratic interpenetration have on policy orientation in an integrating context and, conversely, what impact does this context have on the nature and extent of bureaucratic power? Part of the answer may depend on how one defines the bureaucratic universe—whether one is speaking of all public officials in national administrations exclusive of the minister himself, whether one includes the ministry of foreign affairs or only the "technical" ministries, and so on. The following discussion is focused on the technical ministries but the non-technical administrations will be reincorporated later on.

The phenomenon of bureaucratic interpenetration has been steadily increasing since the inception of the Common Market. As more subject-matter areas have come to be treated in a Community context, more administrators have been drawn into the expanding network of transnational relationships. Bureaucratic influence over the shape and direction of European integration, however, has not followed the same linear progression. Schematically, the impact of administrators has followed a more modest path, possibly even a degressive one over a period of time. In keeping with our earlier caveat concerning generalization, we should bear in mind that there is considerable amount of variation. Bureaucratic influence and impact were relatively high during the euphoric first years of Community life, but they have become subjected to progressively increasing environmental restraints. These restraints derive not only from the chill political atmosphere which first enveloped the EEC when France vetoed the United Kingdom's application for entry in 1963. The chill was exacerbated by the Community crisis of June 1965–February 1966 and the later manifestations of Gaullist hostility to expanding either the membership or the supranational powers of the Community. They also derived from the fact that as the Common Market advanced toward the end of the transition period, more sensitive and difficult problems came to the fore.[24]

The true impact of bureaucratic power on integration and policy-making can be felt best when national and international *fonctionnaires* reach consensus on the nature of the solution to be applied to a given problem. However, it is no simple task to achieve consensus among experts drawn from different environments and operating under the constraints of different economic structures. The notion of an "administrative class," cohesive, continuous, and guided by a common set of ethics and values, has often been taken to task by students of national administrative systems. The clustering together of administrative actors from several countries strains even further the probabilities of technocratically imposed solutions to Community

24. We are referring here to "external" restraints. However, we must not forget "internal" restraints which derive from the growth of the organization itself. There is a lack of cohesion within the EEC administration and a good deal of interservice rivalry. This rivalry not only impedes organizational efficiency but also reduces the ability of the Community bureaucracy to maintain autonomous leadership in policy initiation and development.

problems. Bureaucratic relationships in the Community over the past eight years have been strikingly successful and have led to certain psychological transformations which undoubtedly have simplified management of certain administrative tasks. Overall, however, they have tended to remain fairly constant between the pole of conflict and the pole of collusion, fluctuating in one direction or the other as the interests, problems, and participants have changed. In transport, commercial policy, and certain aspects of competition policy, the tendency has been toward conflict whereas in the sectors of right of establishment and harmonization of legislation, they have been somewhat less strained. In the area of general economic policy (cyclical, monetary, and budgetary policy, for example) they have even tended toward the collusive end of the continuum. One reason for this last situation may be that the dialogue is almost entirely one of *cooperation* among economic experts: there is no immediate question of a transfer of competence; the participants tend to think in the same general analytic patterns; and the Commission has never sought to impose solutions on the member states. Under crisis conditions as occurred in 1965, however, the committees formed in this policy sector are unable to sustain themselves. This is their singular weakness—the inability to convert technocratic skills into viable political leadership in the face of hostility from legitimate national political leaders. Technocratic leadership thus remains dependent on rather than in control of political conditions.

National administrators are by nature protective and conservative and even those who are firmly committed to the principle of economic integration will vigorously defend the systems and policies for which they are responsible. Despite this natural tendency toward administrative conservatism, national administrators are often caught on the horns of a dilemma. On the one hand, they do wish to minimize their sacrifices and to maintain administrative sovereignty, to *bien garder la ficelle.* On the other hand, many national administrators have a considerable interest in "Europe" from the ideological or from the professional point of view. The EEC represents a new dimension of administrative activity, more substantial and meaningful than other transnational economic organizations such as OECD or GATT. Experience would seem to indicate that over the years the system as a whole has been positively affected by the general interest in expanding the dimensions of economic activity. But even as the system shifts, individual administrators tend to incline toward conservatism on individual cases. This is principally true when matters of competence and the division of authority enter the picture—in other words, when institutional questions intrude on substantive issues.

Voluntary change and breaking the cake of custom are not easily achieved and this is one reason why radical innovation, such as in the agricultural sector, requires tactical operations which go beyond the administrative level. Personal friendships, mutual understanding, appreciation for the problems another administration faces, and a more cosmopolitan way of thinking are all fringe benefits derived from frequent and close contact between national and international administrators in the multilateral working-groups of the Commission. The dominant experience of the EEC, however, is that the functional requisites of a man's job invariably will dominate the positions he takes.

Finally, even if consensus is achieved, there is still the critical issue of the effect of this consensus. The answer turns primarily on the political inclination of the government as well, of course, as on the weight carried by the bureaucracy in the political system and on the interplay of such forces as interest groups. If the government line is reasonably clear and either positively inclined toward or not hostile to integration, administrative impact on specific government policies and on overall government orientation will be relatively great and occasionally even definitive. If the government orientation is hostile to integration, if political consensus on progress is lacking, administrative impact will be correspondingly smaller. The changing *marge de manoeuvre* of French administrators who participated in Community activity following the events of June 1965–February 1966 is a good demonstration of this. There is also some evidence that the more receptive attitude toward the Community held by the Pompidou government since mid–1969, but especially following the Hague summit conference of December 1969, has altered the situation somewhat in the direction of broader administrative impact.

There is a generally widespread belief that national administrators who come to Brussels to attend Commission-presided-over working groups are freewheeling, uninstructed delegates who speak officiously and in no way commit their government to any course of action. This is the sort of generalization that often leads to misunderstanding. It is true that governments are not committed, juridically at least, by what their experts say and do in Brussels in the earlier phases of policy preparation. Even at the cost of some embarrassment to the government in question, long-standing commitments by experts have been reversed. It is not true, however, that these administrators come uninstructed. The pattern varies from country to country with Italian experts tending to be the least and West German experts the most instructed, but as the Community has evolved instructions have become more elaborate and restrictive in all countries.[25] The French administrators noted above used to have considerable latitude of action and were frequently able to translate consensual agreements made in Brussels into government instructions and policy at later negotiating stages. Subse-

---

25. This is highly nuanced. French instructions, for example, might be cast in the sense of "don't go beyond this and that limit" with a margin of maneuver left within this framework. Italian instructions, on the other hand, often may be drafted with a view to insisting on one or several points with nothing whatever being said regarding any of the other points to be discussed. Consequently, the Italian delegate may be "free" on these other matters. In any case, the instructions which are given are occasionally challenged by the permanent representatives either because the instructions go too far or because they don't go far enough.

quently they were closely monitored, and even before the 1965–66 Community crisis French administrators were unable and unwilling to take liberties either officially or unofficially. Even with the amelioration of the political climate in the post-de-Gaulle era noted above, the latitude of action continues to be circumscribed. Unfortunately for the Commission, the same attitude and pattern have spread to the other national delegations though in a more modest and less obtrusive manner.

This tendency is not simply a reflection of the changing political climate in the EEC but is also the result of the increased stakes involved in Community decisions. More sensitive economic interests and more far-reaching commitments are now at issue—we have moved from the era of *traité-loi* to the era of *traité-cadre*. Thus it is no longer a question of reducing or eliminating a tariff or paratariff barrier, of treating the nationals of another state on the same basis as a state treats its own citizens, or of allowing free movement of labor within the Community. More and more it is a question of undertaking positive commitments that entail structural, institutional, and psychological changes of far-reaching consequence. Under these conditions governments are rapidly awakening to the increasing importance of even minor "technical" decisions which, when added up, may amount to something quite substantial. In brief, both for political and economic reasons governments have become more concerned with what technicians are saying and doing. A key manifestation of this concern is the tendency to give more and closer instructions to these administrators earlier in the game.

Within the context of the foregoing, the general pattern followed by many of the Commission's services is to try to build consensus among national experts in the Commission-presided-over working groups. What often is sought is the agreement of a Commission-sponsored *avant-project*. There is a wide range of difference, however, between Commission *fonctionnaires* as to how far they will go in seeking to negotiate a consensus among conflicting national views. In the cartels and ententes field, for example, the dialogue often turns into a monologue, the Commission informing the national administrations of what must be done next. Some Community pundits have dubbed the cartel sector as *"l 'Université,"* especially in view of its tendency to draw heavily on independent experts in the academic community. Significantly, this field of activity has not progressed as rapidly or as far as it might have under the "strong" Treaty provisions on competition.[26] In harmonization of legislation, on the other hand, a genuine dialogue obtains and the final project usually has the unanimous or near-unanimous support of the national delegations. For example, the Commission held sixteen working-group meetings over a four-year period on the problem of harmonizing procedures in public works contracting in an effort to hammer out as sound and acceptable a proposal as possible. Not until every avenue of conciliation was explored did the Commission finally "take its responsibility" and submit a proposition.[27]

It is precisely this latter kind of activity that was critized by Arved Deringer, the Parliament's rapporteur whose comments we noted at the outset. However, where unanimity is required in the Council and where the national administrations are currently responsible for the field of activity in question, this would seem to be the pragmatic and realistic approach. Even in an

26. See, however, footnote 15 above.

27. The public contracts case, still not decided by the Council of Ministers, also exemplifies some of the weaknesses of relying on administrative interpenetration to carry policy proposals. In this case the West German administration negotiated a compromise with the Commission which was only to be reversed at home by pressure emanating from the *Laender* and cities which pass most of the contracts and which felt inadequately consulted by Bonn. The Commission eventually redrafted certain provisions to accommodate Germany's federal situation. In fact, it does not appear that the Commission has come to grips either with the issue of West German or Community federalism.

area such as the right of establishment, where a qualified majority suffices to pass a directive in the Council of Ministers, a similar approach usually is used. In both instances, however, when the issue reaches a point where the national administrations are unwilling or unable to go further toward conciliation, the Commission has tended to submit the proposal it felt most representative of the Community interest and most likely to win ultimate approval. Where there has been conflict between what is most likely to succeed and what is in the Community interest, some Community administrators claim to have given priority to the latter but others admit to having followed the path of least resistance. This is a highly significant fact in light of the frequency with which the Commission claims to represent the "Community interest." Moreover, it calls into question the extent to which the integrative process necessarily "upgrades common interests."

Bureaucratic interpenetration is more effective at the technical than at the political level of policy-making. This raises the knotty problem of what constitutes a political as distinguished from a technical issue and the line is often not easy to draw; as we argued earlier the dichotomy implied has a very limited utility. What is technical to one country may be political to another. For the Netherlands, whether the Community oil storage policy is based on a 45- or 60-day supply is simply a technical issue whereas for Italy, an oil importer with no indigenous resources, the same question is quite political given the infrastructure and cost factors involved in oil storage. Furthermore, many technical issues become politicized as they run the course from Commission to Council. This usually occurs either because an attentive interest group perceives a threat in some provision of a proposition, or because, from a government's point of view, something which may be technically sound also may be politically unpalatable. Any issue which is institutionally oriented and which may have a bearing on institutional equilibrium is treated, of course, as political.[28] Once these limitations are realized, however, there still remains a wide range of activity open to technical domination.

National administrators, despite the earlier noted inclination toward increasing the scope of their influence, tend to be circumspect in dealing with such political issues as intrude in their discussions. The Commission *fonctionnaires* have not always been as cautious, and in the earlier years sometimes sought to negotiate with national administrators on some political questions. This could either take the form of seeking to depoliticize the issue by couching it in technical terms—a tactic which rarely escapes the attention of the permanent representatives—or by inserting certain provisions which, while seemingly innocuous, might be politically loaded. In the right of establishment sector, for example, the Commission on several occasions introduced provisions calling for a "right of information" on the part of the Commission. This meant that every national decree, act, or implementing device designed to carry out the directive in issue would first have to be communicated to the Commission which implicitly would have the right to recommend changes, modifications, or alternative solutions. The provisions were quashed before reaching the Council of Ministers, allegedly on the ground of technical complexity but actually because the provisions smacked of institutional imperialism on the part of the Commission and posed the delicate question of Community balance of power. The tendency to negotiage political questions with the national administrations is much less evident today. The Commission has found that to do so sometimes raises unnecessary problems and that in the present political environment of the Community it has limited value. For, even if there are no objections, or even if there is acquies-

28. This does not necessarily mean that the issue is treated at the political level. See, for example, the problem of "right of information" discussed below.

cence by national administrators at the preproposal stage, the latter often are unable to sustain such decisions on behalf of the Commission once the real negotiations begin in the Committee of Permanent Representatives.

INTERPENETRATION AND BUREAUCRATIC POWER

Let us now return to the question of the impact of integration on bureaucratic power. Economic union under the Rome Treaty implies increased administrative activity in the policy-making area, for the economic realm is one in which administrations have typically made the greatest inroads in the political process. As government has expanded to meet increasing socio-economic demands, administrative activity and influence correspondingly have increased. The merging, harmonizing, or coordinating of economic sectors would seem to entail a direct and substantial impact of administration on policy development. It is undeniable that the influence and authority of the executive branch of government in all of the member states have increased as a result of the EEC. Certain traditional restraints on ministers and administrators have been weakened in the face of new and subtle decision-making processes.[29] At the same time certain short-term and long-term *intranational* administrative redistributions are taking place in the executive branch. We earlier noted that bureaucratic influence does not necessarily rise in direct relation to increased bureaucratic interpenetration because of the moderating influence of environmental restraints. It is to the causal role of integration in the creation and nourishment of those restraints that we would like to devote the following comments.

The dominant battle being waged in the member states at the bureaucratic level is between the technical and non-technical ministries for control over the management of integration.

29. We are referring principally to parliamentary controls. However, the influence of interest groups should not be underestimated.

It would be too simple and misleading to say that the economic ministries are in the vanguard of integration, jousting with protectionist foreign ministries, for it is often the case that it is the latter who reach the accommodation necessary to permit integration to move forward. [30] Technicians are not, by nature, more likely to reach agreement than are diplomatic personnel, especially when decisions may involve a shift of competence or a reduction of administrative autonomy. By the same token, however, there is much truth in the contention that foreign ministries are often among the last to appreciate and accept the need for certain integrating decisions. Integration then appears to have affected national bureaucratic power in somewhat the following manner.

The ministries of economic affairs, convinced of the need for developing rational economic growth, have placed great importance on the success of the Common Market. This is strikingly evident in the case of France where many of the ideas now couched in the Rome Treaty originated with *hauts fonctionnaires* in the Ministry of Finance and Economic Affairs. [31] Since foreign economic relations traditionally had been directed primarily from within the ministry of economic affairs or of finance it was assumed that what previously had been done in a bilateral context now should be continued or even expanded in a multilateral context. The ministries of foreign affairs, however, have not shared this view. Except in West Germany where a government mandate lodged authority in the hands of the Ministry of Economic Affairs, the foreign ministries have main-

30. A good example is the issue of association with third states. In the cases of Greece and Turkey the economic experts were much less in favor of reaching an agreement than the political spokesmen. If purely economic criteria were used or if economic technicians dominated the negotiations there probably would not be association agreements with either of these countries.

31. Indeed it has been argued that economic planners in the member states banked on the EEC as a means to ensure fulfillment of national economic development goals. See Zwi Namenwirth, "Bureaucratic Power and European Unification: a Causal Inquiry" (unpub. doc. diss. Harvard University, 1963).

tained a firm hand on the integration tiller.[32] They have sought to exercise surveillance largely through the medium of the permanent representatives who are administratively responsible to the ministry of foreign affairs in all of the member states.

A considerable proportion of the Community work is highly technical in nature and neither the foreign ministries nor the foreign economic divisions in the ministries of economics have adequate personnel to manage the mass of complex materials which daily occupy the national and Community services. The result has been the increasing importance and influence of the technical ministries and services at the expense of both the Ministry of Foreign Affairs and the external relations divisions of the Ministry of Economic Affairs.[33] It is probable in the long run that as the EEC develops and expands, the foreign ministries will continue to lose influence and authority, for as common policies develop they become internal policies no longer the subject of traditional diplomatic negotiators. Eventually, the technical ministries and services will become the dominant actors along with their Commission counterparts in the direction and management of major economic sectors, if not the entire economy. How extensive this will be depends on political will, economic interest, and the fulfillment of spillover potential.

This is the schematic development but in the day-to-day life of the Community matters are more subtle and complex. At

32. In West Germany there is a balance between the Foreign Office and the Ministry of Economic Affairs insofar as the management of common market questions is concerned. Despite this formula of shared responsibility there are always issues which lead to overlapping jurisdictions and consequent tensions.

33. One manifestation is the growth of councils of "technical" ministers such as agriculture, finance, and transport. Although the recent Community crisis retarded this growth, at least for France, the general trend has been in the direction of a sectorial allocation of responsibility. What then becomes crucial is the manner in which the national governments arrive at the positions they will take in the negotiations in Brussels.

present the potential power of the technical expert has been circumscribed not only by the fact that final decisions remain in the hands of politically responsible ministers but also by the assimilation of a certain level of specialized knowledge by the generalist. Furthermore, the technical ministries have been victims of their increased importance and expanding competence in the sense that the dealing with problems multilaterally has reduced the *exclusivity* and *autonomy* of these ministries for the present. Technical ministries now may have a broader scope of action but at the same time what previously might have been done with little or no surveillance from internal political forces is now bruited and subjected to stronger political control. Thus, the multilateral dimension, a key derivative of the integrative process, serves to regulate administrative power at the same time that it broadens the scope of that power.

The structural component of this surveillance and control is found at both the national and Community levels. National control occurs in the coordinating mechanisms established to handle European problems in the member states. Both the mechanism and its effectiveness vary from state to state, with France having the most organized and most effective coordinating mechanism and West Germany having one of the least effective though not the least well-organized coordination committees. In France, for example, the *Secrétariat Général Comité Interministériel* (SGCI), consisting of a ten-man staff, directs the flow of all information between Brussels and Paris. The authority of this institution steadily increased while General de Gaulle was in power in response to a perceived need to exert stronger controls over French administrators who are in liasion with the EEC. Instructions for discussion and negotiation flow from this institution and there is a very high continuity between what a French expert says and what the French government eventually does. The reason is not, however, that the administrator is charting the course of his government. It is rather that under political mandate, the autonomy of French administrators is being closely regulated to allow maximum maneuverability to the political leadership. There is some evidence that previously, French administrators, who were generally outdistancing their government in the development of Community policies, were occasionally "negotiating" compromises with the Commission administration, a situation which helped further integration. To avoid the risks of a *copinage technocratique* and to ensure careful consideration of even minor technical issues, as well as to respond to the political factor noted above, the SGCI, often in conjunction with the Quai d'Orsay, tightened its controls. Under the regime of President Pompidou and probably partly in response to the general easing of tensions of political relations in the Community, the grip of the SGCI has tended to loosen. In the West German situation, on the other hand, coordination between ministries is often lacking until the issue becomes highly political, despite the existence of a coordinating mechanism in the Ministry of Economic Affairs. A political climate favorable to integration and a deep respect for ministerial autonomy in Germany largely account for weaker coordinating controls. However, continuity between what a German administrator says and what his government ultimately does is correspondingly lower than in the case of France. [34]

Structural control at the Community level is exercised through the medium of the Committee of Permanent Representatives. The review and negotiation procedures which take place in this context serve as an effective monitor over technocratic decision-making and sharply curtail the liability of the national administrator to fully commit his government. On the other hand, the permanent representatives often have turned out to be the Commission's best friends and to have labored

34. While there may be poor interministerial coordination in Bonn, this does not mean that within any one ministry things might not be run autocratically, with tight controls over the individual administrator. The problem basically is that a West German administrator may be speaking only for his ministry and not for his government.

hard to overcome technical resistance to politically desirable integration policies. A detailed discussion of the permanent representatives as actors in administrative penetration is beyond the scope of this article, but a few comments regarding this organization are in order.

Activity in the permanent representatives takes place on a *horizontal* plane whereas Commission proposals are evaluated not only in terms of their logic but also in terms of the overall impact of the singular policy decision on the general policy framework. Technically sound proposals have been altered or even rejected at this level because of their incompatibility with greater political interests. The Commission's "prenegotiations," on the other hand, are *vertical* operations largely confined to seeking economically and technically sound solutions often quite aside from their political or social impact. It is the horizontal review which particularly tests the Commission's mettle, for it is here that the fine art of melding economics and politics really begins.

Secondly, although some permanent representative delegations are more influential that others in their home governments and some are closer to the Commission than others, all delegations try to monopolize the relationships between the Commission and their capitals. They seek to minimize direct contact between Commission administrators and national administrations and insist that any written correspondence from Brussels pass through their hands.[35] Without complete information on every dossier, of course, their ability to recommend and to negotiate would be curtailed. Correspondingly, one of the main Community tensions occurs between the permanent representatives and the national administrations for a dominant voice in the management of the development of integration from the nation-state perspective.

35. The French delegations is the most adamant on this point but Italy and the Netherlands follow close behind. The West German delegation takes a more permissive view of the situation but at the same time insists that it be kept informed of all such correspondence and interchange.

Despite the constraints on administrative power and at the risk of complicating the matter even further, it must be stressed that at each of the levels under discussion—Commission "prenegotiation," the preparation of the national government's position, and the final phases of negotiation in Brussels—the administrative expert is always present. His influence is *not* to be underestimated. To the extent that he operates without close instructions or coordination, or to the extent that his government has no strong interest in the question, his ability to commit his government to a particular course of action is increased. The course he chooses to follow under these conditions will have considerable impact on what his government finally does, for where an administrator has been left fairly free to act on behalf of his government the probability is strong that his advice will be accepted by his minister. There also have been many instances where the political authorities, unable or unwilling to come to grips with a problem, will remit it to the experts, and solutions found at this level will be ratified eventually in the Council of Ministers. [36]

RETROSPECT AND PROSPECT

How can we operationally summarize the phenomenon of bureaucratic interpenetration, and what does the EEC experience suggest about the scope and limitations of international administration in the articulation and development of regional

36. Throughout the preceding discussion we have stressed the constraints operating on national bureaucrats. While it is not the purpose of this study to detail the structure and organization of the Commission, it should be noted that parallel constraints operate within the framework of the Commission. The Commission is a collegial body and policy decisions are taken in that framework. The specialist services of the Commission—the Eurocracy—are subject to a hierarchical organization in which low-level initiatives are progressively filtered through such media as the Executive Secretariat, the Juridical Service, and the cabinets of the commissioners. As we shall see in our conclusions, the Eurocracy has during the past several years become increasingly bureaucratized and subject to internal constraints on conduct.

economic integration? These are the questions to which we now turn.

In reaching any conclusions on the relationship of administrative interpenetration to Community policy-making and the process of integration, it is necessary to keep in mind the level of policy about which we are speaking. The EEC is constantly operating at several levels simultaneously—the inner core fulfillment of the customs union provisions of the Rome Treaty and the outer ring development of common policies either on the basis of independent coordinated or cooperative policies or on the basis of a single Community policy. As of this time, except for agricultural policy, the principal progress of the Community has been confined almost exclusively to the inner core customs union. It is precisely in this area that firm commitments, timetables, and the definition of responsibilities have been most clearly spelled out in the Treaty and accepted from the beginning by the member states. Similarly, it is in this relatively technical area, in which the emphasis is on the elimination of barriers and obstacles, that administrative decision-making is most intense and predominant and where the Commission bureaucracy most skillfully exercises its ability to transcribe political issues into technical terms in conjunction with the national administrations.

From the point of view of both levels noted above, it is clear that bureaucratic interpenetration is a singularly important factor in the integrative process. It is equally clear, however, that despite its importance, bureaucratic interpenetration is rarely the decisive factor in major orientation.[37] The interpene-

---

37. There are exceptional occasions, one of which perhaps was the emergence of a common taxing system—the added value tax—where a consensus on the direction of policy was achieved largely in the context of bureaucratic interpenetration in meetings over several years among a member of the Commission, Hans von der Groeben, and the national directors of fiscal services. In fact the French authorities adjusted to the added value tax system even before it became official Community policy and there is good evidence that the interpenetration process largely accounts for this fact.

tration of administrations as an integrative factor depends largely on the political environment. Where governments simply are prepared to abide by the rules of the game, bureaucratic interpenetration can lead and has led to increased governmental parallelism which in turn maximizes the opportunity to bring proposals to a successful conclusion. In the presence of major political support, such as France gave the Commission in the field of agricultural policy, bureaucratic interpenetration plays a more modest role (in basic policy orientation) although bureaucratic influence in operationalizing political decisions obviously is quite great.

To be successful, penetration generally must involve a dialogue between two different types of administration. On the one hand, there is an international administration charged with integrating functions, a process which entails the carrying on of essentially political activities. On the other hand, there are national administrations responsible for the administration of existing political and economic systems. The former is concerned with system transformation; the latter is inclined toward system maintenance. As a result of this difference, the international bureaucracy often seeks to break out of the operational frame of reference while the national administrations seek to stay within it. The Commission cannot afford to discount this psychological factor any more than it can afford to discount national political and social factors in the shaping of Community policy proposals. Where the Commission has failed to take these factors into account, it has also invariably failed to make substantial progress.

When responsible and fairly autonomous administrators come together in a policy-making context, the extremes of collusion, which could lead toward technocratic dominance, and collision, which could lead to the neutralization of bureaucratic power, have rarely, if ever, been found. Collusion is much more probable in the managerial or executory stage, as in the case of the comités de gestion, than in the policy formulation stage.

There also have been occasional incidents of unremitting hostility toward change. In these cases hostilities often have been eliminated by the intercession of individual commissioners or their cabinets at the political level of the national capital in question. Principally, however, national administrations have responded by seeking an accommodation which minimizes sacrifice, change, or loss of autonomy. The EEC experience largely has been one of preparedness of national administrations to accept technical and economic readjustment.

In sum, bureaucratic interpenetration is alone insufficient to bring major policies to bear, but without it progress becomes difficult if not sometimes impossible. The major decisions which have been made thus far in the EEC have been reached at the political level. This is as true for acceleration and for the recent developments in the field of transport policy as it is for agriculture. Bureaucratic interpenetration, however, remains the foundation stone, the *tissu cellulaire* of the system.

The conclusions reached regarding the scope and limits of bureaucratic interpenetration in the process of integration can be elevated to a higher level of generalization. At the very least it can be said that the utilitarian calculation that political union could be forged out of economic-welfare links manipulated by administrative or technocratic elites, although not *definitively* disproven, is yet to be sustained by the events. The inertial forces of technocratic decision-making set in motion by the implementation of the Treaty of Rome are by themselves inadequate to the task of transforming the regional system in which they operate into a qualitatively different political unit. The balance of power at the national level has not so altered to the benefit of national technocratic actors that the cultivation of transnational technocratic linkages suffices to fundamentally reorder intraregional political relationships.

The evolution of the EEC experience reveals a number of features. One is the susceptibility of the system and its institutions to their political environment. Regional administration is a viable leadership force as long as national political leadership maintains support for the enterprise or at least remains neutral. Regional administrative or technocratic forces are not as easily able to cope with a hostile political environment; the regional forces are fundamentally bureaucratic in nature and do not have the means by which to mobilize requisite countervailing political forces.

Second, regional administration is better able to operate without particular concern about the character of the political environment when mainly implementational responsibilities are being pursued. Thus, as long as the central purpose was the elimination of barriers to trade or free movement—i.e. the establishment of a customs union—administrative actors had a wide scope for action. At the level of creating economic union on the other hand one is dealing with matters which touch the very destiny of the nation-state. Here, the political role of the Commission becomes manifest and, simultaneously, curtailed. Lacking the legitimacy normally ascribed to political leaders and operating beyond the point where decisions and their consequences can be quantified and packaged or even subject to cost analysis because of the underlying values that are at stake, the regional administration finds its capacity for action undermined. What is visible in the European Community is a shifting in the balance of power among the Community institutions away from the bureaucratic Commission and toward the more politically controlled organs of the Council of Ministers and the Committee of Permanent Representatives. The bureaucratic system, based on bureaucratic power and interpenetration, falters when activity shifts from the implementation of accepted goals to the determination of new ones.

Finally, the EEC system has been characterized by progressive bureaucratization of its internal structure.[38] We have

38. For a thoughtful and careful examination of these problems see, David Coombes, *Politics and Bureaucracy in the European Community* (Beverly Hills, Calif.: Sage Publications, 1970).

remarked on the dualistic nature of the Eurocracy on a number of occasions—at one and the same time it is called upon to perform political and administrative functions. This in and of itself is a tension-producing phenomenon and as David Coombs correctly asserts, "it may well be that the Initiative and Administrative functions each call for completely different kinds of organization."[39] As the Community has progressed, the scope of its tasks increased, the compartmentalization of its activities intensified, and its political environment shifted from one of highly convergent support to mixed hostility and/or mutual mistrust among the participant states, the Commission's services have tended to shift attention from "making Europe" to "ensuring careers." Features characteristic of traditional bureaucracies increasingly manifest themselves at the level of regional administration. The consequence of this inevitably must be to reduce the political effectiveness of the organization in question, for bureaucracy is the antithesis of the flexibility and dynamism necessary for integration through consensus-building—and this in the last analysis is the keystone in the arch of contemporary regional integration.

39. Ibid., 237.

8

The National Bureaucracies of the EEC Member States and Political Integration: A Preliminary Inquiry

WERNER FELD

The actual and potential role played by the civil service of the European Communities in the process of economic and political integration has been investigated by a number of political scientists.[1] Much less attention, however, has been paid to the part that is played in the integration process by the national bureaucracies of the Community member states.[2] This chapter seeks to shed some additional light on this subject although its conclusions must be preliminary and tentative. As understood in this chapter, political integration refers to the process by which powers and functions are transferred from national

1. See especially Ernst B. Haas, "Technocracy, Pluralism and the New Europe" in Stephen R. Graubard (ed.), *A New Europe?* (Boston: Houghton Mifflin Co., 1964), pp. 62–88; Lawrence Scheinman, "Some Preliminary Notes on Bureaucratic Relationships in the European Economic Community," *International Organization* (Autumn 1966), Vol. XX, No. 4, pp. 750–73; and Werner Feld, "The Civil Service of the European Communities: Legal and Political Aspects," *Journal of Public Law* (1963), Vol. XII, No. 1, pp. 68–85. Cf. also David L. Coombes, *Toward a European Civil Service* (London: Chatham House, PEP, 1968). For pertinent observations regarding the role played by civil servants of the central institutions of LAFTA and the Central American Common Market see Ernst B. Haas, "The Uniting of Europe and the Uniting of Latin America," *Journal of Common Market Studies* (June 1967), Vol. V, No. 4, pp. 315–45.

2. Scheinman, op. cit., discusses this aspect to some extent.

governments to central institutions and which may culminate eventually in political unification.

The findings are mainly based on twenty-three in-depth interviews and conversations. Twenty-two of the persons interviewed were middle- and upper-middle-rank national officials in the economics, agriculture, finance, and foreign ministries of EEC member states, including two officials of a German *Land*. The twenty-third person interviewed was a high official of a national industry association who had close relations with civil servants in the economics and agriculture ministries in his country. The age of the individuals interviewed ranged from thirty-two to sixty years, with the majority being in their middle forties. Admittedly, twenty-three interviews do not provide a scientific basis for definitive conclusions, but they may be considered as sufficient to offer impressions from which provisional inferences can be drawn and upon which subsequent, more extensive, research can be built.

SUPPORT FOR UNIFICATION AND MOTIVATIONS OF BUREAUCRATIC BEHAVIOR

Max Weber, in his study of bureaucracy, stressed that large, long-established state bureaucracies are capable of considerable independence and insulation from the political leadership and are far from being passive tools of those who yield political power in a state.[3] Thus, even if the political leaders in the member states of the Community were fully committed to bringing about political unification, the national civil servants might seek to obviate this goal in the event that they opposed political unity. That this could well be the case is suggested by a statement made by Franz-Joseph Strauss, former West German minister of finance. In an article published in December 1968 he wrote:

3. H. H. Gerth and C. Wright Mills (eds.), *From Max Weber: Essays in Sociology* (New York: Oxford University Press, 1958), pp. 228–35.

Sometimes shortsighted ambition of nationalistically oriented bureaucracies as well as lack of decisiveness on the part of responsible politicians leads to an overgrowth of egocentric interests. We observe not without apprehension that after the dismantlement of the tariff walls new national paper walls are being erected surreptitiously through the issuance of drawn-out indeterminable regulations. The re-nationalization of ideas is followed by the re-nationalization of secret bureaucratic decisions. With the slogan of the sovereignty of the states and the pursuit of their own interests, it is quite easy to manipulate [the bureaucratic schemes].[4]

For the above reasons the first task of our inquiry had to be an exploration of the attitudes and beliefs which the interviewees had regarding political unification as well as the form it should take and methods used to achieve it. Of course, a *caveat* must be immediately inserted here. Support for unification might reflect merely an ideological image of being a "good European" rather than a concrete desire for real political unity. Opinion polls over the last two decades have indicated again and again a high percentage of favorable responses to such questions as "Are you in favor of the unification of Western Europe?" "Do you favor European union?", or "Are you for the evolution of the Common Market toward a political form of a United States of Europe?"[5] But it is doubtful whether the re-

4. "Phrasen schaffen kein Europa," *Europaeische Gemeinschaft* (December 1968), pp. 3–4.

5. For detailed data see Jacques-René Rabier, "The European Idea and National Public Opinion," *Government and Opposition* (April–July 1967), Vol. II, No. 3, pp. 443–54; and *Communauté Européene* (April 1970), No. 141, pp. 11–12. The distribution of the responses to the last question is given below:

	Germ.	Fr.	It.	Bel.	Neth.	Lux.	EEC	G.B.
	%	%	%	%	%	%	%	%
For	69	67	60	60	64	75	65	30
Against	9	11	7	10	17	5	10	48
No Response	22	22	33	30	19	20	25	22

The positive responses to the idea of the political unification of Europe broken down by age are as follows:

spondents had a full understanding of what their replies meant. While it may be comfortable to know that respondents belonging to the upper socio-economic levels manifested a distinctly higher degree of support for unification, Jacques-René Rabier points out that the polls showed overall a perceptible decrease in the percentage of opinion in favor of European union when the question asked became more precise; the respondent in this case appeared to sense a greater extent of commitment and was more cautious. In addition, it seems that those in favor of union based their opinion on rather vague knowledge and somewhat nebulous sensitivity to European problems.[6]

In our own inquiry, twenty-one of the twenty-three individuals expressed support for political unification and two opposed it (one French, one Dutch). With respect to form and method, eleven favored a federal structure, three a "Europe of the fatherlands," eleven wanted to see integration carried out through the full implementation of the Community treaties, while four opted for foreign and defense policy coordination somewhat along the lines envisaged by the Fouchet Plan and the Davignon Committee.[7] We should note that some of the interviewees expressed preferences for more than one of the choices, provided they were not mutually exclusive. Thus, three hoped that the integration process under the Community treaties would eventually lead to a federal structure; three others favored a combination of the implementation of the Community treaties with policy coordination in foreign and

Age	Germ.	Fr.	It.	Bel.	Neth.	Lux.	G.B.
	%	%	%	%	%	%	%
18–34	74	65	60.5	58	65	72.5	36
35–64	64	60	53	59	58	63	29
65 +	52	49	34	39	51.5	59	19

It is interesting but not surprising that the age group between 18 and 34 shows a stronger support for the United States of Europe than the older respondents.

6. Cf. Rabier, op. cit., passim.

7. See *Agence Europe Bulletin,* May 8, 11, 12, and July 20, 1970.

defense policies; one opted for this coordination within a "Europe of the Fatherlands," and one favored the attainment of the last goal as a culmination of the implementation of the Community treaties.

None of the interviewees thought that the objective of political unity as they perceived it could be achieved rapidly. Most believed that it would require a period of thirty to sixty years, if it were possible at all. Naturally, those whose final objective was exclusively the continued integration process under the Community treaties were more optimistic about the period of goal attainment that the others. But it was perhaps symptomatic that almost all regarded the present timetable set by the Communities' Commission and the Council of Ministers for the achievement of the economic and monetary union (1978–80) as unrealistic; in their opinion, ten years would have to be added to that estimate for the attainment of these goals.

THE TRANSFER OF FUNCTIONS TO CENTRAL INSTITUTIONS

To probe deeper into the intensity of support for unification expressed by the individuals interviewed and perhaps to test the sincerity of their statements, the basic motivations and perceptions of bureaucratic behavior as seen by the interviewees were explored briefly. They were asked to rank various motivating factors which they considered to be the most important driving forces for their behavior and attitudes and for those of their colleagues. Table I provides a breakdown of their responses showing the motivations ranked in descending order and the priorities assigned to them. "The work in itself" and "Position of importance and power" hold top honors, but the latter was accorded lower priorities by the respondents than the former. "Possibility for advancement" and "Remuneration" are runners-up.

TABLE I

Motivating Factors	Priority					
	1	2	3	4	5	Total
The work itself	10	2	4		1	17
Position of importance and power	6	6	4	1	1	17
Possibility of advancement	5	5	3	1		14
Remuneration	1	1	2	3	1	8
Prestige	1	1	1	3		6
Desire for supervisory job	1	1	3			5
Desire for responsibility	1	2	1			4
Achievement			2		1	3
Security		1	1			2
Self-respect	1					1
Desire for recognition						0

Do these basic motivations have a bearing on the perception of the public interest? Twenty-one interviewees held that civil servants saw at times the public interest differently from that expressed by the political leadership, and twenty-two of the twenty-three agreed that the private motivations of officials colored their perceptions of the public interest. One official stated bluntly that it is the administrator who makes policy, while a few felt that only technical changes could be made by civil servants against announced policies of the political leadership, especially if the latter was forceful, but that basic political objectives could neither be altered nor subverted. In general, however, the individuals interviewed were conscious that civil servants, especially in upper-middle and upper ranks, could in accordance with Weber's thesis influence the policy-making of the political leadership and modify the implementation of policy following their own perception of what the public interest required.

Anthony Downs, in his book *Inside Bureaucracy*, points out that all officials tend to oppose changes that decrease the number, scope, or relative importance of the functions entrusted to them. He states that like most large organizations, administrative institutions have a powerful propensity to continue doing today whatever they did yesterday. In Down's view the chief cause for this inertia is to be found in the enormous investment in time, effort, and money to build up pertinent administrative processes. Moreover, in many cases a clientele was developed which over time accepted and became used to the behavior pattern of the institution.[8]

With these factors in mind and considering that the process of political integration requires an increasing transfer of functions and competences to the central institution, the following questions were raised with the interviewees. Did they oppose or would they accept any contraction of their functions? Did they perceive themselves and their colleagues as seeking to maintain their organizations as they were? Were they innovation-minded? Except for the first two questions, more than one answer was possible. Table II shows the result of the queries which indicates that a majority opposed any contraction of functions, while a substantial minority would accept such a contingency, and a good number were interested in innovation.

TABLE II
Do you believe that your subordinates and colleagues:

a.	would accept contractions of duties	9
b.	oppose any contraction of duties	12
c.	seek to maintain the organization as is	10
d.	are innovation-minded	10

To evaluate fully these responses, however, requires a number of important qualifications which emerged from the discussion of these questions with the interviewees. First, few really had given full thought to the possibility of an extensive transfer of their functions to central institutions or a central government because realistic progress in political integration

8. Anthony Downs, *Inside Bureaucracy* (Boston: Little, Brown and Co., 1967), pp. 195–204.

still seemed far away and had not to be faced as yet. The probable entry of Great Britain into the Common Market appeared to reinforce the belief that any serious consideration of the consequences of political unification in Europe could be postponed *sine die,* since British membership was seen as having a negative influence on the process of full political integration. Second, officials who were forty-five years and older, who often held influential positions, as well as those engaged primarily in technical jobs, tended to oppose any contraction of their tasks and competences, although the latter category was frequently innovation-minded. Third, civil servants below the age of forty and also those dealing with European Community affairs in their respective ministries seemed to accept the contraction of functions with greater ease.[9] Of course, the duties of the second group may by the very nature of their involvement actually expand as progress in integration is made. This expansion may assume particular significance when finances are made available through the Community institutions for new programs such as the restructuring of national agricultural systems or the establishment of retraining schemes through the Community Social Fund. Fourth, in the agricultural ministries, officials seemed to have fully accepted the transfer of price policies to the Community level, but remain strongly opposed to giving up any functions in connection with the changes to be made in the national farm structures and agricultural systems. German officials in the *Laender* have insisted that they share this task with federal civil servants and in fact play the major role in it. Fifth, it appears that in all EEC member states the bureaucracies of the finance ministries were especially reluctant to part with their fiscal and budgetary authority and that opposition to any contraction of functions was also pronounced in ministries not directly involved in Community affairs (i.e. the interior ministries). Moreover, a number of

9. In this connection see the tables in footnote 5.

foreign office and economics ministry officials were said to oppose giving up their policy prerogatives in the economic foreign policy field, attitudes which reportedly have been strengthened as the common commercial policy functions of the Community have been expanded. Sixth, there seemed to be a particular concern among interviewees that national officials should remain in charge of national regional policies, although others pointed out that a federal structure would lead to greater decentralization and would add functions for regional and local officials.

The reluctance on the part of national civil servants to give up functions and tasks is reinforced by the relationship which many ministries have with their clientele. There was general agreement among the officials interviewed who had such relationships that service to this clientele was a source of satisfaction to themselves and benefited their organization. It provided important information for the tasks they were to perform and at the same time furnished concrete evidence of their position of power and importance when faced with requests for favorable administrative action. Of course, some interviewees disliked the pressure that often accompanied such requests, especially threats to go over their heads directly to the ministers, but they nevertheless thought that the interests of their clientele would be hurt if their institutions were eliminated or their functions reduced. This was one of the main reasons that national officials have insisted on the retention of their authority in restructuring the national agricultural systems and that farm groups have maintained their close relationship with the national ministries of agriculture. For similar reasons, officials of economics ministries have made every effort to continue their close contacts with industrial interest groups and individual enterprises stressing that, in particular, medium-sized and small industries were depending on the assistance of national agencies.

THE RELATIONSHIP BETWEEN NATIONAL
AND COMMUNITY OFFICIALS

It is reasonable to assume that the beliefs and attitudes regarding political unification held by national officials in the EEC member states are influenced by their perceptions and attitudes toward the civil service of the Communities. Moreover, since the EEC system provides manifold contacts between the national officials and the Community civil service not only in Brussels but also to a lesser degree in the national capitals, and since the Eurocrats often are enthusiastic protagonists of the "European" idea, it is conceivable that a political socialization and learning process has been set in motion among the national officials orienting them toward political unification. Therefore, a section of the interviews was devoted to inquiring into the above aspects.

Most of the interviewees who had contacts with civil servants of the Communities considered them competent on the average although some felt that there were more of peaks and valleys in capability than in the national bureaucracies and that Community officials did not work as hard as their national counterparts. Several of those interviewed expressed the opinion that Eurocrats in middle-rank positions were too highly specialized and therefore had too narrow a viewpoint, and two individuals stated that some high Community civil servants lacked the proper qualifications. One reason given for this situation was the reluctance of national governments to recommend for Community positions those national officials who had excelled in their own service. Another reason was that the Community personnel statutes required selection of civil servants from outside the national services and therefore many of the Eurocrats lacked the useful experience which could be gained from understanding the various facets of national administrative processes.

A majority of the interviewees (seventeen) felt that the salaries received by the Eurocrats were too high, particularly when considered in connection with the tax benefits they enjoyed. Some stated that they and many of their colleagues felt an equalization of the national salary scales with that of the Communities was overdue. However, others expressed the opinion that the difference had already been narrowed and that this relatively small difference did not justify "giving up living in Paris or Rome."

While many of the contacts between Community and national officials take place in the form of individual consultation in Brussels and the national capitals, most occur in expert working groups within the framework of the Commission and the Committee of Permanent Representatives. Since these working groups bring together staff members of the Commission and national officials of the various member states, the question was raised whether the interviewees with Community contacts identified themselves professionally more with the Community civil servants or with their colleagues from other national bureaucracies. While it was possible for them to identify with both groups, it was interesting to note that seventeen identified themselves professionally with their national colleagues, and only eleven with the Community officials. On the other hand, seven stated positively that they did not identify themselves with the Eurocrats, but only one said this with respect to his national colleagues. The inference is therefore justified that national civil servants involved in working groups feel themselves to be professionally closer to their national colleagues than to the Community officials. The reason may well be that national officials continue to consider their governments as the main actors in the Community decision-making process and that they share with their national colleagues similar problems when dealing with superiors in their home ministries.

At the same time it is important to point out that thirteen of the interviewees considered themselves as part of an "insider group" in terms of transnational economic and political goals.

These individuals thought that through the increased frequency and range of face-to-face contacts they had contributed to smoothing out differences regarding the value of transnational economic activities held by ministries and bureaucracies in the EEC countries. Ten of these sensed that through their assignment to the working groups and other activities in Brussels they had adopted a more "European" orientation than they had before. Yet, they perceived that their main task in these group meetings was to promote and defend their respective national interests, and most admitted that they and their ministries at times felt obliged to use threats and other competitive measures to bargain for the highest gains for their countries.

The last question in this part of the interview dealt with the desirability of becoming permanent Community civil servants. Of the interviewees only three expressed a desire for a permanent affiliation with the Community civil service. One of them limited his interest to the secretariat of the Council of Ministers, another one was recommended for appointment to the Commission staff, but his ministry vetoed it. The remainder of the interviewees explained their lack of interest by reason of the belief that such an affiliation would reduce the opportunities for advancement in the institution to which they are presently assigned. We should mention here that only the French government, at the end of the 1950s and early 1960s, encouraged their civil servants considered capable to enter the bureaucracy of the Community and provided promotions after their return to the national service. This policy seems to have been discontinued several years ago. None of the governments of the other member states appear to have instituted such a policy; in fact, the Dutch completely separate their officials from the national service if they choose to accept a position with the Community. The officials who returned from the Community to their national services seem to have gradually lost the "European" orientation which they had perhaps acquired during their tenure with the Community civil service. An important cause for this change of attitudes and values is likely to be the influence of the bureaucratic ideologies which permeate the national institutions.

THE U.S. ROLE IN POLITICAL INTEGRATION

The interviews concluded with a somewhat extraneous question regarding the influence of the U.S. in the process of integration in the Community. The officials interviewed were asked whether in their opinion United States policy had contributed to this process, had impeded it, or had had no influence at all. Table III shows the distribution of the responses; however, only twelve of the responses were straight-forward, while the remainder contained various qualifications.

Of the eleven individuals who regarded U.S. policy as aiding in the integration process, six limited this contribution to the 1950s and the periods of the Kennedy administration and, to a lesser degree, the Johnson administration. They perceived the Nixon administration to be aloof to the European integration affairs which, in their view, was harmful. Equally damaging seemed to them the continued battle of the Nixon administration against the protectionistic features of the Community agricultural policy (a battle waged also by the previous administrations), American opposition to the preferential agreements concluded or contemplated by the Community in the Mediterranean area, and the emergence of new American protectionism as evidenced by the Nixon administration's support of the proposed quota legislation for the import of textiles and perhaps other items. However, we should also note a different interpretation which one or two interviewees suggested for these events. These individuals reasoned that similar to the perceived threat of Soviet expansion in the 1950s, which was an important factor for setting the integration process in Western Europe into motion, a pugnacious, "threatening" attitude on the part of the American government in the international trade field could become a new catalyst for moving political integration forward.

TABLE III

Do you consider that the United States has:

		Unqualified	Qualified	Total
a.	helped integration	5	6	11
b.	impeded integration	1	2	3
c.	had no influence on the process of integration	7	2	9
		13	10	23

The three interviewees who thought that American policy impeded integration pointed out that the activistic policy of the U.S. which pushed for European integration had evoked negative reactions, especially among de Gaulle and his followers, and therefore proved to be counter-productive. Two of these individuals believed that since de Gaulle's resignation U.S. policy has had no further influence on the process of integration.

Of the nine interviewees who denied any American influence on European integration, two agreed with the argument that the present American positions regarding protectionism and preferential agreements could produce a sense of threat among Europeans. While they regarded these threat perceptions as affecting the European attitudes toward the U.S. unfavorably, they did not think that they would enhance the process of political integration.

It is noteworthy that all twenty-three persons interviewed were unanimous in their condemnation of the American stand regarding the Community preferential agreements in the Mediterranean although they admitted them to be violations of GATT. This may perhaps suggest a growing "European" chauvinism when it comes to expanding the sphere of influence of the Community and its member states. This phenomenon was already quite apparent to this writer when he conducted interviews during 1965 on elite attitudes in the EEC member states regarding the external relations of the Community.[10] While in

10. Werner Feld, *The European Common Market and the World* (Englewood Cliffs, N.J.: Prentice-Hall, 1967), p. 143.

terms of international politics this new chauvinism is anything but a desirable phenomenon, its development may have favorable long-range implications for the process of political integration in Western Europe.

CONCLUSIONS

When we relate the responses of the interviewees regarding the motivational factors of administrative behavior and the acceptability of the reduction of functions to their expressions of support for unification, their expressions appear to have a hollow ring. Considerations of positions of power and importance as well as possibilities for advancement are prime motivations for civil servants and apprehension about the contraction of functions cannot but militate against support for political integration which by necessity entails a transfer of functions to a higher level and thereby may well reduce the power and importance possessed by national officials. The statements of the officials interviewed to the effect that they do not consider the realization of political unification a likely prospect until thirty to sixty years have passed, may suggest that they have not yet fully faced up to the implications of such an event for their position and future. Or if they are fully aware of these implications, they may want to conceal consciously or subconsciously their understandable concern.

Clearly, a few of the interviewees realize that new programs financed by higher-level, central institutions and decentralization schemes may in fact expand their range of competences, but of course they also recognize that this expansion of functions would be under the direction of a higher authority. If one adds to these factors the definite reluctance of most interviewees to accept a permanent position with the Community civil services, either for fear that it would damage the future of their national careers or for some real or imagined dislike of

Brussels, one cannot escape the impression that little genuine enthusiasm for political integration exists at present among important segments of the national bureaucracies. In this connection, it is also significant that the interviewees assigned to Community working-groups appear to identify themselves professionally more with their colleagues from the EEC countries than with the Eurocrats. The assertion made at times that the number of transactions with Community civil servants can be used as an element of measurement of the integration process,[11] is therefore open to question and needs additional exploration. It becomes even weaker when we consider the influence that bureaucratic ideologies prevailing in the national ministries exert on their employees when they return from their Brussels assignments.

Finally we would like to broaden briefly our perspective to include any regional international organization aspiring expressly or clandestinely to transform the region in which it operates into an economically and politically more integrated unit. Our inquiry suggests that top-level executives of such organizations must guard against the assumption that extensive contacts between the international and national civil servants in the region will automatically enhance the transformation process. In addition, coalitions need to be built with other major elites in the member states of the regional organization to generate broad support for the central institutions and regional ideologies. As experience in the European Community has shown, these are very formidable undertakings whose success remains highly questionable at this time. Nevertheless they are necessary if the integration process is to move forward. These considerations also apply *mutatis mutandis* to the situation in the East African Community, LAFTA, and the Central

11. Leon N. Lindberg, "Political Integration as a Multi-dimensional Phenomenon Requiring Multivariate Measurement," *International Organization* (Autumn 1970), Vol. XXIV, No. 4, pp. 690–91.

American Common Market although much more research is needed to determine similarities and differences of interactions between international and national bureaucracies in various integration-oriented regional organizations. [12]

---

12. See for example James D. Cochrane, "The Politics of Regional Integration: The Central American Case," *Tulane Studies in Political Science*, Vol. XII; and Philippe C. Schmitter, "Central American Integration: Spill-Over, Spill-Around or Encapsulation?" *Journal of Common Market Studies* (September 1970), Vol. IX, No. 1.

EPILOGUE

The International Civil
Servant in Law and in Fact

DAG HAMMARSKJÖLD

I

In a recent article Mr. Walter Lippmann tells about an interview in Moscow with Mr. Khrushchev. According to the article,
Chairman Khrushchev stated that "while there are neutral
countries, there are no neutral men," and the author draws
the conclusion that it is now the view of the Soviet Government "that there can be no such thing as an impartial civil servant in this deeply divided world, and that the kind of political
celibacy which the British theory of the civil servant calls for,
is in international affairs a fiction.[1]

Whether this accurately sums up the views held by the
Soviet Government, as reflected in the interview, or not, one
thing is certain: the attitude which the article reflects is one
which we find nowadays in many political quarters, communist
and non-communist alike, and it raises a problem which cannot
be treated lightly. In fact, it challenges basic tenets in the
philosophy of both the League of Nations and the United Nations, as one of the essential points on which these experiments
in international co-operation represent an advance beyond

1. *New York Herald Tribune,* Apr. 17, 1961, pp. 1 and 2.

A lecture delivered to Congregation, University of Oxford on May 30,
1961. Reprinted by permission of the Clarendon Press, Oxford.

traditional "conference diplomacy" is the introduction on the international arena of joint permanent organs, employing a neutral civil service, and the use of such organs for executive purposes on behalf of all the members of the organizations. Were it to be considered that the experience shows that this radical innovation in international life rests on a false assumption, because "no man can be neutral," then we would be thrown back to 1919, and a searching reappraisal would become necessary.

II

The international civil service had its genesis in the League of Nations but it did not spring full-blown in the Treaty of Versailles and the Covenant. The Covenant was in fact silent on the international character of the Secretariat. It contained no provisions comparable to those of Article 100 of the Charter, and simply stated:

> The permanent Secretariat shall be established at the Seat of the League. The Secretariat shall comprise a Secretary-General and such secretaries and staff as may be required.[2]

In the earliest proposals for the Secretariat of the League, it was apparently taken for granted that there could not be a truly international secretariat but that there would have to be nine national Secretaries, each assisted by a national staff and performing, in turn, the duties of Secretary to the Council, under the supervision of the Secretary-General. This plan, which had been drawn up by Sir Maurice Hankey, who had been offered the post of Secretary-General of the League by the Allied Powers, was in keeping with the precedents set by the various international Bureaux established before the war which were staffed by officials seconded by Member countries on a temporary basis.

---

2. Article 6 of the Covenant of the League of Nations.

It was Sir Eric Drummond, first Secretary-General of the League, who is generally regarded as mainly responsible for building upon the vague language of the Covenant a truly international secretariat. The classic statement of the principles he first espoused is found in the report submitted to the Council of the League by its British member, Arthur Balfour:

> By the terms of the Treaty, the duty of selecting the staff falls upon the Secretary-General, just as the duty of approving it falls upon the Council. In making his appointments, he had primarily to secure the best available men and women for the particular duties which had to be performed; but in doing so, it was necessary to have regard to the great importance of selecting the officials from various nations. Evidently, no one nation or group of nations ought to have a monopoly in providing the material for this international institution. I emphasize the word "international," because the members of the Secretariat once appointed are no longer the servants of the country of which they are citizens, but become for the time being the servants only of the League of Nations. Their duties are not national but international.[3]

Thus, in this statement, we have two of the essential principles of an international civil service: (1) its international composition, and (2) its international responsibilities. The latter principle found its legal expression in the Regulations subsequently adopted which enjoined all officials "to discharge their functions and to regulate their conduct with the interests of the League alone in view" and prohibited them from seeking or receiving "instructions from any Government or other authority external to the Secretariat of the League of Nations."[4]

Along with the conception of an independent, internationally responsible staff, another major idea was to be found: the international Secretariat was to be solely an administrative organ, eschewing political judgements and actions. It is not at

3. *League of Nations Official Journal* (June 1920), Vol. I, p. 137.
4. Article I of the Staff Regulations of the Secretariat of the League of Nations, 1945 edition.

all surprising that this third principle should have originated with a British Secretary-General. In the United Kingdom, as in certain other European countries, a system of patronage, political or personal, had been gradually replaced in the course of the nineteenth century by the principle of a permanent civil service based on efficiency and competence and owing allegiance only to the State which it served. It followed that a civil service so organized and dedicated would be non-political. The civil servant could not be expected to serve two masters and consequently he could not, in his official duties, display any political allegiance to a political party or ideology. Those decisions which involved a political choice were left to the Government and to Parliament; the civil servant was the non-partisan administrator of those decisions. His discretion was a limited one, bound by the framework of national law and authority and by rules and instructions issued by his political superiors. True, there were choices for him, since neither legal rules nor policy decisions can wholly eliminate the discretion of the administrative official, but the choices to be made were confined to relatively narrow limits by legislative enactment, Government decisions and the great body of precedent and tradition. The necessary condition was that there should exist at all times a higher political authority with the capacity to take the political decisions. With that condition it seemed almost axiomatic that the civil service had to be "politically celibate" (though not perhaps politically virgin). It could not take sides in any political controversy and, accordingly, it could not be given tasks which required it to do so. This was reflected in the basic statements laying down the policy to govern the international Secretariat. I may quote two of them:

> We recommend with special urgency that, in the interests of the League, as well as in its own interests, the Secretariat should not extend the sphere of its activities, that in the preparation of the work and the decisions of the various organizations of the League, it should regard it as its first duty to collate the relevant

documents, and to prepare the ground for these decisions with-out suggesting what these decisions should be; finally, that once these decisions had been taken by the bodies solely responsible for them, it should confine itself to executing them in the letter and in the spirit.[5]

Une fois les décisions prises, le rôle du Secrétariat est de les appliquer. Ici encore, il y a lieu de faire une distinction entre ap-plication et interprétation, non pas, à coup sûr, que je demande au Secrétariat de ne jamais interpréter; c'est son métier! Mais je lui demande, et vous lui demanderez certainement tous, d'interpréter le moins loin possible, le plus fidèlement possible, et surtout de ne jamais substituer son interprétation à la vôtre.[6]

Historians of the League have noted the self-restraining role played by the Secretary-General.[7] He never addressed the Assembly of the League and in the Council "he tended to speak . . . as a Secretary of a committee and not more than that."[8] For him to have entered into political tasks which involved in any substantial degree the taking of a position was regarded as compromising the very basis of the impartiality essential for the Secretariat.

True, this does not mean that political matters as such were entirely excluded from the area of the Secretariat's interests. It had been reported by Sir Eric Drummond and others that he played a role behind the scenes, acting as a confidential chan-nel of communication to Governments engaged in controversy

5. Report of Committee No. 4 ("Noblemaire Report"), League of Nations, Records of the Second Assembly, Plenary Meetings, p. 596.

6. Statement by M. Noblemaire at the 26th plenary meeting of the League Assembly, Oct. 1, 1921, League of Nations, Records of the Second Assembly, Plenary Meetings, p. 577.

7. F. P. Walters, A History of the League of Nations (London: Oxford University Press, 1952), pp. 559 ff.; Egon F. Ranshofen-Wertheimer, The In-ternational Secretariat (Washington, D.C.: Carnegie Endowment for Inter-national Peace, 1945), pp. 48–49; Stephen M. Schwebel, The Secretary-General of the United Nations (Cambridge: Harvard University Press, 1952), pp. 6 ff.

8. Proceedings of the Conference on Experience in International Adminis-tration, (Washington: Carnegie Endowment, 1943), p. II.

or dispute, but this behind-the-scenes role was never extended to taking action in a politically controversial case that was deemed objectionable by one of the sides concerned.

III

The legacy of the international secretariat of the League is marked in the Charter of the United Nations. Article 100 follows almost verbatim the League regulations on independence and international responsibility barring the seeking or receiving of instructions from States or other external authority. This was originally proposed at San Francisco by the four sponsoring powers—China, the USSR, the United Kingdom, and the United States—and unanimously accepted.[9] The League experience had shown that an international civil service, responsible only to the Organization, was workable and efficient. It had also revealed, as manifested in the behaviour of German and Italian Fascists, that there was a danger of national pressures corroding the concept of international loyalty. That experience underlined the desirability of including in the Charter itself an explicit obligation on officials and Governments alike to respect fully the independence and the exclusively international character of the responsibilities of the Secretariat.

It was also recognized that an international civil service of this kind could not be made up of persons indirectly responsible to their national governments. The weight attached to this by the majority of members was demonstrated in the Preparatory Commission London, when it was proposed that appointments of officials should be subject to the consent of the government of the Member State of which the candidate was a national.[10] Even in making this proposal, its sponsor explained that it was only intended to build up a staff adequately representative of

9. Documents of the U.N. Conference on International Organization (hereinafter referred to as UNCIO), Vol. VII, p. 394. See also summary record of 18th meeting, Committee I/2, (June 2, 1945) in UNCIO, Vol. VII, pp. 169–70.

10. Report of U.N. Preparatory Commission (1946), UN doc. PC/AD. 54.

the governments and acceptable to them. He maintained that prior approval of officials was necessary, in order to obtain the confidence of their governments which was essential to the Secretariat, but once the officials were appointed, the exclusively international character of their responsibilities would be respected. However, the great majority of Member States rejected this proposal, for they believed that it would be extremely undesirable to write into the regulations anything that would give national governments particular rights in respect of appointments and thus indirectly permit political pressures on the Secretary-General. [11]

Similarly, in line with Article 100, the Preparatory Commission laid emphasis on the fact that the Secretary-General "alone is responsible to the other principal organs for the Secretariat's work," and that all officials in the Organization must recognize the exclusive authority of the Secretary-General and submit themselves to rules of discipline laid down by him. [12]

The principle of the independence of the Secretariat from national pressures was also reinforced in the Charter by Article 105, which provides for granting officials of the Organization "such privileges and immunities as are necessary for the independent exercise of their functions in connexion with the Organization." It was in fact foreseen at San Francisco that in exceptional circumstances there might be a clash between the independent position of a member of the Secretariat and the position of his country, and consequently that an immunity in respect of official acts would be necessary for the protection of the officials from pressure by individual governments and to permit them to carry out their international responsibilities without interference. [13]

11. Report of U.N. Preparatory Commission, Committee 6, 22nd and 23rd meetings, Assembly records, pp. 50–51.

12. Report of UN Preparatory Commission (1946), p. 85, para. 5, and p. 86, para. 9.

13. Report of Rapporteur of Committee I/2, UNCIO, Vol. VII, p. 394.

In all of these legal provisions, the Charter built essentially on the experience of the League and affirmed the principles already accepted there. However, when it came to the functions and authority of the Secretary-General, the Charter broke new ground.

In Article 97 the Secretary-General is described as the "chief administrative officer of the Organization," a phrase not found in the Covenant, though probably implicit in the position of the Secretary-General of the League. Its explicit inclusion in the Charter made it a constitutional requirement—not simply a matter left to the discretion of the organs—that the administration of the Organization shall be left to the Secretary-General. The Preparatory Commission observed that the administrative responsibility under Article 97 involves the essential tasks of preparing the ground for the decisions of the organs and of "executing" them in co-operation with the Members.[14]

Article 97 is of fundamental importance for the status of the international Secretariat of the United Nations, and thus for the international civil servant employed by the Organization, as, together with Articles 100 and 101, it creates for the Secretariat a position, administratively, of full political independence. However, it does not, or at least it need not, represent an element in the picture which raises the question of the "neutrality" of the international civil servant. This is so because the decisions and actions of the Secretary-General as chief administrative officer naturally can be envisaged as limited to administrative problems outside the sphere of political conflicts of interest or ideology, and thus as maintaining the concept of the international civil servant as first developed in the League of Nations.

However, Article 97 is followed by Article 98, and Article 98 is followed by Article 99. And these two Articles together open

14. Report of UN Preparatory Commission, p. 86, para. 12.

the door to the problem of neutrality in a sense unknown in the history of the League of Nations.

In Article 98 it is, thus, provided not only that the Secretary-General "shall act in that capacity" in meetings of the organs, but that he "shall perform such other functions as are entrusted to him by these organs." This latter provision was not in the Convenant of the League. It has substantial significance in the Charter, for it entitles the General Assembly and the Security Council to entrust the Secretary-General with tasks involving the execution of political decisions, even when this would bring him—and with him the Secretariat and its members—into the arena of possible political conflict. The organs are, of course, not required to delegate such tasks to the Secretary-General but it is clear that they may do so. Moreover, it may be said that in doing so the General Assembly and the Security Council are in no way in conflict with the spirit of the Charter—even if some might like to give the words "chief administrative officer" in Article 97 a normative and limitative significance—since the Charter itself gives to the Secretary-General an explicit political role.

It is Article 99 more than any other which was considered by the drafters of the Charter to have transformed the Secretary-General of the United Nations from a purely administrative official to one with an explicit political responsibility. Considering its importance, it is perhaps surprising that Article 99 was hardly debated; most delegates appeared to share Smuts's opinion that the position of the Secretary-General "should be of the highest importance and for this reason a large measure of initiative was expressly conferred."[15] Legal scholars have observed that Article 99 not only confers upon the Secretary-General a right to bring matters to the attention of the Security Council but that this right carries with it, by necessary implica-

15. Letter from Field-Marshal Jan Christian Smuts to Mr. H. W. A. Cooper, Dec. 15, 1949, quoted in Schwebel, op. cit., p. 18.

tion, a broad discretion to conduct inquiries and to engage in informal diplomatic activity in regard to matters which "may threaten the maintenance of international peace and security."[16]

It is not without some significance that this new conception of a Secretary-General originated principally with the United States rather than the United Kingdom. It has been reported that at an early stage in the preparation of the papers that later became the Dumbarton Oaks proposals, the United States gave serious consideration to the idea that the Organization should have a President as well as a Secretary-General.[17] Subsequently, it was decided to propose only a single officer, but one in whom there would be combined both the political and executive functions of a President with the internal administrative functions that were previously accorded to a Secretary-General. Obviously, this is a reflection, in some measure, of the American political system, which places authority in a chief executive officer who is not simply subordinated to the legislative organs but who is constitutionally responsible alone for the execution of legislation and in some respects for carrying out the authority derived from the constitutional instrument directly.

The fact that the Secretary-General is an official with political power as well as administrative functions had direct implications for the method of his selection. Proposals at San Francisco to eliminate the participation of the Security Council in the election process were rejected precisely because it was recognized that the role of the Secretary-General in the field of political and security matters properly involved the Security Council

16. Ibid., p. 25. See summary record of 48th meeting of Committee of Experts of the Security Council, UN doc. S/Procedure/103, particularly statement of the representative of Poland. Also Virally, "Le Rôle politique du Secrétaire général des Nations Unies," Annuaire Français de Droit International, (1958), Vol. IV, p. 363 and footnote 2; Simmonds, "Good Offices and the Secretary-General, Nordisk Tidsskrift for International Ret (1959), Vol. XXIX, fasc. 4, pp. 332, 340, and 341.

17. Schewebel, op. cit., p. 17.

and made it logical that the unanimity rule of the permanent Members should apply.[18] At the same time, it was recognized that the necessity of such unanimous agreement would have to be limited only to the selection of the Secretary-General and that it was equally essential that he be protected against the pressure of a Member during his term in office.[19] Thus a proposal for a three-year term was rejected on the ground that so short a term might impair his independent role.

The concern with the independence of the Secretary-General from national pressures was also reflected at San Francisco in the decision of the Conference to reject proposals for Deputies to the Secretary-General appointed in the same manner as the Secretary-General. The opponents of this provision maintained that a proposal of this kind would result in a group of high officials who would not be responsible to the Secretary-General but to the bodies which elected them.[20] This would inevitably mean a dilution of the responsibility of the Secretary-General for the conduct of the Organization and would be conducive neither to the efficient functioning of the Secretariat nor to its independent position.[21] In this action and other related decisions, the drafters of the Charter laid emphasis on the personal responsibility of the Secretary-General; it is he who is solely responsible for performing the functions entrusted to him for the appointment of all Members of the Secretariat and for assuring the organ that the Secretariat will carry out their tasks under his exclusive authority. The idea of a "Cabinet system" in which responsibility for administration and political functions would be distributed among several individuals was squarely rejected.

It is also relevant in this connexion that the provision for "due regard to geographical representation" in the recruitment of the

18. UNCIO, Vol. II, pp. 691-93.

19. Report of Rapporteur of Committee I/2, ibid., Vol. VII, pp. 343–47, 387–89.

20. Ibid., p. 386.

21. Ibid. See also summary record of 12th meeting of Committee I/2, ibid., p. 106.

Secretariat was never treated as calling for political or ideological representation. It was rather an affirmation of the idea accepted since the beginning of the League Secretariat that the staff of the Organization was to have an international composition and that its basis would be as "geographically" broad as possible.[22] Moreover, as clearly indicated in the language of Article 101, the "paramount consideration in the employment of the staff" should be the necessity of securing the highest standards of efficiency, competence, and integrity. This terminology is evidence of the intention of the drafters to accord priority to considerations of efficiency and competence over those of geographical representation, important though the latter be.

To sum up, the Charter laid down these essential legal principles for an international civil service:

It was to be an international body, recruited primarily for efficiency, competence, and integrity, but on as wide a geographical basis as possible;

It was to be headed by a Secretary-General who carried constitutionally the responsibility to the other principal organs for the Secretariat's work;

And finally, Article 98 entitled the General Assembly and the Security Council to entrust the Secretary-General with tasks going beyond the *verba formalia* of Article 97 — with its emphasis on the administrative function — thus opening the door to a measure of political responsibility which is distinct from the authority explicitly accorded to the Secretary-General under Article 99 but in keeping with the spirit of that Article.

This last-mentioned development concerning the Secretary-General, with its obvious consequences for the Secretariat as such, takes us beyond the concept of a non-political civil service

22. UNCIO, Vol. II, pp. 505, 510–11.

into an area where the official, in the exercise of his functions, may be forced to take stands of a politically controversial nature. It does this, however, on an international basis and, thus, without departing from the basic concept of "neutrality"; in fact, Article 98, as well as Article 99, would be unthinkable without the complement of Article 100 strictly observed both in letter and spirit.

Reverting for a moment to our initial question, I have to emphasize the distinction just made. If a demand for neutrality is made, by present critics of the international civil service, with the intent that the international civil servant should not be permitted to take a stand on political issues, in response to requests of the General Assembly or the Security Council, then the demand is in conflict with the Charter itself. If, however, "neutrality" means that the international civil servant, also in executive tasks with political implications, must remain wholly uninfluenced by national or group interests or ideologies, then the obligation to observe such neutrality is just as basic to the Charter concept of the international civil service as it was to the concept once found in the Covenant of the League. Due to the circumstances then prevailing the distinction to which I have just drawn attention probably never was clearly made in the League, but it has become fundamental for the interpretation of the actions of the Secretariat as established by the Charter.

The criticism to which I referred at the beginning of this lecture can be directed against the very Charter concept of the Secretariat and imply a demand for a reduction of the functions of the Secretariat to the role assigned to it in the League and explicitly mentioned in Article 97 of the Charter; this would be a retrograde development in sharp conflict with the way in which the functions of the international Secretariat over the years have been extended by the main organs of the United Nations, in response to arising needs. Another possibility would be that the actual developments under Articles 98 and 99 are accepted but that a lack of confidence in the possibility of personal "neutrality" is considered to render necessary administrative arrangements putting the persons in question under special constitutional controls, either built into the structure of the Secretariat or established through organs outside the Secretariat.

IV

The conception of an independent international civil service, although reasonably clear in the Charter provisions, was almost continuously subjected to stress in the history of the Organization. International tensions, changes in governments, concern with national security, all had their inevitable repercussions on the still fragile institution dedicated to the international community. Governments not only strove for the acceptance of their views in the organs of the Organization, but they concerned themselves in varying degrees with the attitude of their nationals in the Secretariat. Some governments sought in one way or another to revive the substance of the proposal defeated at London for the clearance of their nationals prior to employment in the Secretariat; other governments on occasion demanded the dismissal of staff members who were said to be inappropriately representative of the country of their nationality for political, racial, or even cultural reasons.

In consequence, the Charter Articles underwent a continual process of interpretation and clarification in the face of pressures brought to bear on the Secretary-General. On the whole the results tended to affirm and strengthen the independence of the international civil service. These developments involved two complementary aspects: first, the relation between the Organization and the Member States in regard to the selection and employment of nationals of those States, and second, the relation between the international official, his own State, and the international responsibilities of the Organization. It is apparent that these relationships involved a complex set of obligations and rights applying to the several interested parties.

One of the most difficult of the problems was presented as a result of the interest of several national governments in passing upon the recruitment of their nationals by the Secretariat. It was of course a matter of fundamental principle that the selection of staff should be made by the Secretary-General on his own responsibility and not on the responsibility of the national governments.[23] The interest of the governments in placing certain nationals and in barring the employment of others had to be subordinated, as a matter of principle and law, to the independent determination of the Organization. Otherwise there would have been an abandonment of the position adopted at San Francisco and affirmed by the Preparatory Commission in London.

On the other hand, there were practical considerations which required the Organization to utilize the services of governments for the purpose of obtaining applicants for positions and, as a corollary of this, for information as to the competence, integrity, and general suitability of such nationals for employment. The United Nations could not have an investigating agency comparable to those available to national governments, and the Organization had therefore to accept assistance from governments in obtaining information and records concerning possible applicants. However, the Secretary-General consistently reserved the right to make the final determination on the basis of all the facts and his own independent appreciation of these facts.[24]

It may be recalled that this problem assumed critical proportions in 1952 and 1953 when various authorities of the United

23. Report of UN Preparatory Commission, p. 86, para. 15; General Assembly resolution 13 (I), Feb. 13, 1946.

24. Report of the Secretary-General on Personnel Policy (Jan. 30, 1953), UN doc. A/2364, para. 7 and Annex 1.

States Government, host to the United Nations Headquarters, conducted a series of highly publicized investigations of the loyalty of its nationals in the Secretariat.[25] Charges were made which, although relating to a small number of individuals and largely founded upon inference rather than on direct evidence or admissions, led to proposals which implicitly challenged the international character of the responsibilities of the Secretary-General and his staff.[26] In certain other countries similar proposals were made and in some cases adopted in legislation or by administrative action.

In response, the Secretary-General and the Organization as a whole affirmed the necessity of independent action by the United Nations in regard to selection and recruitment of staff. The Organization was only prepared to accept information from governments concerning suitability for employment, including information that might be relevant to political considerations such as activity which would be regarded as inconsistent with the obligation of international civil servants.[27] It was recognized that there should be a relationship of mutual confidence and trust between international officials and the governments of Member States. At the same time, the Secretary-General took a strong position that the dismissal of a staff member on the basis of the mere suspicion of a Government of a Member State or a bare conclusion arrived at by that Government on evidence which is denied the Secretary-General would amount to receiving instructions in violation of his obligation under Article 100, paragraph 1 of the Charter "not to receive in the performance of his duties instructions from any Government."[28] It should be said that, as a result of the stand taken by

25. See Hearings of the Sub-Committee of the Committee on the Judiciary of the U.S. Senate on "Activities of U.S. Citizens employed by the United Nations" (1952).

26. Ibid., pp. 407–11. See also Bill S. 3, 83rd Cong. 1st Sess.

27. Report of the Secretary-General on Personnel Policy, UN doc. A/2533, paras. 69–70.

28. UN doc. A/2364, para. 94.

the Organization, this principle was recognized by the United States Government in the procedures it established for hearings and submission of information to the Secretary-General regarding U.S. citizens.[29]

A risk of national pressure on the international official may also be introduced, in a somewhat more subtle way, by the terms and duration of his appointment. A national official, seconded by his government for a year or two with an international organization, is evidently in a different position psychologically—and one might say, politically—from the permanent international civil servant who does not contemplate a subsequent career with his national government. This was recognized by the Preparatory Commission in London in 1945 when it concluded that members of the Secretariat staff could not be expected "fully to subordinate the special interests of their countries to the international interest if they are merely detached temporarily from national administrations and dependent upon them for their future."[30] Recently, however, assertions have been made that it is necessary to switch from the present system, which makes permanent appointments and career service the rule, to a predominant system of fixed-term appointments to be granted mainly to officials seconded by their governments. This line is prompted by governments which show little enthusiasm for making officials available on a long-term basis, and, moreover, seem to regard—as a matter of principle or, at least, of "realistic" psychology—the international civil servant primarily as a national official representing his country and its ideology. On this view, the international civil service should be recognized and developed as being an "intergovernmental" secretariat composed principally of national officials assigned by their governments, rather than as an "international"

29. UN doc. A/2364, pp. 35–36, containing Executive Order No. 10422; as amended by Executive Order No. 10459, UN doc. A/2533, appendix to Annex 1.

30. Report of UN Preparatory Commission, p. 92, para. 59.

secretariat as conceived from the days of the League of Nations and until now. In the light of what I have already said regarding the provisions of the Charter, I need not demonstrate that this conception runs squarely against the principles of Articles 100 and 101.

This is not to say that there is not room for a reasonable number of "seconded" officials in the Secretariat. It has in fact been accepted that it is highly desirable to have a number of officials available from governments for short periods, especially to perform particular tasks calling for diplomatic or technical backgrounds. Experience has shown that such seconded officials, true to their obligations under the Charter, perform valuable service but as a matter of good policy it should, of course, be avoided as much as possible to put them on assignments in which their status and nationality might be embarrassing to themselves or the parties concerned. However, this is quite different from having a large portion of the Secretariat — say, in excess of one-third — composed of short-term officials. To have so large a proportion of the Secretariat staff in the seconded category would be likely to impose serious strains on its ability to function as a body dedicated exclusively to international responsibilities. Especially if there were any doubts as to the principles ruling their work in the minds of the governments on which their future might depend, this might result in a radical departure from the basic concepts of the Charter and the destruction of the international civil service as has been developed in the League and up to now in the United Nations.

It can fairly be said that the United Nations has increasingly succeeded in affirming the original idea of a dedicated professional service responsible only to the Organization in the performance of its duties and protected so far as possible from the inevitable pressures of national governments. And this has been done in spite of strong pressures which are easily explained in terms of historic tradition and national interests. Obviously, however, the problem is ultimately one of the spirit of service shown by the international civil servant and respected by Member Governments. The International Secretariat is not what it is meant to be until the day when it can be recruited on a wide geographical basis without the risk that then some will be under—or consider themselves to be under—two masters in respect of their official functions.

V

The independence and international character of the Secretariat required not only resistance to national pressures in matters of personnel, but also—and this was more complex—the independent implementation of controversial political decisions in a manner fully consistent with the exclusively international responsibility of the Secretary-General. True, in some cases implementation was largely administrative; the political organs stated their objectives and the measures to be taken in reasonably specific terms, leaving only a narrow area for executive discretion. But in other cases—and these generally involved the most controversial situations—the Secretary-General was confronted with mandates of a highly general character, expressing the bare minimum of agreement attainable in the organs. That the execution of these tasks involved the exercise of political judgement by the Secretary-General was, of course, evident to the Member States themselves.

It could perhaps be surmised that virtually no one at San Francisco envisaged the extent to which the Members of the Organization would assign to the Secretary-General functions which necessarily required him to take positions in highly controversial political matters. A few examples of these mandates in recent years will demonstrate how wide has been the scope of authority delegated to the Secretary-General by the Security Council and the General Assembly in matters of peace and security.

One might begin in 1956 with the Palestine armistice problem, when the Security Council instructed the Secretary-General "to arrange with the parties for adoption of any measures" which he should consider "would reduce existing tensions along the armistice demarcation lines."[31] A few months later, after the outbreak of hostilities in Egypt, the General Assembly authorized the Secretary-General immediately to "obtain compliance of the withdrawal of foreign forces."[32] At the same session he was requested to submit a plan for a United Nations Force to "secure and supervise the cessation of hostilities," and subsequently he was instructed "to take all . . . necessary administrative and executive action to organise this Force and dispatch it to Egypt."[33]

In 1958 the Secretary-General was requested "to despatch urgently an Observation Group . . . to Lebanon so as to ensure that there is no illegal infiltration of personnel or supply of arms or other matériel across the Lebanese borders."[34] Two months later he was asked to make forthwith "such practical arrangements as would adequately help in upholding the purposes and principles of the Charter in relation to Lebanon and Jordan."[35]

Most recently, in July 1960, the Secretary-General was requested to provide military assistance to the Central Government of the Republic of the Congo. The basic mandate is contained in a single paragraph of a resolution adopted by the Security Council on 13 July 1960 which reads as follows:[36]

The Security Council
. . . .

2. *Decides* to authorize the Secretary-General to take the necessary steps, in consultation with the Government of the Republic of the Congo, to provide the Government with such military assistance, as may be necessary, until, through the efforts of the

31. Security Council resolution S/3575 of Apr. 4, 1956.
32. General Assembly resolution 999 (ES-I) of Nov. 4, 1956.
33. General Assembly resolutions 998 (ES-I) of Nov. 4, 1956 and 1001 (ES-I) of Nov. 7, 1956.
34. Security Council resolution S/4023 of June 11, 1958.
35. General Assembly resolution 1237 (ES-III) of Aug. 21, 1958.
36. Security Council resolution S/4387 of July 13, 1961.

> Congolese Government with the technical assistance of the
> United Nations, the national security forces may be able, in the
> opinion of the Government, to meet fully their tasks.

The only additional guidance was provided by a set of principles concerning the use of United Nations Forces which had been evolved during the experience of the United Nations Emergency Force.[37] I had informed the Security Council[38] before the adoption of the resolution that I would base any action that I might be required to take on these principles, drawing attention specifically to some of the most significant of the rules applied in the UNEF operation. At the request of the Security Council I later submitted an elaboration of the same principles to the extent they appeared to me to be applicable to the Congo operation.[39] A report on the matter was explicitly approved by the Council,[40] but naturally it proved to leave wide gaps; unforeseen and unforeseeable problems, which we quickly came to face, made it necessary for me repeatedly to invite the Council to express themselves on the interpretation given by the Secretary-General to the mandate. The needs for added interpretation referred especially to the politically extremely charged situation which arose because of the secession of Katanga and because of the disintegration of the central government which, according to the basic resolution of the Security Council, were to be the party in consultation with which the United Nations activities had to be developed.[41]

37. See "Summary Study of the Experience Derived from the Establishment and Operation of the Force: Report of the Secretary-General," UN doc. A/3943, General Assembly, Official Records, 13th session, annexes, agenda item 65.

38. See Security Council, Official Records, 15th year, 873rd meeting, para. 28.

39. First report by the Secretary-General dated July 18, 1960 on the implementation of the Security Council resolution of July 13, 1960, UN doc. S/4389, p. 4

40. See para. 3 of Security Council resolution S/4405 of July 22, 1960.

41. See Memorandum on implementation of Security Council resolution of Aug. 9, 1960, UN doc. S/4417 and addenda; Security Council, Official Records, 15th year, 884th and following meetings.

These recent examples demonstrate the extent to which the Member States have entrusted the Secretary-General with tasks that have required him to take action which unavoidably may have to run counter to the views of at least some of these Member States. The agreement reached in the general terms of a resolution, as we have seen, no longer need to obtain when more specific issues are presented. Even when the original resolution is fairly precise, subsequent developments, previously unforeseen, may render highly controversial the action called for under the resolution. Thus, for example, the unanimous resolution authorizing assistance to the Central Government of the Congo offered little guidance to the Secretary-General when that Government split into competing centres of authority, each claiming to be the Central Government and each supported by different groups of Member States within and outside the Security Council.

A simple solution for the dilemmas thus posed for the Secretary-General might seem to be for him to refer the problem to the political organ for it to resolve the question. Under a national parliamentary regime, this would often be the obvious course of action for the executive to take. Indeed, this is what the Secretary-General must also do whenever it is feasible. But the serious problems arise precisely because it is so often not possible for the organs themselves to resolve the controversial issue faced by the Secretary-General. When brought down to specific cases involving a clash of interests and positions, the required majority in the Security Council or General Assembly may not be available for any particular solution. This will frequently be evident in advance of a meeting and the Member States will conclude that it would be futile for the organs to attempt to reach a decision and consequently that the problem has to be left to the Secretary-General to solve on one basis or another, at his own risk but with as faithful an interpretation of the instructions, rights, and obligations of the Organization as possible in view of international law and the decisions already taken.

It might be said that in this situation the Secretary-General should refuse to implement the resolution, since implementation would offend one or another group of Member States and open him to the charge that he has abandoned the political neutrality and impartiality essential to his office. The only way to avoid such criticism, it is said, is for the Secretary-General to refrain from execution of the original resolution until the organs have decided the issue by the required majority (and, in the case of the Security Council, with the unanimous concurrence of the permanent members) or he, maybe, has found another way to pass responsibility over on to Governments.

For the Secretary-General this course of action—or more precisely, non-action—may be tempting; it enables him to avoid criticism by refusing to act until other political organs resolve the dilemma. An easy refuge may thus appear to be available. But would such refuge be compatible with the responsibility placed upon the Secretary-General by the Charter? Is he entitled to refuse to carry out the decision properly reached by the organs, on the ground that the specific implementation would be opposed to positions some Member States might wish to take, as indicated, perhaps, by an earlier minority vote? Of course the political organs may always instruct him to discontinue the implementation of a resolution, but when they do not so instruct him and the resolution remains in effect, is the Secretary-General legally and morally free to take no action, particularly in a matter considered to affect international peace and security? Should he, for example, have abandoned the operation in the Congo because almost any decision he made as to the composition of the Force or its role would have been contrary to the attitudes of some Members as reflected in debates, and maybe even in votes, although not in decisions.

The answers seem clear enough in law; the responsibilities of the Secretary-General under the Charter cannot be laid aside merely because the execution of decisions by him is likely to be politically controversial. The Secretary-General remains under the obligation to carry out the policies as adopted by the organs; the essential requirement is that he does this on the basis of his exclusively international responsibility and not in the interest of any particular State or groups of States.

This presents us with the crucial issue: is it possible for the Secretary-General to resolve controversial questions on a truly international basis without obtaining the formal decision of the organs? In my opinion and on the basis of my experience, the answer is in the affirmative; it is possible for the Secretary-General to carry out his tasks in controversial political situations with full regard to his exclusively international obligation under the Charter and without subservience to a particular national or ideological attitude. This is not to say that the Secretary-General is a kind of delphic oracle who alone speaks for the international community. He has available for his task varied means and resources.

Of primary importance in this respect are the principles and purposes of the Charter which are the fundamental law accepted by and binding on all States. Necessarily general and comprehensive, these principles and purposes still are specific enough to have practical significance in concrete cases. [42]

The principles of the Charter are, moreover, supplemented by the body of legal doctrine and precepts that have been accepted by States generally, and particularly as manifested in the resolutions of UN organs. In this body of law there are rules and precedents that appropriately furnish guidance to the Secretary-General when he is faced with the duty of applying a general mandate in circumstances that had not been envisaged by the resolution.

42. See, for example, references to the Charter in relation to the establishment and operation of UNEF: UN doc. A/3302, General Assembly, Official Records, first emergency special session, annexes, agenda item 5, pp. 19–23; UN doc. A/3512, General Assembly, Official Records, eleventh session, annexes, agenda item 66, pp. 47–50. See also references to the Charter in relation to the question of the Congo: UN doc. S/PV.887, p. 17; UN doc. S/PV.920, p. 47; UN doc. S/PV.942, pp. 137–40; UN doc. S/4637 A.

Considerations of principle and law, important as they are, do not of course suffice to settle all the questions posed by the political tasks entrusted to the Secretary-General. Problems of political judgement still remain. In regard to these problems, the Secretary-General must find constitutional means and techniques to assist him, so far as possible, in reducing the element of purely personal judgement. In my experience I have found several arrangements of value to enable the Secretary-General to obtain what might be regarded as the representative opinion of the Organization in respect of the political issues faced by him.

One such arrangement might be described as the institution of the permanent missions to the United Nations, through which the Member States have enabled the Secretary-General to carry on frequent consultations safeguarded by diplomatic privacy. [43]

Another arrangement, which represents a further development of the first, has been the advisory committee of the Secretary-General, such as those on UNEF and the Congo, composed of representatives of Governments most directly concerned with the activity involved, and also representing diverse political positions and interests. [44] These advisory committees have furnished a large measure of the guidance required by the Secretary-General in carrying out his mandates relating to UNEF and the Congo operations. They have provided an essential link between the judgement of the executive and the consensus of the political bodies.

43. See Introduction to the Annual Report of the Secretary-General on the Work of the Organization, June 16, 1958–June 15, 1959, p. 2, UN doc. A/4132 add. 1, General Assembly, Official Records, fourteenth session, Supplement No. 1 A.

44. UNEF Advisory Committee, established by General Assembly resolution 1001 (ES-I). The Advisory Committee on the Congo was established by the Secretary-General and recognized by the General Assembly and in the Security Council's various resolutions.

VI

Experience has thus indicated that the international civil servant may take steps to reduce the sphere within which he has to take stands on politically controversial issues. In summary, it may be said that he will carefully seek guidance in the decisions of the main organs, in statements relevant for the interpretation of those decisions, in the Charter and in generally recognized principles of law, remembering that by his actions he may set important precedents. Further, he will submit as complete reporting to the main organs as circumstances permit, seeking their guidance whenever such guidance seems to be possible to obtain. Even if all of these steps are taken, it will still remain, as has been amply demonstrated in practice, that the reduced area of discretion will be large enough to expose the international Secretariat to heated political controversy and to accusations of a lack of neutrality.

I have already drawn attention to the ambiguity of the word "neutrality" in such a context. It is obvious from what I have said that the international civil servant cannot be accused of lack of neutrality simply for taking a stand on a controversial issue when this is his duty and cannot be avoided. But there remains a serious intellectual and moral problem as we move within an area inside which personal judgement must come into play. Finally, we have to deal here with a question of integrity or with, if you please, a question of conscience.

The international civil servant must keep himself under the strictest observation. He is not requested to be a neuter in the sense that he has to have no sympathies or antipathies, that there are to be no interests which are close to him in his personal capacity, or that he is to have no ideas or ideals that matter for him. However, he is requested to be fully aware of those human reactions and meticulously check himself so that they are not permitted to influence his actions. This is nothing unique. Is not every judge professionally under the same obligation?

If the international civil servant knows himself to be free from such personal influences in his actions and guided solely by the common aims and rules laid down for, and by the Organization he serves and by recognized legal principles, then he has done his duty, and then he can face the criticism which, even so, will be unavoidable. As I said, at the final test, this is a question of integrity, and if integrity in the sense of respect for law and respect for truth were to drive him into positions of conflict with this or that interest, then that conflict is a sign of his neutrality—and not of his failure to observe neutrality—then it is in line, not in conflict with his duties as an international civil servant.

Recently it has been said, this time in Western circles, that as the International Secretariat goes forward on the road of international thought and action, while Member States depart from it, a gap develops between them and they grow into mutually hostile elements; and this is said to increase the tension in the world which it was the purpose of the United Nations to diminish. From this view the conclusion has been drawn that we may have to switch from an international Secretariat, ruled by the principles described in this lecture, to an intergovernmental Secretariat, the members of which obviously would not be supposed to work in the direction of an internationalism considered unpalatable to their governments. Such a passive acceptance of a nationalism rendering it necessary to abandon present efforts in the direction of internationalism symbolized by the international civil service—somewhat surprisingly regarded as a cause of tension—might, if accepted by the Member Nations, well prove to be the Munich of international co-operation as conceived after the First World War and further developed under the impression of the tragedy of the Second World War. To abandon or to compromise with principles on which such co-operation is built may be no less dangerous than to compromise with principles regarding the rights of a nation. In both cases the price to be paid may be peace.

Bibliography

(Items marked with an asterisk are of special relevance to this book.)

AGHNIDES, H. E. T., "Standards of Conduct of the International Civil Servant," *International Review of Administrative Sciences*, No. 1, 1953.

ALKER, HAYWARD R., JR., *Mathematics and Politics*, New York: Macmillan, 1965.

ANSTEE, MARGARET J. *The Administration of International Development Aid*. Syracuse, New York: The Maxwell School of Citizenship and Public Affairs, 1969.

ASCHER, CHARLES S. *Program-Making in UNESCO, 1946–1951: A Study in the Processes of International Administration*. Chicago: Public Administration Service, 1951.

AUFRICHT, HANS. *The International Monetary Fund: Legal Bases, Structure, Functions*. London: Stevens and Sons, 1964.

BAILEY, SYDNEY D. *The Secretariat of the United Nations*. New York: Frederick A. Praeger, 1964.

BAKER, RAY STANNARD. *Woodrow Wilson and World Settlement*. New York: Doubleday, 1925.

* BARROS, JAMES. *Betrayal from Within*. New Haven: Yale University Press, 1969.

BASCH, ANTONIN, "International Bank for Reconstruction and Development, 1944–1949," *International Conciliation*, November 1949.

BAUMANN, CAROL E. *Political Cooperation in NATO*. Madison: University of Wisconsin Press (for the National Security Studies Group), 1960.

BEAUFRE, ANDRE. *NATO and Europe.* New York: A. A. Knopf, 1966.

* BEER, FRANCIS A. *Integration and Distintegration in NATO: Processes of Alliance Cohesion and Prospects for Atlantic Community.* Columbus: Ohio State University Press, 1969.

BELOFF, MAX. *New Dimensions in Foreign Policy: A Study in British Administrative Experience, 1947–59.* New York: Macmillan, 1961.

BEYEN, J. W., "The International Bank for Reconstruction and Development," *International Affairs,* October 1948.

BIRRENBACH, KURT, "The Reorganization of NATO," *Orbis,* Summer 1962.

BLACK, EUGENE R. *The Diplomacy of Economic Development.* New York: Atheneum, 1963.

———, "The World Bank at Work," *Foreign Affairs,* April 1952.

BLOOMFIELD, LINCOLN P. *International Military Forces.* Boston: Little, Brown, 1964.

———. *Outer Space: Prospects for Man and Society.* New York: Frederick A. Praeger (for the American Assembly), 1968.

BOLLES, BLAIR. *The Armed Road to Peace: An Analysis of NATO.* New York: Foreign Policy Association, 1952.

———, "Residual Nationalism: A Rising Threat to Projected European Union," *Annals,* July 1963.

BOWETT, D. W. *United Nations Forces: A Legal Study.* New York: Frederick A. Praeger, 1964.

BRAIBANTI, RALPH (ed.). *Asian Bureaucratic Systems Emergent from the British Imperial Tradition.* Durham: Duke University Press, 1966.

BRYSON, L., L. FINKELSTEIN, and R. W. MacIVER. *Approaches to World Peace.* New York: Harper and Bros., 1944.

BUCHAN, ALASTAIR. *Crisis Management: The New Diplomacy.* Boulogne-sur-Seine: The Atlantic Institute, 1966.

———. *NATO in the 1960's: The Implications of Interdependence.* New York: Frederick A. Praeger, 1963.

———, "The Reform of NATO," Foreign Affairs, January 1962.

BURNS, SIR ALAN. In Defence of Colonies: British Colonial Territories in International Affairs. London: George Allen and Unwin, 1957.

BURNS, ARTHUR L. and NINA HEATHCOTE. Peacekeeping by U.N. Forces, from Suez to Congo. New York: Frederick A. Praeger, 1963.

BURNS, MAJ. GEN. E. L. M., "The Withdrawal of UNEF and the Future of Peacekeeping," International Journal, Winter 1967–68.

CAIRNCROSS, ALEXANDER K. The International Bank for Reconstruction and Development. Princeton: Princeton University Press (for International Finance Section, Department of Economics and Sociology), 1959.

CERNY, KARL H. and HENRY W. BRIEFS (eds.). NATO in Quest of Cohesion. New York: Frederick A. Praeger (for the Hoover Institute), 1965.

CHAMBERLAIN, SIR AUSTEN, "Civil Service Traditions and the League of Nations," Public Administration, Vol. VIII, 1928.

CHAMBERLAIN, WALDO, "Strengthening the Secretariat," (with comments by Wolfgang Friedmann, et. al.), The Annals, November 1954.

CHARLESWORTH, JAMES C. (ed.). Contemporary Political Analysis. New York: The Free Press, 1967.

CHEEVER, DANIEL and H. FIELD HAVILAND, JR., Organizing for Peace: International Organization in World Affairs. Cambridge: Harvard University Press, 1954.

CITRIN, JACK. United Nations Peacekeeping Activities: A Case Study in Organizational Task Expansion. Denver: University of Denver Press, 1965.

CLAUDE, INIS L., JR., "United Nations Use of Military Force," Journal of Conflict Resolution, June 1963.

———. Swords into Plowshares: The Problems and Progress of International Organization. New York: Random House, 1964 (rev. ed.).

CODDING, GEORGE. The International Telecommunications Union. Leyden: A. W. Sijthoff, 1952.

COHEN, MAXWELL, "The Demise of UNEF," International Journal, Winter 1967–68.

COHEN, MORRIS R. and ERNEST NAGEL. *An Introduction to Logic and Scientific Method*. New York: Harcourt, Brace and Co., 1934.

COX, ROBERT W. (ed.). *International Organisation: World Politics*. London: Macmillan, 1969.

* CROCKER, WALTER R. *On Governing Colonies, Being an Outline of the Real Issues and a Comparison of the British, French, and Belgian Approach to Them*. London: George Allen and Unwin, 1947.

* CROWDER, MICHAEL. *West Africa Under Colonial Rule*. Evanston: Northwestern University Press, 1968.

DAALDER, HANS. *Cabinet Reform in Britain, 1914–1963*. Stanford: Stanford University Press, 1963.

DETTER, INGRID. *Lawmaking by International Organizations*. Stockholm: P. A. Norstedt, 1965.

DRUMMOND, SIR ERIC, "The Secretariat of the League of Nations," *Public Administration*, Vol. IX, 1933.

* EAGLETON, CLYDE. *International Government*. New York: The Ronald Press, 1948.

* EGGER, ROWLAND and WILLIAM C. ROGERS. *Introduction to the Study of International Administration*. Charlottesville: University of Virginia Press, 1949.

EHRMAN, JOHN. *Cabinet Government and War, 1890–1940*. Cambridge: Cambridge University Press, 1958.

EVANS, LUTHER H., "Some Management Problems of UNESCO," *International Organization*, February 1963.

* FABIAN, LARRY L. *Soldiers Without Enemies: Preparing the United Nations for Peacekeeping*. Washington, D.C.: The Brookings Institution, 1971.

FABIAN SOCIETY. *International Action and the Colonies*. London: Fabian Publications, 1943.

FAIRLEI, JOHN A. *British War Administration*. London: Oxford University Press, 1919.

FELD, WERNER. *The European Common Market and the World*. Englewood Cliffs, N. J.: Prentice-Hall, 1967.

FOOTE, WILDER (ed.). *Servant of Peace: A Selection of the Speeches and Statements of Dag Hammarskjöld.* New York: Harper & Row, 1962.

FOSDICK, RAYMOND. *Letters on the League of Nations.* Princeton: Princeton University Press, 1966.

FRIEDMAN, WOLFGANG C., GEORGE KALMANOFF, and ROBERT MEAGHER. *International Financial Aid.* New York: Columbia University Press, 1966.

FRUTKIN, ARNOLD. *International Cooperation in Space.* Englewood Cliffs, N. J.: Prentice-Hall, 1965.

FRYDENBURG, PER (ed.). *Peacekeeping, Experience and Evaluation.* Oslo: Norwegian Institute of International Affairs, 1964.

FRYE, WILLIAM R. *A United Nations Peace Force.* Dobbs Ferry, N. Y.: Oceana, 1957.

FURNISS, EDGAR S., JR. (ed.). *The Western Alliance: Its Status and Prospects.* Columbus: Ohio State University Press, 1965.

GARDNER, RICHARD and MAX F. MILLIKAN (eds.). *The Global Partnership: International Agencies and Economic Development.* New York: Frederick A. Praeger, 1968.

GAUDEMET, P. M., "The Status of International Civil Servants in National Law," *International Review of Administrative Sciences,* No. 1, 1959.

GIBBS, N. H. *Keith's British Cabinet System.* London: Stevens and Sons, 1952.

———. *The Origins of Imperial Defence.* Oxford: The Clarendon Press, 1955.

GOODRICH, LELAND M. and ANNE P. SIMONS. *The United Nations and the Maintenance of International Peace and Security.* Washington, D.C.: The Brookings Institution, 1955.

GOORMAGHTIGH, JOHN, "European Coal and Steel Community," *International Conciliation,* May 1955.

———, "European Integration," *International Conciliation,* February 1953.

GORDENKER, LEON. *The United Nations and the Peaceful Unification of Korea: The Politics of Field Operations, 1947–1950.* The Hague: M. Nijhoff, 1959.

* ———. *The UN Secretary-General and the Maintenance of Peace.* New York: Columbia University Press, 1967.

GORVINE, A., "Socio-Cultural Factors in the Administration of Technical Assistance Programs," *International Review of Administrative Sciences,* No. 3, 1962.

GREGOIRE, ROGER. *National Administration and International Organization.* Paris: UNESCO, 1960

HAAS, ERNST B. *Beyond the Nation State.* Stanford: Stanford University Press, 1964.

* ———. *Collective Security and the Future International System.* Denver: University of Denver Press, 1968.

———, "International Integration: The European and the Universal Process," *International Organization,* Summer 1961.

———, "Regionalism, Functionalism, and Universal International Organization," *World Politics,* January 1956.

HAEKKERUP, PER, "Scandinavia's Peace-Keeping Forces for U.N.," *Foreign Affairs,* July 1964.

HAILEY, LORD. *An African Survey.* New York: Oxford University Press, 1957.

* HALLSTEIN, WALTER, "The EEC Commission: A New Factor in International Life," *International and Comparative Law Quarterly,* July 1965.

———, "The European Economic Community," *Political Science Quarterly,* June 1963.

———. *United Europe: Challenge and Opportunity.* Cambridge Harvard University Press, 1962.

HAMILTON, WILLIAM B. (ed.). *The Transfer of Institutions.* Durham: Duke University Press, 1964.

* HANKEY, SIR MAURICE (later Lord). *Diplomacy by Conference.* London: Ernest Benn, 1946.

———. *Government Control in War* (The Lees Knowles Lectures). Cambridge: Cambridge University Press, 1945.

———, "The Origins and Development of the Committee of Imperial Defence," *Army Quarterly,* July 1927.

———. *The Science and Art of Government.* Oxford: The Clarendon Press, 1950.

———. *The Supreme Command 1914–1918* London: George Allen and Unwin, 1961.

HANSON, SIMON. *Five Years of the Alliance for Progress: An Appraisal.* Washington, D.C.: Inter-American Affairs Press, 1967.

HOLMES, JOHN, "The United Nations in the Congo," *International Journal*, Winter 1960–61.

HORSEFIELD, J. KEITH. *The International Monetary Fund 1945–1965* (3 vols.). Washington, D.C.: International Monetary Fund, 1969.

INTERNATIONAL BANK FOR RECONSTRUCTION AND DEVELOPMENT. *International Bank for Reconstruction and Development, 1946–1953.* Baltimore: Johns Hopkins Press, 1954.

———. *Uses of Consultants by the World Bank and its Borrowers.* Washington, D.C.: IBRD, 1965.

———. *The World Bank: Policies and Operations.* Washington, D.C.: IBRD, 1957.

INTERNATIONAL INSTITUTE OF ADMINISTRATIVE SCIENCES AND UNESCO. *National Administration and International Organization: A Comparative Study of Fourteen Countries.* (Sharp-Godchot Report). Brussels: UNESCO, 1951.

ISMAY, HASTINGS L. (later Lord), "The Machinery of the Committee of Imperial Defence," *The Journal of the Royal United Service Institute*, May 1939.

*JACKSON, SIR ROBERT. *A Study of the Capacity of the United Nations Development System.* Geneva: United Nations Document DP/5, 1969.

JAMES, ALAN. *The Politics of Peacekeeping.* New York: Frederick A. Praeger, 1969.

*JAMES, ROBERT RHODES. *Staffing the United Nations Secretariat.* Sussex: University of Sussex (for the Institute for the Study of International Organisation), 1970.

JEFFRIES, SIR CHARLES J. *The Colonial Empire and its Civil Service.* Cambridge: Cambridge University Press, 1938.

JENKS, C. WILFRED. *International Immunities*. Dobbs Ferry, N. Y.: Oceana, 1961.

———. *The World Beyond the Charter*. London: Allen and Unwin, 1969.

JENNINGS, SIR W. I., *Cabinet Government*. Cambridge: Cambridge University Press, 1959.

* JENSEN, FINN B. and INGO WALTER. *The Common Market: Economic Integration in Europe*. Philadelphia: Lippincott, 1965.

JESSUP, PHILIP C. *International Regulation of Economic and Social Questions*. New York: Carnegie Endowment for International Peace, 1955.

JOHNSON, FRANKLYN A. *Defence by Committee: The British Committee of Imperial Defence, 1885–1959*. London: Oxford University Press, 1960.

JOHNSON, RICHARD A., "The Origin of UNESCO," *International Conciliation*, October 1946.

JORDAN, ROBERT S. *Government and Power in West Africa*. London: Faber and Faber, 1969.

———(ed.). *Multinational Cooperation: Economic, Social, and Scientific Development*. New York: Oxford University Press, 1972.

* ———. *The NATO International Staff/Secretariat, 1952–1957: A Study in International Administration*. London: Oxford University Press, 1967.

KAPLAN, MORTON A. (ed.). *New Approaches to International Relations*. New York: St. Martin's Press, 1968.

KASH, DON. *The Politics of Space Cooperation*. Purdue, Ind.: Purdue University Studies, 1967.

KEENLEYSIDE, HUGH L. *International Aid: A Summary with Special Reference to Programmes of the United Nations*. Toronto: McClelland and Stewart, 1966.

KELMAN, HERBERT C. (ed.). *International Behavior, A Social-Psychological Analyses*. New York: Holt, Rinehart and Winston, 1966.

KERLINGER, FRED N. *Foundations of Behavioral Research, Educational and Psychological Inquiry*. New York: Holt, Rinehart and Winston, 1966.

KING, JOHN A., JR. *Economic Development Projects and their Appraisal: Cases and Principles from the Experience of the World Bank.* Baltimore: Johns Hopkins Press, 1967.

KITZINGER, UWE W. *The Challenge of the Common Market.* Oxford: B. Blackwell, 1962.

*———. *The European Common Market and Community.* London Routledge and Kegan Paul, 1967.

KNOWLTON, WILLIAM A., "Early Stages in the Organization of SHAPE," *International Organization,* Winter 1959.

*LANGROD, GEORGES. *The International Civil Service.* Dobbs Ferry, N. Y.: Oceana, 1963.

LaPALOMBARA, JOSEPH. *Bureaucracy and Political Development.* Princeton: Princeton University Press, 1963.

LAVES, WALTER H. C. and CHARLES A. THOMSON. *UNESCO: Purpose, Progress, Prospects.* Bloomington: Indiana University Press, 1957.

LAYTON, CHRISTOPHER. *European Advanced Technology, A Programme for Action.* London: George Allen and Unwin (for P.E.P.), 1969.

LEE, JOHN M. *Colonial Development and Good Government: A Study of the Ideas Expressed by the British Official Classes in Planning Decolonization, 1939–1964.* Oxford: The Clarendon Press, 1967.

*LEWIS, ROY. *Colonial Development and Welfare, 1946–1955.* London: H.M.S.O., 1956.

LIE, TRYGVE. *In the Cause of Peace.* New York: Macmillan, 1954.

LINDBERG, LEON, "Decision Making and Integration in the European Community," *International Organization,* February 1965.

———. *The Political Dynamics of European Economic Integration.* Stanford: Stanford University Press, 1963.

*LINDBERG, LEON and STUART SCHEINGOLD. *Europe's Would-Be Polity.* Englewood Cliffs, N. J.: Prentice-Hall, 1970.

LISKA, GEORGE. *Nations in Alliance: The Limits of Interdependence.* Baltimore: Johns Hopkins Press, 1968.

LOEWENSTEIN, KARL. *British Cabinet Government.* New York: Oxford University Press, 1967.

LOOPER, R. B., "Federal States and International Organizations," *British Yearbook of International Law, 1955–56.*

LOURIE, SYLVAIN, "The United Nations Military Observer Group in India and Pakistan," *International Organization,* February 1955.

*LOVEDAY, ALEXANDER. *Reflections on International Administration.* Oxford: The Clarendon Press, 1956.

*LUARD, EVAN (ed.). *The Evolution of International Organizations.* New York: Frederick A. Praeger, 1966.

LUGARD, LORD. *The Dual Mandate in British Tropical Africa.* London: William Blackwood, 1922.

MACK, R. J., JR. *Raising the World's Standard of Living: The Coordination and Effectiveness of Point Four United Nations Technical Assistance and Related Programs.* New York: Citadel Press, 1953.

MACKINTOSH, JOHN P. *The British Cabinet.* London: Stevens and Sons, 1962.

MANGER, WILLIAM. *Pan America in Crisis: The Future of the OAS.* Washington, D.C.: Public Affairs Press, 1961.

*MANGONE, GERARD J. (ed.). *United Nations Administration of Economic and Social Programs.* New York: Columbia University Press, 1966.

MARSHALL, CHARLES B., "Character and Mission of a United Nations Peace Force, Under Conditions of General and Complete Disarmament," *American Political Science Review,* June 1965.

MARTELLI, GEORGE. *Experiment in World Government: An Account of the UN Operation in the Congo, 1960–1964.* London: Johnson Publications, 1966.

MARTIN, PAUL, "Peace-Keeping and the United Nations—The Broader View," *International Affairs,* April 1964.

MILLER, DAVID HUNTER. *The Drafting of the Covenant.* New York: G. P. Putnam's Sons, 1928.

*MITRANY, DAVID, "The Functional Approach to International Organization," *International Affairs,* July 1948.

———. *The Progress of International Government.* New Haven: Yale University Press, 1933.

———. *A Working Peace System.* Chicago: University of Chicago Press, 1966.

MOATS, HELEN M. *The Secretariat of the League of Nations: International Civil Service or Diplomatic Conference?* Chicago: University of Chicago Press, 1939.

MOHN, PAUL, "Problems of Truce Supervision," International Conciliation, February 1952.

MOORE, FREDERICK J. *The Failures of the World Bank Missions.* Santa Monica, Calif.: The Rand Corp., 1958.

MORRIS, JAMES. *The Road to Huddersfield: A Journey to Five Continents* (also called: *The World Bank: A Prospect*). London: Faber and Faber, 1963.

MULLEY, FRED W. *The Politics of Western Defense.* New York: Frederick A. Praeger, 1962.

MURRAY, D. J. (ed.). *Studies in Nigerian Administration.* London: Hutchinson, 1970.

———. *The Work of Administration in Nigeria.* London: Hutchinson, 1969.

MYRDAL, GUNNAR. *Realities and Illusions in Regard to Intergovernmental Organization.* London: Oxford University Press, 1955.

NICHOLAS, HERBERT. *The United Nations as a Political Institution.* New York: Oxford University Press, 1967.

NICOLSON, HAROLD. *Peacemaking 1919.* New York: Grosset & Dunlap, 1965.

NYE, JOSEPH L., JR. (ed.). *International Regionalism.* Boston: Little, Brown, 1968.

O'BRIEN, CONOR CRUISE. *To Katanga and Back: A UN Case History.* New York: Simon and Schuster, 1963.

OSGOOD, ROBERT S. *NATO: The Entangling Alliance.* Chicago: University of Chicago Press, 1962.

PADELFORD, NORMAN J. and LELAND M. GOODRICH (eds.). *The United Nations in the Balance.* New York: Frederick A. Praeger, 1955.

PEARSON, LESTER B., "Force for U.N.," Foreign Affairs, April 1957.

————. *Partners in Development* (Report of the Commission on International Development). New York: Frederick A. Praeger, 1969.

*PELT, ADRIAN, "International Secretariat: A Dream or a Necessity," *Ecumenical Review*, April 1967.

PHELAN, E. J., "The New International Civil Service," *Foreign Affairs*, January 1933.

————. *Yes and Albert Thomas*. London: Cresset Press, 1936.

POLSBY, NELSON W., ROBERT A. DENTLER, and PAUL A. SMITH (eds.). *Politics and Social Life, An Introduction to Political Behavior*. Boston: Houghton Mifflin, 1963.

PURVES, CHESTER. *The Internal Administration of an International Secretariat*. London: Royal Institute of International Affairs, 1945.

RANSHOFEN-WERTHEIMER, EGON F. *The International Secretariat*. Washington: Carnegie Endowment for International Peace, 1945.

*RAPHAELI, NIMROD. *Readings in Comparative Public Administration*. Boston: Allyn and Bacon, 1967.

RAPPARD, WILLIAM E., "The Evolution of the League of Nations," *Problems of Peace*, Geneva Institute of International Relations, 1928 (2nd series).

REID, ESCOTT. *The Future of the World Bank*. Washington, D.C.: IBRD, 1965.

REINSCH, PAUL S. *Colonial Government, An Introduction to the Study of Colonial Institutions*. New York: Macmillan, 1926.

————. *Public International Unions: Their Work and Organization: A Study in International Administrative Law*. Boston: Ginn and Co., 1911.

RIKER, WILLIAM. *The Theory of Political Coalitions*. New Haven: Yale University Press, 1962.

ROBERTSON, A. H. *European Institutions: Cooperation, Integration, Unification*. New York: Frederick A. Praeger, 1966.

ROBINSON, KENNETH (ed.). *Essays in Imperial Government*. Oxford: B. Blackwell, 1963.

ROSENAU, JAMES N. (ed.). *International Politics and Foreign Policy, A Reader in Research and Theory*. New York: The Free Press, 1969 (rev. ed.).

ROSENTHAL, ALBERT H. *Administration in the Establishment of UNESCO*. Washington, D.C.: U.S. Department of State, 1948.

ROSKILL, STEPHEN. *Hankey, Man of Secrets*. London: Collins, 1970.

*ROSNER, GABRIELLA. *The United Nations Emergency Force*. New York: Columbia University Press, 1963.

*ROVINE, ARTHUR W. *The First Fifty Years: The Secretary-General in World Politics*. Leyden: A. W. Sijthoff, 1971.

ROYAL INSTITUTE OF INTERNATIONAL AFFAIRS. *The British Empire: A Report on Its Structure and Problems by a Study Group of Members of the Royal Institute of International Affairs*. London: Oxford University Press, 1938.

―――. *Colonial Administration by European Powers* (A Series of Papers read at King's College, London, November–December 1946). London: Royal Institute of International Affairs, 1947.

ROYAL INSTITUTE OF PUBLIC ADMINISTRATION. *United Kingdom Administration and International Organization: A Report by a Study Group*. London: Royal Institute of International Affairs, 1951.

*RUSSELL, RUTH B. *United Nations Experiences with Military Forces: Political and Legal Aspects*. Washington, D.C.: The Brookings Institution, 1964.

―――. *The United Nations and United States Security Policy*. Washington, D.C.: The Brookings Institution, 1968.

SALTER, SIR ARTHUR, "From Combined War Agencies to International Administration," *Public Administration Review*, Winter 1944.

SATHYAMURTHY, J. V., "Functional Cooperation: UNESCO," *International Studies*, April 1967.

―――, "Twenty Years of UNESCO: An Interpretation," *International Organization*, Summer 1967.

SAYRE, FRANCIS B. *Experiments in International Administration*. New York: Harper and Co., 1919.

SCHECTER, ALAN H. *Interpretation of Ambiguous Documents by International Administrative Tribunals*. London: Stevens and Sons, 1964.

*SCHEINMAN, LAWRENCE, "EURATOM: Nuclear Integration and Europe," *International Conciliation*, May 1967.

SCHUYLER, ROBERT L., "The British Cabinet, 1916–1919," *Political Science Quarterly*, March 1920.

*SCHWEBEL, STEPHEN M. *The Secretary-General of the United Nations*. Cambridge: Harvard University Press, 1952.

SEWELL, JAMES P. *Functionalism and World Politics*. Princeton: Princeton University Press, 1966.

SHARP, WALTER R. *Field Administration in the United Nations System* New York: Frederick A. Praeger, 1961.

——. *The United Nations Economic and Social Council*. New York: Columbia University Press, 1969.

SHONFIELD, ANDREW. *The Attack on World Poverty*. New York: Vintage Books, 1962.

SHUSTER, GEORGE. *UNESCO: Assessment and Promise*. New York: Harper & Row, 1963.

SINGER, J. DAVID (ed.). *Quantitative International Politics: Insights and Evidence*. New York: The Free Press, 1968.

SIOTIS, JEAN, "The Secretariat of the United Nations Economic Commission for Europe and European Economic Integration: The First Ten Years," *International Organization*, February 1965.

SLATER, JEROME. *The OAS and United States Foreign Policy*. Columbus: Ohio State University Press, 1967.

STANLEY, TIMOTHY W. *NATO in Transition: The Future of the Atlantic Alliance*. New York: Frederick A. Praeger (for Council on Foreign Relations), 1965.

STOETZER, O. CARLOS. *The OAS: An Introduction*. New York: Frederick A. Praeger, 1965.

STIKKER, DIRK U. *Men of Responsibility*. New York: Harper & Row, 1966.

SYMONDS, RICHARD. *The British and Their Successors*. London: Faber and Faber, 1966.

——(ed.). *International Targets for Development*. New York: Harper & Row, 1970.

TANDON, YASHPAL, "Consensus and Authority Behind United Nations Peacekeeping Operations," *International Organization*, Spring 1967.

———, "UNEF, the Secretary-General, and International Diplomacy in the Third Arab-Israeli War," *International Organization*, Spring 1968.

TEAD, ORDWAY, "The Importance of Administration in International Action," *International Conciliation*, January 1945.

TEW, BRIAN. *The International Monetary Fund: Its Present Role and Future Prospects*. Princeton: Princeton University Press (for International Finance Section, Department of Economics and Sociology), 1961.

UNITED NATIONS. *The United Nations Development Decade: Proposals for Action*. UN Sales No. 62.II.B.2.

UN OFFICE OF PUBLIC INFORMATION. *The United Nations in West New Guinea: An Unprecedented Story*. New York: The United Nations, 1963.

VANDEVANTER, EDWARD, JR. *Some Fundamentals of NATO Organization*. Santa Monica: The Rand Corporation, 1963.

* ———. *Studies on NATO: An Analysis of Integration*. Santa Monica: The Rand Corporation, 1966.

WAINHOUSE, DAVID W., et. al. *International Peace Observation*. Baltimore: Johns Hopkins Press, 1966.

WALTERS, F. P. *A History of the League of Nations*. London: Oxford University Press, 1952.

WEAVER, JAMES. *The International Development Association: A New Approach to Foreign Aid*. New York: Frederick A. Praeger, 1965.

WEHBERG, NANS. *Theory and Practice of International Policing*. London: Constable, 1935.

WILLSON, F. M. G. *The Organization of British Central Government, 1914–1956*. London: George Allen and Unwin, 1957.

WRONG, MARGARET, "The Evolution of Local Government in British African Colonies," *International Affairs*, July 1946.

YOUNG, ORAN R. *The Intermediaries: Third Parties in International Crises.* Princeton: Princeton University Press, 1967.

YOUNG, TIEN CHENG. *International Civil Service: Principles and Problems.* Brussels: International Institute of Administrative Sciences, 1958.

The Contributors

JOHN A. BALLARD holds a law degree from Harvard, and a doctorate from the Fletcher School of Law and Diplomacy. After lecturing and conducting research in Nigerian universities, most recently as reader in government at Ahmadu Bello University, he currently holds a Rockefeller grant as visiting fellow at the Institute of Commonwealth Studies, University of London, where he is completing work on a study of the transfer of institutions in Nigeria. He has also carried out research in French-speaking Africa and has published several articles and longer studies on both Equatorial and West African politics and administration.

FRANCIS A. BEER is associate professor of political science, University of Texas. He had his first book published under the auspices of the Mershon Program in National Security Studies at Ohio State University. It is: *Integration and Disintegration in NATO: Processes of Alliance Cohesion and Prospects for Atlantic Community*. His latest book, of which he is the editor, is: *Alliances: Latent War Communities in the Contemporary World*. His doctorate was taken at the University of California (Berkeley).

LARRY L. FABIAN is presently research associate, Foreign Policy Studies Program, The Brookings Institution. He has just completed a book for The Brookings Institution: *Soldiers Without Enemies: Preparing the United Nations For Peacekeeping*. He also is contributor to *Vietnam after the War: Peacekeeping and Rehabilitation*. Previously, he served on the staff of the Carnegie Endowment for International Peace. His doctorate is from Columbia University.

WERNER FELD is professor of political science, and chairman of the department of political science, Louisiana State University in New Orleans. He has traveled widely in Europe, and has written: *The Court of the European Communities: New Dimension in International Adjudication; Reunification and West German-Soviet Relations; The European Common Market and the World.* He took his doctorate at Tulane University, and is a member of the Committee on Atlantic Studies.

DAG HAMMARSKJÖLD is the late Secretary-General of the United Nations.

ROBERT RHODES JAMES is director of the Institute for the Study of International Organization at the University of Sussex, England. He was formerly an official of the House of Commons, a Fellow of All Souls College, Oxford, and Kratter professor of European history at Stanford University. He has also held a NATO research fellowship and professorship. He has written *Lord Randolph Churchill: A Study in Failure,* along with having edited two major collections of political papers, and a study of the 1968 Czechoslovak crisis. His most recent work is *Staffing the United Nations Secretariat,* published as a monograph by the Institute for the Study of International Organization. He is a member of the Committee on Atlantic Studies.

ROBERT S. JORDAN is professor of political science, and chairman of the department of political science, State University of New York at Binghamton. For the previous nine years he was at George Washington University, Washington, D.C., except for two years as Littauer Visiting Professor of Political Science and International Politics, Fourah Bay College, University of Sierra Leone. He has doctorates from Princeton University and Oxford University. His publications include: *The NATO International Staff/Secretariat, 1952–57: A Study in International Administration; Government and Power in West Africa; Europe and the Superpowers: Perceptions of European International Politics* (editor and contributor); and *Multinational Cooperation: Economic, Social, and Scientific Development* (editor). He is a member of the Committee on Atlantic Studies.

DAVID J. MURRAY is professor of government, The Open University, England. During the previous ten years he has been teaching and conducting research at different universities in East, Central, and West Africa. His final appointment was as director of research in the Institute of Administration, University of Ife, Ibadan, Nigeria. His doctorate is from Oxford University. He has published many books and articles in the fields of public and comparative administration, the most recent of which are *The Governmental System in Southern Rhodesia;* and *Studies in Nigerian Administration* (editor).

LAWRENCE SCHEINMAN is associate professor of political science, University of Michigan, where he took his doctorate. He was for several years previously at the University of California (Los Angeles), and in 1966–67, was a research fellow at the Center for International Affairs, Harvard University. He has published widely in journals, as well as having written: *Atomic Energy Policy in France Under the Fourth Republic.* Most recently, under a fellowship with the Carnegie Endowment for International Peace, he has studied the growth of the bureaucracies of the European Communities.

RICHARD SYMONDS has had extensive experience in international organizations, having served with UNRRA in Austria, with the UN Commission for India and Pakistan, with the UN Technical Assistance Board, and as a regional representative. He took his degree at Oxford, and has served at the Institute of Commonwealth Studies at Oxford as a fellow, with the Institute of Commonwealth Studies in London as a fellow, and has been at the University of Sussex as a professorial fellow. He is now representative in Europe, UN Institute for Training and Research. He has published: *The Making of Pakistan; The British and Their Successors; International Targets for Development* (editor).

RICHARD W. VAN WAGENEN is training officer, projects department, International Bank for Reconstruction and Development (World Bank). Before joining the World Bank, he was dean of the graduate school and professor of international organization at The American University, Washington, D.C.; director of the Center for Research on World Political Institutions and associate professor of politics, Princeton University; and a member of the faculties of Columbia University and Duke University. He took his doctorate at Stanford University. He served for many years on the board of editors of *International Organization,* and has published: *The Iranian Case: Research in the International Organization Field; An International Police Force and Public Opinion* (co-author); *Political Community and the North Atlantic Area* (co-author).

INDEX

A

Acheson, Dean, 173
Adamolekun, O., 97(n)
Adedeji, Adebayo, 97(n)
Africa (general), 74ff, 98ff, 179
Algeria, 175
Allied Maritime Transport Council,
        see World War I, inter-
        Allied Cooperation
Amery, L. S., 33, 35, 36(n)
Arab League, see League of Arab
        States
Asia, 98ff, 179ff
Asian Development Bank (ADB), 4
Asquith, Lord, 34
Atlantic Community, see NATO
Austin, Dennis, 79
Australia-New Zealand-United States
        Security Treaty (ANZUS),
        169, 186

B

Bailey, Sidney, 17
Balfour, Arthur, 247
Ballard, J. A., 97(n)
Balogh, Lord, 108
Barros, James, 50(n)
Beer, Francis A., 168(n)
Belgium, 5
    and EEC, 199ff
    and NATO, 181ff
Beloff, Max, ix
Berg, Elliot J., 82(n)
Berlin, 173, 175, 180
    blockade of, 52, 92, 105

Bloomfield, Lincoln, 124, 150(n)
Boer War, 27
Bourgeois, Leon, 139
Bowett, D. W., 128(n)
Bowman, Edward H., 156
Boyd, Andrew, 23, 125(n)
Bozeman, Adda B., 132(n)
Brasbanti, R., 96
Brind, J., 137(n)
Britain, see Great Britain
British Cabinet, 29ff, 33, 36, 53
    Cabinet Office, 36, 39ff
British colonial administration, 74ff
    Colonial Development and Welfare
        Act (CD&W), 82, 88, 92
    community development, 94
    indirect administration in, 91–93,
        96
    institutional transfer, 95–97
    Journal of Local Administration,
        88
    and native administration, 92, 93
British West Africa, see British
        colonial administration
Broadley, Sir Herbert, 112
Brokensha, David, 86(n)
Brosio, Manlio, 171
Bruce, Lord (Bruce Report), 101–2
Bunche, Ralph, 64, 155
Burne, Col. A. H., 137(n)

C

Cabinet Office, see British Cabinet
Cameron, Sir Donald, 91, 92(n)
Canada, 159–60

Canadian International Development
    Agency (CIDA), 4
Carey, Joyce, 81
Carroll, Thomas, H., vii
Central Treaty Organization
    (CENTO; also called Bagh-
    dad Pact), 169, 185–86
Centre Africain de formation et de
    recherche administratives
    pour le developpement
    (Tangier, Morocco), 91
China (Communist), 185
Churchill, Winston, 146, 171
Clarke, Sir George (later Lord
    Sydenham), 30–31
Claude, I. L., Jr., 24, 54, 58, 129(n),
    130(n), 131(n), 146(n), 148(n)
Clemenceau, Georges, 41
Coastwith, R., 84(n)
Cochrane, James D., 244(n)
Codding, George, 103(n)
Cold War, 146, 149, 168
Collective security, 129ff, 145ff
Colonial administration, 74ff
Committee of Imperial Defense
    (CID), 28ff, 32, 34, 53
    secretariat of, 31ff
Commonwealth Conferences, 38
Coombs, David, 226(n), 227, 228(n)
Cooper, W. A., 253(n)
Cornford, Francis M., 131(n)
Council of Europe, 170
Cox, David, 149(n)
Cox, Robert, 15
Crocker, Walter R., 62(n)
Crowder, Michael, 81(n), 95(n)
Cuba, 173, 175
Czechoslovakia, 173, 178

D

Dardanelles Committee (Great
    Britain), 28, 34, 36
Deakin, F. W. D., ix
de Gaulle, Charles, 219, 241
Denmark, 143
    and NATO, 180ff

Deringer, Arved, 213
de Sá, Hernane Tavares, 15
Deschamps, Hubert, 95(n)
Downs, Anthony, 233, 234(n)
Drummond, Sir Eric, 43, 47ff, 52,
    54ff, 109, 140, 247
Dunant, Henri, 99
Dutch, see the Netherlands

E

Eastern Europe, 179; see also War-
    saw Treaty Organization
Eden, Anthony (later Lord Avon),
    140
Ehrman, John, 25
Eicher, Carl, 88(n)
Eisenhower, Dwight D., 171, 174
Emir (Northern Nigeria), 78
English-speaking Africa, see British
    colonial administration
Equatorial Africa, 95
Esher Report, 31, 32(n)
Ethiopia, 143
Eurocrats, 195
"Europe of the Fatherlands," 232
European Atomic Energy Community
    (EURATOM), 193
European Communities, 170, 187ff
    bureaucratic interpenetration in,
        189ff
    Commission, 232
    Council of Ministers, 187, 232,
        237
    relation with national administra-
        tion, 237ff
European Defense Community
    (EDC), 180
European Economic Community
    (EEC), 187ff
    and cartels, 196ff
    Commission, 188ff
    Committee of Permanent Repre-
        sentatives, 220, 226
    common agricultural policy of,
        200–201
    Council of Ministers, 226

European Economic Community
(cont.)
and Eurocrats, 195
and Rome Treaty, 195ff
and public opinion, 230ff
European Free Trade Association
(EFTA), 170
European Political Community (EPC),
180

F

Fabian, Larry L., 128(n)
Fanning, James E., 156
Feld, Werner, 228(n), 241(n)
Finkelstein, Lawrence S., 130(n)
Finnegan, Ruth, 81(n)
Fishback, David, ix
Fisher, H. A. L., 51
Foch, Marshal Ferdinand, 139
Food and Agriculture Organization
(FAO), 7, 102ff
Foote, Wilder, 159(n)
Ford Foundation, 84
Fosbrooke, Henry A., 84(n)
Fouchet Plan, 231; see also Euro-
pean Political Community
France
and European Communities, 187ff,
193
and League of Nations, 145
and NATO, 181ff
and peace-keeping, 136ff, 151
Frederick the Great, 132
French colonial administration, 74ff
Centre de Hautes Études de
l'Administration Musul-
man, 89
community development by, 94
École Nationale de la France
d'Outre-Mer, 89
Fonds d'Investissement de Developpement Economique
et Sociale (FIDES), 82, 88
institutional transfer in, 95–97
French West Africa, see French
colonial administration

Functional international cooperation, 27, 99, 109ff, 113ff
Functionalism, 27, 99

G

General Agreement on Tariffs and
Trade (GATT), 189(n),
210, 241
Germany (West)
and EEC, 199ff
and NATO, 181ff
Gerth, H. H., 229(n)
Ghana, 79
Ashanti Confederacy Council, 79
Gold Coast, 79–80
Gibbs, N. H. ix
Gold Coast, see Ghana
Goodpaster, General Andrew, 172
Goodrich, L. M., 53(n), 125(n)
Gordenker, Leon, 20, 46, 125(n),
153(n)
Graubard, Stephen R., 228(n)
Great Britain
administrative flexibility of, 20, 72
colonial expansion of, 27, 28
contribution to international
administration, 34ff, 45,
54–55, 57, 247ff
and NATO, 181ff
and peace-keeping, 136ff, 151
Greece, 131
Athens, 132
Delian League, 131
and NATO, 180ff
Peloponnesian Conferation, 131
Sparta, 132
Grey, Sir Edward, 32(n)
Griffith, Ernest R., vii
Gruenther, General Alfred, 172
Guinea, 119

H

Haas, Ernst, 99(n), 190(n), 191(n),
228(n)
Hailey, Lord, 76, 89, 92

Hamilton, Alexander, 132
Hamilton, William B., 96
Hammarskjöld, Dag, 8, 64ff, 124ff, 155, 159ff
Hankey, Sir Maurice (later Lord), 28ff, 32(n), 43(n), 50, 53(n)
  at Paris Peace Conference (1919), 41–42, 53, 246
  personality and influence of, 33–34, 35
  as secretary to the Cabinet, 31, 34, 53–54
  views of administration, 36, 54
Hapsburg Empire, 5
Hazzard, Shirley, 73(n)
Heussler, Robert, 78(n)
Hicks, Ursula, 96
Hinsley, F. H., 132(n)
Hitler, Adolph, 140, 142
Holmes, John, 126(n)
House, Col. Edward H., 46(n), 48(n)
Howard-Ellis, C., 43(n)

I

Iceland
  and NATO, 181ff
Imperial War Cabinet, see World War I
Imperial War Conference, see World War I
India, 111
Indirect rule, see British colonial administration, indirect administration
Indonesia, 119
Inglehart, Ronald, 202(n)
Institute of Administration (University of Ife), 91
Inter-American Development Bank (IDB), 4
Inter-American Treaty of Reciprocal Assistance (Rio Pact), 169
International African Institute, 89

International Bank for Reconstruction and Development (IBRD), see World Bank
International Civil Aviation Organization (ICAO), 104
International civil service, 6, 9, 11, 13–14, 15, 20, 23
  administrative style of, 19–20
  bureaucratic interpenetration in, 191ff
  career failure in, 11, 233
  conflict of loyalty or interest in, 17–18, 67–68, 258ff
  and EEC, 191ff, 230ff
  and Eurocrats, 195
  geographical distribution, see nationality question (below)
  integration of, 207ff, 234
  morale of, 9, 233
  and nationality question, 6–7, 11–12, 13ff, 60, 65–66, 111, 113
  and NATO, 182ff
  ofjectivity and neutrality of, 7–8, 58–59, 245ff
  peace-keeping, 134ff, 139, 147, 150ff
  promotion by merit in, 11–12, 233
  recruitment, 21–22, 60–61
  respect for, 11, 233
  social isolation in, 8ff, 58–59, 245ff
  skills of communication of, 6, 19
  standard of living of, 11
  tendency toward fragmentation, 14, 17
International Civil Service Advisory Board, 68–69
International Institute of Agriculture, 99
International Labor Organization (ILO), 8, 14, 55, 57, 62, 101ff
International Monetary Fund (IMF), 103–4

International Red Cross, 99, 160
International Telecommunications
        Union (ITU), 100, 103
Ismay, Sir Hastings (later Lord),
        31, 171, 174(n)
Italy
    and EEC, 199ff
    and NATO, 181ff
Ivory Coast, 97

J

Jackson, Sir Robert, 105, 116
James, Alan, 128(n), 144(n)
Jenks, Wilfred, 14, 56, 57(n), 59
Johnson, Franklyn, 29, 30(n), 31(n),
        32(n), 37(n)
Johnson, Lyndon, 240
Jordan, Robert S., 31(n), 44(n)

K

Karamojong (Uganda), 85
Kennedy, John F., 174, 240
Khrushchev, Nikita, 111, 173, 245
Kikuyu (Kenya), 77
Kirk-Greene, A. M., 92(n)
Korea, 149ff, 173

L

Langrod, Georges, 3, 124(n), 147(n)
Lasch, Christopher, 176(n)
League of Arab States (also Arab
        League), 169, 186
League of Nations, 3–4, 7ff, 28, 52,
        75, 100–101, 168, 245ff
    Assembly, 249
    Council, 44, 45–47, 127, 139, 142
    Covenant, 45, 46(n), 47, 100,
        130, 145, 246
    Mandate Commission, 90
    Secretariat, 7, 28, 43ff, 47, 52, 54,
        59–60, 62, 136ff, 246ff
    Secretary-General, 28, 43, 45ff,
        52, 109, 136ff, 246ff
Lee, John M., 96
Lemnitzer, General Lyman, 172

Lennard, Jeffrey, ix, 27
Liddell Hart, Captain B. H., 137(n)
Lie, Trygve, 49(n), 63, 153, 156, 161
Lindberg, Leon, 191(n), 200(n),
        243(n)
Lippmann, Walter, 245
Lithuania, 139ff
Lloyd George, David, 35, 38, 41,
        42(n), 53
Loveday, Alexander, 3ff, 8, 15–16,
        18, 20–21, 108(n), 123
Luard, Evan, 121
Lubin, David, 100, 116
Lugard, Lord, 91, 93, 95
Luxembourg
    and EEC, 199ff
    and NATO, 181ff
Lyons, F. S. L., 99(n)

M

McDonald, J. Kenneth, ix
Mackintosh, John P., 37
Macmillan, Harold, 174
Madison, James, 132
Makarios, Archbishop, 142
Mansholt, Sicco L., 200
Mantoux, Pierre, 56
Mills, C. Wright, 229(n)
Milner, Lord, 56
Mitrany, David, 99(n)
Monnet, Jean, 56
Morocco, 95
Morris, James, 18
Morse, David, 8
Multinational organization, 28
Multinational staff, 13; see also
        International civil service
Murray, D. J., 77(n), 79(n), 81(n),
        86(n), 97(n)
Myrdal, Gunnar, 20

N

Nairn, R., 109(n)
Namenwirth, Zwi, 217(n)

National administration, 5, 28–29, 215
    and bureaucratic interpenetration,
        193ff
    and EEC, 237ff
National civil service, 13, 237ff
    and bureaucratic interpenetration,
        193ff
    and EEC, 237
Ndebele (southern Rhodesia), 85
Nehru, J., 149
Netherlands, the, 143
    and EEC, 199ff
    and NATO, 181ff
Nicholas, Herbert, 52
Nicolson, Sir Harold, 41
Niculescu, Barbu, 82(n)
Nigeria, 5, 76, 78, 84–85, 91, 92, 97
Nixon, Richard, 240
Nkrumah, Kwame, 80
Noblemaire, M. (also Noblemaire
        Report), 249
Non-political international organiza-
        tions, 3, 23
Nordic Council, 170
Norstad, General Lauris, 171, 174(n)
North Atlantic Treaty Organization
        (NATO), 142, 149, 169ff,
        189
    and Atlantic Community, 180ff
    Council, 181
    infrastructure of, 172–73, 175
    International Staff/Secretariat of,
        171, 177
    North Atlantic Assembly, 182
    and nuclear affairs, 174, 177, 180
    SACEUR, 171, 181
    SHAPE, 171
    Three Wise Men, 170, 181
Northcote-Trevelyan reforms, 58
Norway, 143
    and NATO, 180ff

O

O'Brien, Conor Cruise, 7
Organization of African Unity (OAU),
        169

Organization of American States
        (OAS), 186
Organization for Economic Coopera-
        tion and Development
        (OECD), 170, 184, 190, 210
Orlando, Vittorio Emanuele, 41
Ottley, Sir Charles, 31
Owen, David, 108(n)

P

Padelford, N. J., 53(n), 125(n)
Pakistan, 111
Paris Peace Conference (1919)
    conduct of, 40–42
    contribution to international ad-
        ministration, 44–46, 53–54,
        246
    organization of, 38–39
    peace-keeping, 145
    Supreme Council, 28
Pearson, Lester, 126, 160, 162–63
Phelan, E. J., 55, 56(n)
Poland, 139ff
Pompidou, Georges, 211
Pope Paul VI, 7
Portugal
    and NATO, 181ff
Purves, Chester, 60

R

Rabier, Jacques-René, 230(n), 231
Ranshofen-Wertheimer, Egon, 6,
        47(n), 56(n), 123(n), 138(n),
        249(n)
Regional administration, 225–26;
        see also European Eco-
        nomic Community
Rhodes Scholars, 15
Riddell, Lord, 33(n), 44
Ridgway, General Mathew, 171
Roosevelt, Elliot, 103(n)
Roosevelt, Franklin D., 102, 146
Roskill, Stephen, 30(n), 35(n), 37(n),
        54(n)

Royal Institute of International
     Affairs, 89
Rublee, George, 40(n)
Russell, Ruth, ix, 128(n), 144(n),
     158(n)

S

Saar plebescite, 137ff
Salter, Sir Arthur, 56
Scheingold, Stuart, 191(n)
Scheinman, Lawrence, 187(n), 228(n)
Schlesinger, Arthur, 176(n)
Schmitter, Philippe C., 191(n), 244(n)
Schwebel, Stephen M., 49(n), 50(n),
     249(n), 254(n)
Senegal, 95
Sewell, James P., 99(n), 102(n)
Sierra Leone, 86
Smith, Sir Bryan Sharwood, 77, 78(n)
Smith, John, 78(n)
Smuts, Jan C., 46(n), 62, 253(n)
Southeast Asia Collective Defense
     Treaty (SEATO), 169,
     185–86
Soviet Union, 149, 151, 160, 166, 240
  and NATO, 179
  and reform of UN Secretariat,
     162ff
Spaak, Paul-Henri, 171
Spain, 118
Stalin, Josef, 126, 161
Stikker, Dirk, 171, 172(n)
Stone, Julius, 149(n)
Strauss, Franz-Joseph, 229
Suez War (1956), 124
Supreme War Council, see World
     War I
Sweden, 143
Swedish International Development
     Authority (SIDA), 4
Symonds, Richard, 27, 107(n), 113(n)

T

Tanzania, 84
Thomas, Albert, 55–56, 109–10, 114
Tiv (Nigeria), 85

Torre, Mottram, 9
Tunisia, 175
Turkey
  and NATO, 180ff
Tyrell, William (later First Baron),
     32

U

Uganda, 84–86, 87
Unilateral Declaration of Indepen-
     dence (Rhodesia, 98, 118
United Kingdom, see Great Britain
United Nations, 4, 7ff, 11, 98, 102,
     105, 115, 123, 168, 186, 245
  Administrative Committee on
     Coordination, 104
  Capacity Study, 72, 105ff, 113(n),
     114ff
  Capital Development Fund, 113
  Charter, 102, 111, 123, 131, 145,
     147–48, 153, 159, 161, 250ff
    Article 19 crisis, 162–63
  Civilian Operations Component,
     154
  Development Program (UNDP),
     72, 105ff, 114–15
  Economic Commission for Africa
     (ECA), 91
  Economic Commission for Europe
     (ECE), 118
  Economic, Scientific, and Cultural
     Organization (UNESCO),
     101, 103, 108, 110, 115, 118
  Economic and Social Council
     (ECOSOC), 102, 104, 109,
     115
  Emergency Force (UNEF), 125,
     127ff, 165, 265ff
  General Assembly, 104, 124, 127,
     136, 148, 151, 253
  Military Staff Committee, 144ff,
     159, 161
  peace-keeping, 8, 63–65, 123ff,
     131ff
    ONUC (Congo), 128, 134, 141,
     153, 159ff, 175, 264ff

United Nations *(cont.)*
UNCI (Indonesia), 127, 150
UNFICYP (Cyprus), 128, 141,
152, 154, 163, 175
UNIPOM (India-Pakistan), 128,
163
UNMOGIP (Kashmir), 127, 152
UNOGIL (Lebanon), 128, 264
UNSCOB (Greece), 127, 150
UNTEA (West Irian), 128, 141
UNTSO (Palestine), 127, 150,
264
UNTSO-expanded (Suez Canal),
128, 143, 153, 163, 173, 185
UNYOM (Yemen), 128
Preparatory Commission, 57,
61–62, 69, 250ff, 261
Secretariat, 15, 19, 52–53, 59ff,
115, 125ff, 144, 150
future of, 252ff
peace-keeping, 152ff
proposals for peace-keeping,
164ff
and secondment, 261–62
Secretaries-General, 8, 52, 63, 73,
104, 110, 124ff, 134, 137,
148, 152ff
and peace-keeping, 265ff
powers of office, 251ff
proposals for peace-keeping,
164ff
Security Council, 127, 136, 146,
148–49, 151ff, 253
peace-keeping, 163
Special Fund, 104–5
Specialized agencies, 98, 100,
103, 108–9
Technical Assistance Board
(TAB), 98, 104–5
Trusteeship Council, 90
Uniting for Peace, 144ff, 149, 159,
161
Urquhart, Brian E., 150(n)
United States, 101
administrative system of, 19
Agency for International Development (AID), 4, 78
Constitutional Convention (1787),
133
contribution to international administration, 254
McCarthy period in, 8, 63, 153,
260
and political integration in Western Europe, 240ff
Universal Postal Union (UPU), 100

V

Versailles, see Paris Peace Con-
ference
Vietnam, 175
Vilna dispute (1920), 136, 139
Vishinsky, A., 161
Voltaire, 132(n)
von der Groeben, Hans, 223(n)

W

Wahlen, F. T., 115
Wainhouse, David, 128(n)
Walters, F. P., 55(n), 58(n), 101(n),
249(n)
Wambaugh, Sarah, 137(n)
War Cabinet (Great Britain), 28,
34ff, 38–39
War Committee (Great Britain),
34, 36
War Council (Great Britain), 28, 34,
36
Warsaw Treaty Organization (also
Warsaw Pact), 169, 178,
185–86
Weber, Max, 229
Wehberg, Hans, 135(n)
Wells, H. G., 102
Western Europe, 23, 62, 170, 176ff,
230, 240ff
Western European Union (WEU),
170, 180–81

Wheat Executive, see World War I, inter-Allied cooperation
Willson, F. M. G., 86(n)
Wilson, Harold, 185
Wilson, J. V., 49(n)
Wilson, Woodrow, 41, 46(n)
Winchmore, Charles, 53(n), 57(n), 125(n), 164(n)
Woodruff, A. M., vii
Woolf, Leonard, 102
World Bank, 3, 11–12, 14ff, 17–18, 21–22, 104
   Bank Group, 3–4, 6
World Health Organization (WHO), 14, 101, 103
World Meteorological Organization (WMO), 107
World War I, 27–28
   and Imperial War Cabinet, 38–39
   and Imperial War Conference, 38–39
   inter-Allied cooperation in, 39–40
   Supreme War Council, 41–42, 44
World War II, 77, 79, 81, 88, 92, 146, 168, 173

Y

Ydit, Meir, 135(n)
Young, Oran R., 133(n)
Young, Roland, 84(n)
Yugoslavia, 5

Z

Zambia, 87
Zimmern, Sir Alfred, 102